A GUIDE TO EARLY AMERICAN HOMES

North

A Guide to

EARLY

AMERICAN

HOMES

North

DOROTHY & RICHARD PRATT

McGraw-Hill Book Company, Inc.

NEW YORK TORONTO LONDON

Published by the McGraw-Hill Book Company, Inc.
Printed in the United States of America

PREFACE

It would be a slight exaggeration to say that nothing could be less alike than the early houses of the North and those of the South. Yet it is striking what differences do appear as from either direction you break through the boundaries marked out by Mason and Dixon and the Ohio River. Here in this book the early homes in the fourteen states that lie above those boundaries and between the Atlantic Seaboard and the valley of the Mississippi furnish the explanation of how and why they are different from the houses down south. Even more interesting will be their demonstration of how they happened to be different from one another. And it isn't merely that the various types of early houses in Massachusetts are different from those of Michigan. They are different even from those of the next-door states of New Hampshire, Vermont, New York, Connecticut, and Rhode Island. Pennsylvania houses are quite remarkably different from those of New Jersey. And the early houses of Ohio have a mood and manner very much their own. All this will appear as you pick your way through the pages of this book.

In the South the early houses are mainly to be found in the country; in the North they are mainly to be found in the cities, towns, and villages, thus explaining to some extent the essential nature of the two regions—the one a rural, the other a town economy. That may or may not be the reason why there are so many restoration communities in the North, such as Shelburne in Vermont; Sturbridge, Deerfield and Storrowton in Massachusetts; Mystic Seaport in Connecticut; the Farmer's Village in Cooperstown, among many others

in New York; Hopewell and Old Economy in Pennsylvania; Greenfield Village in Michigan, and a dozen or more others here and there. In the South, on the other hand, aside from Old Salem in North Carolina, there is only one other of any stature, namely Colonial Williamsburg, the most stunning of them all, of course, anywhere in the country.

And while, again, there are any number of organized house tours in the North, hardly any can even begin to compare in scope and attendance with a good half-dozen famous ones in the South.

As against the nearly seven hundred houses that can be visited in the South, there are well over nine hundred in the North, as described herein. Approximately two-thirds of these are houses that are open to the public and maintained for that purpose. The remaining one-third are private homes. We believe you will find in this book, for the first time anywhere, virtually every open early house of any merit in the North. We *know* that you will find here, for the first time anywhere, the hundreds of private homes whose owners, through the *Guide,* have generously agreed to let their homes be visited under conditions set down in each case. The authors are as pleased to have helped make possible this unprecedented privilege as they are grateful to all the various owners involved for granting it. Readers will readily appreciate that to abuse this privilege will be to run the risk of ending it for others.

The order in which the states are arranged gives the same precedence to Massachusetts here as is given to Virginia in the South. After Massachusetts it is merely a matter of working your way through the rest of New England and striking down through New York, New Jersey, and Pennsylvania. From the seaboard states you start westward as the pioneers did before you. When it seemed to us an advantage for the reader that the localities in any given state should be arranged regionally, this was done—just as an alphabetical order was followed when that seemed better.

¶ Things to remember

Automobile road maps are accurate, up to date, and free. We believe that with the *Guide* and a good road map you can find every house listed herein, except some of the *private houses*. For these, which are often isolated, get explicit directions from the owners when making appointments by letter or phone.

For further local guidance, we suggest that the town or county historical societies, the chambers of commerce, the public libraries, the post office, and even sometimes the gas station or the police, will prove helpful—more or less in the order given.

It goes without saying that days, hours, and entrance fees are subject to change. Advance inquiries sometimes save disappointments. When two fees are given, the first is for adults, the second for children. If no fee is mentioned, no fee is required. Voluntary contributions are suggested in many cases but not obligatory.

¶ To those who helped

Mention of all the individuals who have given helpful information, and all the books which have been consulted, would fill a volume in themselves. We have tried the patience of countless homeowners, of house custodians and curators, of endless officers of state and local historical societies, of development commissions, of landmark and antiquarian societies, of pilgrimage and house-tour people, of chambers of commerce, women's clubs, librarians, town clerks, of the Colonial Dames and the D.A.R.—and we thank them all for the time they have taken in our behalf during the more than three years we have been working intensively on the books. For expert assistance on the manuscripts, we wish to give sincere thanks in particular to Miss Lorinda Ballard and Mrs. Anthony Salisbury—bless their hearts!

To the LADIES' HOME JOURNAL *and its editors, Bruce and Beatrice Blackmar Gould, and to the parent organization, the Curtis Publishing Company, a special note of appreciation for putting picture material at our disposal, along with indispensable facilities and advantages of many kinds, without which it would have been impossible to produce these Guides.*

CONTENTS

A GUIDE TO EARLY AMERICAN HOMES

North

Here at the fascinating Saugus Ironworks restoration, of which this is the Ironmaster's house, you are in one of the richest seventeenth-century regions of Massachusetts (see page 22), with both the Parson Capen and Scotch Boardman houses nearby. This many-gabled and weather-darkened house was restored some forty years ago by Wallace Nutting, a pioneer in promoting public appreciation of our heritage homes. Across the page is a typical interior of the Wayside Inn at South Sudbury, celebrated by Longfellow, and forming part of an extensive restoration by Henry Ford.

Massachusetts

*T*HERE is great equality in the people of this state. Few or no opulent men—and no poor—great similitude in their buildings, the general fashion of which is a chimney (always of stone or brick) and door in the middle, with a staircase fronting the latter . . . two flush doors with a very good show of sash and glass windows. The size generally is from 30 to 50 feet in length, and from 20 to 30 feet in width, exclusive of a back shed, which seems to be added as the family increases."

Thus did the man who slept in probably more early American homes than anyone else in our history put down in his Journal his impressions of Massachusetts houses as he passed among them in the peaceful golden autumn of 1790, on his first great Presidential tour. He had driven that particular morning through the village of Longmeadow with its lovely green, and he could have had the Storrs Parsonage in mind because of its "two flush doors with a very good show of sash and glass windows."

But he should have known better than to mention "similitude," for even at this early date the houses of Massachusetts were outstanding for their wide variety. With one house of a very elegant variety Washington had reason to be well familiar, for with his unerring eye for the best, the General had chosen it for his Cambridge headquarters back in 1775—a big Georgian beauty of a house that nearly everyone now knows as the "Longfellow Home."

The gap between Storrs Parsonage

and the Cambridge mansions was great enough, but there were many Massachusetts houses in 1790 that were much earlier than the parsonage—a good hundred and fifty years earlier, represented now by those dark, brooding Elizabethan dwellings, like the "Ward," the "Witch," and the "Seven Gables" group in Salem; the "Boardman" and the "Capen"; and a whole collection at Ipswich. And after Washington's time the variety was to be enriched by houses, still early in our terms, as different as Gore Place at Waltham, the fine foursquare Federal houses in Newburyport, the McIntire masterpieces in Salem, and the Bulfinch houses on Beacon Hill.

Nor is any other state a match for Massachusetts in the total number of houses that can be visited. And because a great majority of the early houses are located in the eastern portion of the state, a concentration of early houses here is something to consider.

The density is greatest in the crescent of land which lies back from the borders of Massachusetts Bay. On your road map you will see that Newburyport would be the tip of the crescent, Plymouth the toe, and the landward curve would cut right through Concord. Between that outward sweeping line and the waters of the Bay there are, of early American houses that matter, more to the square mile than in any other area of similar extent in the country.

Another situation exists, namely the peculiar perplexity that confronts the stranger endeavoring to find his way from one place to another. We suggest the planned approach. To that end, instead of attempting to relate the towns geographically to each other, which would have been pure madness, we have taken the more or less accepted geographical areas of the state, as indicated above, and in these areas have simply arranged the towns in alphabetical order. The reader now merely marks on his road map the towns he wishes to visit, and works out his own itinerary to fit. It couldn't be simpler!

IN & OUT OF BOSTON

On & off Beacon Hill; Arlington; Brookline; Cambridge; Chelsea;
Dorchester; Medford; Watertown & Waltham; Winthrop

¶ On & off Beacon Hill

Up on Beacon Hill there is a profusion of fine Federal architecture. Credit much of its beauty and abundance to Charles Bulfinch, who crowned the Hill in 1795 with his golden-domed State House. He was a darling of his day, famous for the purity of his façades. He made a fashion of shallow recessed arches in his walls, and his Adam details were always done with wit, taste, and delicacy.

Down the Hill, in the direction of Dock Square, Faneuil Hall brings you face to face with your Revolutionary past, as does the elegant old State House around on State Street, its Dutch gables adorned with the unicorn and lion of the Crown. Take in the spiral staircase of the State House and the grasshopper weathervane of Faneuil Hall.

PAUL REVERE HOUSE (*1680*)
19 North Square; daily 10 to 4 except Sundays and holidays; 25 cents; Paul Revere Memorial Association.

There couldn't be a better house to begin with here than Paul Revere's. Down below Beacon Hill on ground hallowed by history in what is now Boston's "Little Italy," this dark, medieval dwelling, close-clapboarded,

Hemmed in as it is, the Paul Revere house stands out from its surroundings with an aura of history and age.

with corbeled overhang, leaded diamond panes, and peek-hole shutters, has the Elizabethan look that early Boston builders brought here in memory from England. The house was already a hundred years old when Revere moved in before the Revolution, and it is furnished now as it must have been when Paul occupied it, and the house was bursting at the seams with sixteen little Reveres. Four rooms and attic are filled with mementos of the famous silversmith and midnight rider, who was descended from the French Huguenot family of Rivoire. He worked in copper as well as silver, and became one of the most successful craftsmen of his day. He was also accounted very skillful at fashioning false teeth from ivory.

MOSES PIERCE-HICHBORN HOUSE (c. 1676)

29 North Square adjacent to Paul Revere House; weekdays 10 to 4 and Sundays 2 to 4 November 1 to April 30, (closed Tuesday and holidays), daily 10 to 6 except Mondays May 1 to October 31; 25 cents.

Hichborn was a prosperous cousin of Paul Revere's who occupied this nearby fine red-brick residence with big chimneys, fireplaces in every room, and one of the first cove ceilings in the Colonies. If the date is correct, it is one of the rare remaining pre-Georgian brick houses in New England. Unfortunately, the most remarkable one in the country (the Foster-Hutchinson House) was torn down here as long ago as 1833.

HARRISON GRAY OTIS HOUSE (1795)

141 Cambridge Street; daily, 9 to 4:45, except Saturdays and holidays; 25 cents; S.P.N.E.A.

Bulfinch undoubtedly did this one, the only "open" house on the Hill today. Don't dream of missing it. Otis was a wealthy politician with a passion for stylish houses. This was his first one, but there is a second and a third. The dining room here is a special delight. There are fine collections of silver, glass, pewter, ceramics, costumes, and Shaker pieces. The house is also the home today of an organization dear to the hearts of early-house devotees, the Society for the Preservation of New England Antiquities, whose good works are duly noted most happily on many occasions in this *Guide*. They administer more than half a hundred old New England houses; many, like this one, of great distinction.

The first Harrison Gray Otis house has one of the finest Adam dining rooms in America.

THE SECOND HARRISON GRAY OTIS HOUSE (*1800*)

85 Mt. Vernon Street; on request by letter, December through April; Miss Evelyn Sears.

Furnished and used as a lived-in home, with pieces of many periods and countries, this house offers a rare opportunity without and within to enjoy at first hand the Bulfinch flavor and distinction.

TOWNSEND HOUSE (*1820*)

48 Chestnut Street; by appointment; Mr. and Mrs. Charles Townsend.

Built on land that was once a terraced garden, this house has two flights of stairs below the first floor. A tall, handsome Federal-style dwelling, with stunning interiors, furnishings of museum quality, and one of the finest small city gardens in the country.

At Numbers 54 and 55 BEACON STREET you pass a pair of houses by Asher Benjamin, now occupied by the Colonial Dames; at 45 the THIRD HARRISON GRAY OTIS HOUSE, by Bulfinch; at Number 39 and Number 40 two beauties, most probably by Bulfinch, now the WOMEN'S CITY CLUB. The big gray wood-and-brick 1805 house, with its black shutters, at 14 Walnut Street, was the home of Ellery Sedgwick, famous editor. Two notable houses on Mt. Vernon Street, in addition to the "Otis Number Two," are Number 57 and Number 59, once the homes of Charles Francis Adams, Civil War Ambassador to England, and of Thomas Bailey Aldrich, respectively. As for privately maintained LOUISBURG SQUARE, with its cobbled paving, there is nothing quite like it this side of London.

There is a galaxy of early rooms to be seen at the MUSEUM OF FINE ARTS, among them two McIntire rooms from Peabody, with the master's exquisite carving; a wonderfully paneled fireplace wall from Fiskdale; and seventeenth-century rooms with massive medieval framing from Ipswich and West Box-

ford—a good introduction to the many wonders you will walk into throughout Massachusetts.

¶ *Arlington (out past Cambridge)*

JASON RUSSELL HOUSE (*1680*)

7 Jason Street; daily 2 to 5 except Mondays, April to November; contribution; Arlington Historical Society.

The bloodiest fighting on April 19, 1775, in what is now this Boston suburb between Cambridge and Lexington, took place in and about the Jason Russell House, when a group of Minute Men were caught off guard by the British. Jason Russell and eleven others were killed and lie together in a common grave in the Arlington burying ground. The house has been put into pre-Revolutionary shape, as a well-to-do farmer's home. Many relics, some Paul Revere silver, and plenty of bullet holes.

¶ *Brookline (out Beacon Street to Harrow)*

EDWARD DEVOTION HOUSE (*c. 1680*)

347 Harvard Street; Saturday afternoons 2 to 4, other times by appointment; 25 cents.

This is one of the few remaining houses that Paul Revere passed on his midnight ride, and on the annual reenactment of the ride a stop is made at the doorstep.

¶ *Cambridge*

(out Memorial Drive)

In addition to the houses listed below, after you leave the Longfellow House you will certainly want to stroll down Brattle Street, once known as "The King's Highway" and for a long time as "Tory Row." It is a street of ample lawns and ancient trees, and many of its houses still breathe the opulent yet conservative living habits of their early inhabitants. At 153 stands the handsome THOMAS LEE HOUSE (1685), at 159 the NICHOLAS LEE HOUSE, an interesting oblong mass painted brown, set off by ivory-colored corner quoins and broad doorway and a central chimney twelve feet in width. At 94 Brattle is the massive BELCHER HOUSE, an impressive yellow frame mansion with main entrances at either end; the east end, dated 1700, retains its fine features. The READ HOUSE (1725) is at Number 55, and at 76 is the SAMUEL LONGFELLOW HOUSE (1725), of the brother of the poet.

In addition to the houses listed below, you may want to stroll past the following. The large yellow mansion with the balustraded roof at the corner of Mt. Auburn Street and Elmwood Avenue (1767) was the HOME OF JAMES RUSSELL LOWELL, built for an Englishman named Oliver, the last of the King's deputies here.

BRATTLE HOUSE (c. 1735)

42 Brattle Street; Monday to Saturday, 9 to 5 (except when rooms are being used for courses); Cambridge Social Union.

The first of the stylish eighteenth-century houses still standing here has quite a lot of its style still remaining; a three-story clap-boarded gambrel with dormers, it has some fine paneling and a handsome staircase. Brattle was one of the prominent royalists who left Cambridge in a hurry when Boston was evacuated by the British. Then for a while in the Emersonian era, when it was occupied by Margaret Fuller, brilliant editor, teacher, and critic, the house was aglow with the literary lights who clustered where today the Cambridge Social Union holds its classes.

LONGFELLOW HOUSE (*1759*)

105 Brattle Street; daily 10 to 5, Saturdays 12 to 5, Sundays 1 to 5; 30 cents; Longfellow Memorial Trust.

The last and most elegant of this Cambridge triumvirate is the great square white and yellow mansion in which the poet Longfellow lived. A royalist, Maj. Henry Vassall, built it, but, like Mr. Brattle mentioned above, left it suddenly one night fifteen years later with all his Tory neighbors. The next occupant was Gen. George Washington, who managed to pick some very handsome headquarters here and there. The side piazzas and other additions were made right after the Revolution by Dr. Andrew Craigie, Apothecary General

Long before this famous old house became the home of Longfellow, it served as Washington's headquarters during the early days of the Revolution.

of the Army, whose widow, following the doctor's financial failure and death, rented out rooms to Harvard students and other eligibles—among the latter Longfellow, in 1837, when he was a young professor. When the poet married after a seven-year courtship, the bride's father gave the pair the house as a wedding present; and here Longfellow lived until he died in 1882. Still lived in by his grandson, the house has been kept exactly as it was during the poet's lifetime.

COOPER-FROST-AUSTIN HOUSE (*1657*)

21 Linnaean Street 1 mile from Harvard Square, to left of Massachusetts Avenue; Mondays, Thursdays, and Fridays 2 to 5 June to October, Mondays and Thursdays 2 to 5 November to May; 25 cents; S.P.N.E.A.

This earliest house in Cambridge is a seventeenth-century beauty, of size and substance, with great modesty of manner, built by Deacon John Cooper. It is a two-story, foursquare white clapboard structure with monumental central chimney. Expertly maintained to set it all off to the best advantage both inside and out.

WADSWORTH HOUSE (*1726*)

Open during office hours, except during commencements; Harvard Alumni Association.

This big yellow house, full of Cambridge character (for yellow-painted clapboards, green shutters, and white trim combined to make a favorite Cambridge color scheme, as you can see), was built by Benjamin Wadsworth, the first of nine Harvard presi-

The Royall house in Medford is adorned with a great variety of architectural delights.

dents to live in it; Wadsworth's tenure was 1725–1737, while Edward Everett's (the last one to live here) was 1846–1849. A Stuart portrait of E. E. as a young man hangs in the Board Room to the right of the front door. The visiting preacher used to have his rooms here; students have lived here in the past, among them Emerson and "Light Horse Harry" Lee. The interior woodwork (and it is very handsome) has been well preserved, and there are eighteenth-century furnishings in most of the rooms and offices. The house is now used mainly as the alumni center.

¶ Chelsea (out across the Mystic River Bridge past Bunker Hill and the Constitution)

GOVERNOR BELLINGHAM-CARY HOUSE (*1659*)

34 Parker Street; by appointment; Mr. Charles W. Bennett, 20 Lawrence Street.

This is the house built here by a seventeenth-century colonial governor named Richard Bellingham, whose eccentricities you will hear about at the house. In the siege of Boston it was the last outpost of the Continental Army's left wing. Later the original frame structure was somewhat refashioned, but from the two periods there is some fine paneling, much original hardware, and a secret passage.

¶ Dorchester (southeast section of city)

CLAPP HOUSE (*1806*) *or* EMMA M. E. REED MEMORIAL

195 Boston Street; by appointment with caretaker; Dorchester Historical Society.

CLAPP HOUSE (*seventeenth century*)

Adjoining on Willow Street; same as above; librarian in charge.

The two adjoining Clapp Houses—one early, one late—here in this southeast section of Boston, give a good opportunity to compare the building manners of the late seventeenth and early nineteenth centuries. The later one is being restored with furnishings of the Federal period; the earlier has an interesting contemporary in the James Blake House (1648) on Edward Everett Square, where the caretaker lives.

The country seat of Governor Gore out Waltham way is once again a wonder of the opulence and sophistication of the early 1800s hereabouts.

¶ *Medford (north on Route 1)*

This northerly suburb, where some of the first New England bricks were baked and the first rum was distilled, has two "open" houses of particular and contrasting interest: the seventeenth-century Tufts House, and the eighteenth-century Royall House, the former built as a garrison house, and the latter as a wealthy merchant's establishment.

PETER TUFTS HOUSE, *formerly*
CRADDOCK HOUSE (*1678*)

> *350 Riverside Avenue, near Spring Street; Mondays, Thursdays, and Fridays 2 to 5 June to October, Mondays and Thursdays 2 to 5 November to May; 25 cents; S.P.N.E.A.*

A big gambrel-roof house of early brick, with a pair of first- and second-story portholes at either end of the front face that are architecturally delightful. Beautiful oak beams and furnishings to fit.

ISAAC ROYALL HOUSE (*1732*)

> *15 George Street; daily 2 to 5 except Mondays and Fridays, May 1 to October 1; 50 cents and 25 cents; Royall House Association.*

Be prepared to see quite a house when you visit the mansion Col. Isaac Royall built for himself around a seventeenth-century farmhouse after he came here from the West Indies, with twenty-seven slaves, to live in style. The brick ends gable up into great chimneys. The full three-story eastern façade is filled with richly framed windows, corniced and quoined; the western façade has one of the first rusticated wooden walls in the Colonies, with end pilasters to the eaves. From a lookout in the attic roof, Mollie Stark kept her eye on the British troops over on the Mystic shore, while Gens. Washington, Charles Lee, Sullivan, and Stark held councils of war in the richly paneled and furnished rooms below —rooms that are once more as they were. There are commodious slave quarters on the grounds. It was Gen. Charles Lee who left Washington at the Vassall House (some say in a huff) and made this mansion his headquarters.

¶ *Watertown & Waltham*
(*out Route 20*)

ABRAHAM BROWNE, JR., HOUSE
(*1698, addition 1720*)

> *562 Main Street; daily 2 to 5, except Saturdays; 25 cents; S.P.N.E.A.*

The first and by far the oldest of the three important houses in this area contains rooms and furnishings from both seventeenth- and eighteenth-century times, and a fireplace whose heroic dimensions make you wish we had the courage to do things this way today. The house is rightly proud of its three-part casements of rare early design. And while you are here, ask the custodians to show you the McIntire stable brought from the Derby farm at Peabody. It contains a nice collection of early carriages.

GORE PLACE (*1804*)

Main and Gore Streets; daily 10 to 5 except Mondays, Sundays 2 to 5; 50 cents; Gore Place Society, Inc.

Next, where Watertown and Waltham meet, you come to the showpiece of Massachusetts, a country mansion of princely appearance. And so it is, as you will see— in its scope and scale, its park, its style (very English in the Regency or Adam manner), its furnishings. It is filled with fascinating contrasts. Along with rooms for entertaining in the grand manner, there are family rooms of true intimacy, the Gores being people whose home provided as well for their private life as their public one. Christopher Gore was obviously a very wealthy personage—lawyer, diplomat, and a Governor of Massachusetts. Daniel Webster was a law clerk in Gore's office, and the elegant chandelier in the state dining room of Gore Place today is from the later law offices of the great orator. The whole effect is choice; the banquet hall impressive, and the staircase stunning.

LYMAN HOUSE *or* THE VALE (*1795*)

Lyman and Beaver Streets; Wednesday through Saturday 11 to 5, May 19 to September 11; 50 cents; S.P.N.E.A.

Farther along, and off to the right, the Lyman House is of equal eloquence in its own way, having been designed by the great Samuel McIntire of Salem. This was the farthest from Salem that the celebrated woodcarver ever worked. The master's carving is, as ever, a joy. The ballroom is one of his best, and the bow parlor has some rare McIntire furniture. The setting is delightful; the McIntire stable and the old greenhouses and gardens are reminders of the style in which the Lymans lived.

As an indication of Gore house glamour, the circular staircase leading up from the marble-floored entrance hall will do very nicely.

Out beyond Gore Place, the Lyman house by McIntire stands up imposingly from its lovely sylvan setting; fine interiors, fascinating dependencies.

¶ *Winthrop (out past airport; bear right on Bennington and Saratoga Streets)*

DEANE WINTHROP HOUSE (*1637*)
> *40 Shirley Street; Wednesday and Friday afternoons, 3 to 5; 10 cents; Winthrop Historical and Improvement Association.*

This old peninsular community of the metropolitan area lies just across the harbor waters from the airport, and the little unassuming Deane Winthrop House here just happens to be one of the very first salt boxes in America. At 49 Siren Street you can see, in passing, the red-brick house that John Hancock built as his summer home in 1756. Frequent partakers of the famous fish-and-game dinners served at the old Tufts Inn were four old friends named Emerson, Lowell, Holmes, and Longfellow.

NORTH OF BOSTON

Amesbury; Andover; Beverly; Boxford; Danvers; Gloucester; Groton; Haverhill & East Haverhill; Ipswich; Lowell; Lynn; Marblehead; Melrose; Manchester; Newbury; Newburyport; North Andover; Peabody; Reading; Rockport; Rowley; Salem; Saugus; Topsfield; Wakefield; Wenham; Woburn

¶ *Amesbury (up near the New Hampshire corner on Route 110)*

MACY-COLBY HOUSE (*1654*)
> *259 Main Street; Wednesdays 2 to 5, June 1 to August 31; contributions; Bartlett Cemetery Association.*

A fine little salt box, delightfully kept up. It has a fireplace ten feet wide. The house figures in Whittier's poem *The Exile*, describing how Thomas Macy was banished to Nantucket in 1655 for sheltering Quakers here in a storm.

In the 1860s Mary Baker Eddy lived and worked practically next door in the SQUIRE BAGLEY HOMESTEAD.

JOHN GREENLEAF WHITTIER HOUSE (*before 1836*)
> *86 Friend Street; daily 10 to 5, Sundays by appointment; Whittier Home Association.*

The house where the poet lived for fifty-six years is special mostly for its Whittier associations—associations that permeate the town and the countryside all the way to Haverhill.

¶ *Andover* (*23 miles up from Boston on Route 28*)

DEACON AMOS BLANCHARD HOUSE (*1819*)

> *97 Main Street; daily; contribution; Miss Caroline Underhill.*

A big foursquare house in the Federal style, attractively fenced, and fittingly furnished with local pieces from as far back as the late 1600s.

A mile away, on Argilla Road, is the 1680 BENJAMIN ABBOTT FARMSTEAD, weathered and worn, but soon to be restored. Don't miss it.

¶ *Beverly* (*turn south off 128 onto 97*)

BALCH HOUSE (*1638, later additions*)

> *448 Cabot Street; daily 10 to 4 and Sundays 2 to 4 June 15 to September 15, other times by appointment; 25 cents and 10 cents; Beverly Historical Society.*

Said to be the oldest New England house with a recorded history, both the house and its history worth looking into. It is part of the record that John Balch built it for the bride he went all the way back to England to fetch.

HALE HOUSE (*1694*)

> *39 Hale Street; daily 10:30 to 4:30 except Sundays, Mondays, and holidays June 15 to September 15, other times by appointment; Beverly Historical Society.*

This place clearly shows how radically styles had begun to change even before the seventeenth century was over. Under its gambrel roof the goodly wife of the Reverend John Hale, an early ancestor of the patriot Nathan and of Edward Everett, was accused of witchcraft—a canard so preposterous as finally to cause the persecutions, one and all, to collapse.

JOHN CABOT MANSION-HOUSE (*1781*)

> *117 Cabot Street; daily 10 to 4 July and August, Saturdays 10 to 4 rest of year; Beverly Historical Society.*

A full-blown foursquare Georgian mansion of brick, with monumental chimneys, captain's walk, and the formality that went with a wealthy merchant's town house of the time. A very handsome sight, with some finely furnished rooms.

¶ *Boxford* (*left on Topsfield Road off Route 1*)

HOLYOKE-FRENCH HOUSE (*1760*)

> *Elm Street and Topsfield Road; Sundays 3 to 5 May 1 to November 1, or on request to custodian; 25 cents; Boxford Historical Society.*

The proportions of this great gambrel-roof house are truly impressive. Mt. Holyoke College was named after the great-grandfather of its builder, and in it are many heirlooms of the French family who followed the Holyoke occupancy—some good primitives, dolls, and toys, and in the barn a fine collection of early farm tools.

¶ *Danvers*
(*turn north off 128 onto 97*)

There are many good early houses here which are private homes to be visited only on special occasions, but at the Historical Society in the Page House readers of the *Guide* will be furnished with directions for seeing them. It was from Danvers, by the way, that "The Lindens" was removed in 1927 to Washington, D.C.

PAGE HOUSE (*antique shop*) (*1754*)

> *11 Page Street; Saturday afternoons and by appointment; small charge.*

This place shows comparatively recent modifications through which the good original gambrel-roof house emerges. Contains collections of antiques and historical relics.

JUDGE SAMUEL HOLTEN HOUSE (*1670*)

> *Holten and Center Streets; preferably by appointment; contribution; General Israel Putnam Chapter, D.A.R.*

A seventeenth-century house now grown into a dwelling of considerable substance, containing many early furnishings and features of interest including the partitioned privy at the rear, with two doors and seven seats.

REBECCA NURSE HOUSE (*1678*)

> *149 Pine Street; daily 10 to 5 or by appointment, mid-June to mid-October; 25 cents; S.P.N.E.A.*

The wife of Francis Nurse was taken from her house here and hanged in Salem as a witch. A fine old clapboard house, filled with much honest workmanship of a simple, primitive nature. The tragic circumstances of its early history are in striking contrast to its present serenity.

SAMUEL FOWLER HOUSE (*1810*)

166 High Street; Wednesdays 3 to 5 and Saturdays 10 to 5, other times by appointment; 25 cents; S.P.N.E.A.

This is a real beauty of a large brick house, designed with uncommon restraint and immensely rewarding within for such features as its notable woodwork and the Zuber wallpapers of 1829. It is furnished in excellent style and there are fine collections of good china and pewter. The Fowlers were an old family hereabouts, an ancestor, Philip Fowler, having settled at Ipswich in 1632.

¶ *Gloucester* (*out past the end of Route 128*)

BEAUPORT (*1907*)

Eastern Point Boulevard; weekday afternoons for guided tours only (2:30, 3:30, and 4:30), June through September (closed Sundays and holidays); $1.00 and 50 cents; S.P.N.E.A.

This is an extraordinary museum out here by the sea, containing a surprising assortment of period rooms assembled by a collector named Henry Sleeper, which are housed in this late château-like structure made up of many parts and pieces of architecture. It has been called the most fascinating house in America, and not without some justification. There is plenty of color and variety, and no matter what your taste, you are almost certain to find it entertaining.

SARGENT-MURRAY-GILMAN-HOUGH HOUSE (*1768, remodeled 1916*)

49 Middle Street; weekdays 11 to 5, July 1 to September 25; 30 cents; Sargent-Murray-Gilman-Hough House Association.

The handsome hip-on-gambrel house that Winthrop Sargent built as a pre-Revolutionary wedding present for his daughter Judith brings you back from the theatrical to the serene. It discloses with dignity and warmth, and with just a pleasant touch of ostentation in its heroic corner pilasters, how homelike a stylish early house could be.

CAPE ANN HISTORICAL HOUSE (*c. 1805*)

27 Pleasant Street; daily 11 to 4, June to September; 25 cents; Cape Ann Scientific, Literary and Historical Association.

This place reflects without and within the typical seaport town house of Federal times. It is simple, straightforward, and nautical in its neatness; even the quoins that decorate its corners do so with crisp and clean restraint. Inside, it is furnished in a way that old seafarers would admire.

RIGGS HOUSE (*1638–1700*)

By appointment; 50 cents.

The oldest dwelling in the vicinity, it was the first schoolhouse of the town, and there are collections of early household equipment.

¶ *Groton* (*turn right on Route 110, then 40 miles out on Route 2*)

GOVERNOR BOUTWELL HOUSE (*1851, remodeled 1938*)

Main Street; Saturday afternoons 3 to 5, June to November; Groton Historical Society.

An interesting frame house of a late but fascinating period, painted yellow with green trim. A nice piece of preservation, portraying the background of a notable of this community.

¶ *Haverhill & East Haverhill* (*up near the New Hampshire line*)

THE BUTTONWOODS (*1814*)

240 Water Street; Tuesdays, Thursdays, and Saturdays, 2 to 5; contribution; Haverhill Historical Society.

"The Buttonwoods" is one of those orderly, square two-story hip-roof houses that the builders who used the books of Asher Benjamin did so well in the early 1800s. The rooms are foursquare and capacious, well lighted by four large windows apiece. Some of them here are finely furnished and filled with items of local historical interest.

JOHN WARD HOUSE (*before 1645*)

240 Water Street; Tuesdays, Thursdays, and Saturdays, 2 to 5; voluntary contribution; Haverhill Historical Society.

The little white Ward House next door is twice as old as "The Buttonwoods."

The bedroom of the grand old Whipple house in Ipswich.

The SPILLER HOUSE, at Groveland and Water Streets, and the AYER HOMESTEAD, overlooking the green, are both seventeenth-century houses worthy of attention.

JOHN GREENLEAF WHITTIER HOMESTEAD (*1688*)

> *Route 110 just off Amesbury Road; daily 10 to 6 except Mondays, Sundays 1 to 6; 25 cents and 15 cents; Trustees of the John Greenleaf Whittier Homestead.*

Three miles out on Route 110, the Whittier birthplace is architecturally a much more enjoyable house than the one at Amesbury in which the poet spent so much of his later life. This is a typical New England farmhouse in the best tradition—a fitting birthplace for this particular poet. Also, as you might know, it is the scene of *Snowbound.* Filled with Whittier belongings.

¶ Ipswich

The assortment of seventeenth-century houses here is probably as large as any in the country. Eight houses in all can be visited. One is a sea captain's house from the mid-1800s and one a wealthy merchant's mansion from the century before that; but all the rest are of the 1600s. If you come here on Seventeenth Century Day in August (write the Waters Memorial for dates), you will hit the jackpot, for many more will be open.

LAKEMAN-JOHNSON HOUSE (*before 1850*)

> *16 East Street; Tuesdays, Thursdays, and Saturdays, 10 to 5, mid-June through September; contribution; S.P.N.E.A.*

This is the sea captain's house, the first but by far the latest in our Ipswich listing. It is being kept up in character simply and attractively.

THOMAS FRANKLIN WATER MEMORIAL, *formerly* JOHN HEARD HOUSE (*1795*)

> *Daily 10 to 5, except Mondays, Sundays 1 to 5, April to November; 75 cents; Ipswich Historical Society.*

Likewise late for Ipswich, this foursquare three-story house also belonged to an old seafaring family. It has many attractive features like the Chinese Chippendale stair rail and the furnishings of its period.

JOHN WHIPPLE HOUSE (*1640, 1670, and 1700*)

> *53 South Main Street; daily 10 to 5, except Mondays, Sundays 1 to 5, April to November; 50 cents; Ipswich Historical Society.*

This famous and venerable house is able to show off to wonderful advantage the character of our home-building pioneers. The way they worked those massive oaken beams and girders and posts into an everlasting frame makes it plain that these people felt they were here to stay. And, of course, what time has done to the color and feel of that oak is a treat to the senses of sight and touch. Fortunately, the house has not been made into a piece of period perfectionism. The furnishings are complete in all that matters—possessions that any ancient house would acquire, with discrimination, in the course of several centuries.

THE HOUSE OF THE ORANGE SHUTTERS (*1680 and 1715*)

106 High Street; by written or phone appointment; may be seen 11 to 12 and 1 to 4 (phone: 889M); 50 cents; Mr. and Mrs. Roy Lee Bulger.

This house offers a rare opportunity to see how well these ancient dwellings can be adapted to modern living.

EMERSON-HOWARD HOUSE (c. *1648*)

Turkey Shore Road at eastern end of Green Street bridge; Monday through Thursday June 15 to October 15, other times by appointment; contribution; S.P.N.E.A.

The house that Thomas Emerson built here more than a hundred and fifty years before his famous philosopher descendant was born in Boston has the narrow, weathered siding, hewn overhang, and vast framing members that become a familiar sight in Ipswich. Sparsely but expertly furnished.

PRESTON-FOSTER HOUSE (c. *1640*)

6 Water Street; daily 10 to 5 except Mondays June 15 to October 15, rest of year by appointment; contribution; S.P.N.E.A.

The pitch of the roof of the Preston-Foster House has been left as it was when thatching was still the habit, showing how much steeper a roof had to be before shingles superseded straw. Very simply maintained at the moment, but many things about the house itself claim your attention.

HART HOUSE (*an inn*) (*1640*)

Line Brook Road, 0.7 mile off Route 1A; April to December; Mrs. Elizabeth L. Marr.

No doubt the oldest house in the country now used as an inn. A first-floor room is at the Metropolitan, and a second-floor room at Winterthur—a rather wry kind of recognition; but both rooms have been faithfully reconstructed here. It is all furnished with feeling. An excellent inn.

Ipswich itself and the Whipple house here make a real seventeenth-century combination.

STRAWBERRY HILL *or* PROCTOR HOUSE (*c. 1670*)

> *Jeffrey's Neck Road, 2 miles from center of town; by appointment only; Mr. and Mrs. Daniel S. Wendell.*

The Wendells rescued this from its town site and took it to its present hilltop location two miles out of town. There, as "Strawberry Hill," today very much a home, it stands as one of the most remarkable examples in America of the seventeenth-century style and structure which followed Elizabethan lines. It is a great privilege to see it and one of the choice pleasures of a *Guide*-d visit to Ipswich.

¶ *Lowell*

WHISTLER HOUSE (*an art gallery*) (*1823*)

> *243 Worthen Street; daily 1 to 5, except Mondays; Lowell Art Association.*

This simple and retiring birthplace of the painter—who was anything but—is primarily interesting for its Whistleriana and for its art exhibits.

¶ *Lynn*

HYDE-MILLS HOUSE (*c. 1838*)

> *125 Green Street; by appointment with custodian there part of every day except Sundays; Lynn Historical Society.*

Exhibits in this good-looking house include an early Lynn shoeshop, early household objects, a few period rooms, and a McIntire eagle. The lack of lengthy and elaborate descriptions, we might reiterate here, does not indicate lack of excellence or things of interest. To this general rule the Hyde-Mills House is no exception.

¶ *Marblehead*

Just to pick your way through the tangled streets and lanes of this famous and delightful old harbor town is a pleasure. And every now and then you will be stopped in your tracks by the style and polish of a fine old mansion from the days when commerce by sea was a paying proposition here.

This extraordinary example of a seventeenth-century house was moved from Ipswich to its present location outside the town, restored to perfection, and named Strawberry Hill.

COL. JEREMIAH LEE MANSION
(*1768*)
161 Washington Street; weekdays May 15 to October 15, Sundays 2 to 5 July and August; 50 cents; Marblehead Historical Society, Miss Gretchen Girdler.

This ranks among the finest old homes in America. The stateliness of its rusticated exterior is more than matched by its inside. One of the most monumental of domestic staircases mounts from the immense hall, the walls dramatically covered by paper painted in England. Although Lee lived in princely fashion here, his death was due to exposure: having been ambushed by the British while on a Revolutionary mission out beyond Boston, he was forced to flee his lodging in very little clothing.

KING HOOPER MANSION
(*1728–1745*)
Hooper Street; daily 2 to 5, except Mondays; 30 cents; Marblehead Arts Association.

This is another luxurious home, of nearly the same scale. Its formal front, beautifully quoined and corniced, almost conceals an earlier tall Hooper House that had to be turned endwise on its lot to make street room for this more imposing addition. The ballroom is used for art exhibitions.

HOOPER-PARKER HOUSE
(*before 1775*)
181 Washington Street; Mondays, Wednesdays, and Fridays 2 to 4, June 15 to September 15; 25 cents; S.P.N.E.A.

This other Hooper House has once again that stateliness and charm which mark these fine Marblehead mansions.

As you walk around, keep your eyes open for the PEDRICK MANSION, at 52 Washington Street; for the COL. WILLIAM R. LEE, at 185; and the MANSION HOUSE, at 187.

¶ Melrose

PHINEAS UPHAM HOUSE (*1703*)
225 Upham Street; by appointment with Mrs. W. C. Rogers (phone: Melrose 4-3335); contribution; The Upham Family Society, Inc.

The weather-darkened siding of the house that Phineas Upham built in what is now this Boston suburb has been saved by a society formed by his present-day descend-

The picturesque town of Marblehead has a wonderful collection of Early American homes, but none with quite the nobility of the Lee mansion, or one with such impressive interiors and handsome furnishings.

ants to restore and perpetuate their family heirloom.

¶ Manchester

TRASK HOUSE (*1830*)
12 Union Street; Wednesdays 2 to 5, July 1 to August 31; Manchester Historical Society.

A Late Federal house, prettily fenced and balustraded as becomes this attractive North Shore town, containing exhibits of a nautical nature, including a sailor-made model of the frigate *Constitution*.

¶ Newbury

TRISTRAM COFFIN HOUSE (*original ell c. 1651, later additions in the same century*)
14 High Road; Mondays, Wednesdays, and Fridays 2 to 5, other times by appointment; S.P.N.E.A.

Of the three listed here, the Coffin House probably depicts best the household life in those early days. It remained in the Coffin family almost three hundred years—possibly a record in this country.

SHORT HOUSE (*1733*)

33 High Road; daily 10 to 5, Tuesdays and Thursdays 2 to 5, mid-June through September, other times by appointment; 25 cents; S.P.N.E.A.

Recommended are the red door and window trim on the weathered face of the Short House. The ends are brick; inside there is a lot of excellent paneling.

SWETT-ILSLEY HOUSE (*1670*)

4 and 6 High Road; Tuesday through Saturday, 12 to 7; S.P.N.E.A.

This place has at one time been a tavern, a chocolate works, and is now, at least in part, a tearoom—recommended along with the house.

¶ *Newburyport*

High Street here is a picture of the prosperity that came to the town in the days when this was a shipbuilder's paradise.

PETTINGILL-FOWLER HOUSE (*1793*)

High and Winter Streets; daily, except Sundays and holidays, June through September; 10 cents; Historical Society of Old Newbury.

In outward appearance this is an exception to the general run of tall, square, three-story High Street houses—shallower, lower, with a hip-on-gambrel roof. Its date would account for the difference; most of the others came along twenty-five years later. There is nothing better in town than its drawing-room mantel.

TRACY HOUSE (*1771*)

94 State Street, 9 to 9, daily except Sunday; city of Newburyport.

This is still earlier—Late Georgian in character. It is the public library, and the directors' room with its carving and its alcove windows is something to look at.

BRADBURY-SPALDING HOUSE

(*1788–1791*)

28 Green Street; Mondays, Wednesdays, and Fridays 10 to 5, other times by appointment; S.P.N.E.A.

Except for its roof, which is a regular and very good gambrel, the Bradbury-Spalding House has much in common with the Pettingill House, its contemporary. Compare, for instance, the drawing-room mantels.

The collections and the furnishings are of special interest.

¶ *North Andover (turn off Route 28 at Andover)*

THE COTTAGE *or* SAMUEL DALE STEVENS MEMORIAL (*1790*)

153 Academy Road; Mondays, Wednesdays, and Saturdays, 2 to 5; North Andover Historical Society.

They don't come any neater and trimmer than this, inside or out.

BRADSTREET HOUSE (*1666–1667*)

179 Osgood Street; Wednesdays and by appointment; North Andover Historical Society, Mrs. Woodbury K. Howe (custodian and tenant).

This is an unusually interesting house, not only as a dwelling, but because of those whom it housed. Simon and Anne Bradstreet, ardent Puritans, came here in Governor Winthrop's party on the *Arabella* in 1630. Simon Bradstreet, as the first secretary of the colony and later its Governor, was a man of importance in his day, but it remains for time to tell that it was his fragile wife, Anne, who will best be remembered. Anne, the mother of eight children, lived to be only sixty. But she left a small body of poetry which has increasingly redounded to her fame. She is the first American poet. Her poetry was published in England in 1650, and there became so popular that the bookseller catalogued it as "the most vendible book." Conrad Aiken, in his *Comprehensive Anthology of American Poetry* (1944), devotes twelve pages to her poems, four to Lowell, six to Whittier, and eight to Longfellow.

¶ *Peabody (at intersection of Routes 1 and 128)*

GEN. GIDEON FOSTER HOUSE

(*between 1808 and 1815*)

35 Washington Street; Wednesdays 2 to 5, July 1 to September 30; Peabody Historical Society.

A pleasant example of the tall, three-story, hip-roof house so numerous hereabouts. They vary in distinction; this one being not quite the equal of the High Street houses in Newburyport, though they vary too.

¶ *Reading* (*just north of Route 128 on Route 28*)

PARKER TAVERN (*1694*)

103 Washington Street; Sundays 2 to 5 June 1 to October 1, and by appointment with Mrs. Robert Barclay; contribution; Reading Antiquarian Society.

It is the unusual claim of this weather-darkened salt box that "no famous people have either lived or visited here." It is preserved simply as a typical early homestead, and filled with fascinating collections of woodenware, lighting devices, children's toys, and early household paraphernalia.

¶ *Rockport* (*out on the point of Cape Ann*)

OLD GARRISON HOUSE *or* WITCH HOUSE (*possibly c. 1675*)

188 Granite Street; open to students of architecture by written request, May to November; Mrs. Oliver Williams and daughter Mrs. McKinney.

The Garrison House, built of logs hewn square to resist attack, with a second-story overhang, was used as a garrison during King Philip's War, but is now a summer home.

OLD CASTLE (*1715–1792*)

Castle Lane; Saturdays and Sundays 2 to 5, July and August; Pigeon Cove Village Improvement Society.

How the fine old shingled house with its overhang and added lean-to came to be called the "Old Castle" is worth a question when you call to see its collections of early household equipment.

¶ *Rowley* (*between Ipswich and Newburyport*)

CHAPLIN-CLARK-WILLIAMS HOUSE (*1671*)

Route 133, Bradford Street between Newburyport Turnpike and Old Bay Road; by appointment with custodian; contribution; S.P.N.E.A.

PLATTS-BRADSTREET HOUSE

(*c. 1670; restored in eighteenth century and again in 1919*)

Main Street; on request, June 1 to October 1; contribution; Rowley Historical Society.

The unpretentious Chaplin farmhouse has features of historical and structural interest, and, together with the larger Platts-

Bradstreet House, which has a beautiful setting, makes a pleasant pause on the way.

¶ Salem

Largely because of the work of the master craftsman, Samuel McIntire, connoisseurs consider this the treasure town of the state. And when you have taken in the Peirce and Pingree Houses, walked back and forth a few times on Chestnut Street, and made your way around Washington Square, very likely you will come to the same conclusion.

But there is still the fine Georgian Derby House to visit down by the Derby wharf. And to get way back to the Salem version of the dark Elizabethan look, there are still the ancient House of Seven Gables group and other houses like the Ward and the Witch to investigate.

After the austerity of pioneer days, and the passion of witchcraft in the seventeenth century, the eighteenth century brought something that was a welcome relief in a wonderful, swashbuckling way: namely, trade with Europe and the West Indies, in fleet little ships that were Salem-built to fit snug Salem harbor. And from the wealth that began piling up on the Derby wharf was built the lovely Georgian house right across the way from the wharf; a house, however, not to be compared in size and glamour with the great Derby Mansion by McIntire that went up on Essex Street forty years later, only to be torn down fifteen years after it was finished.

Then, all of a sudden, a new kind of Yankee ship was created that could outsail and outcarry the little Salem craft. What was worse, these new, deep-draft clippers needed deep-water harbors, and Salem simply didn't have one that would accommodate them. But Salem had her houses. And in time she became a big bustling modern industrial city. But by some miracle a lot of Old Salem still stands, and with it some of the finest old houses in America.

ROPES MANSION
(1719, additions 1804 and 1894)
318 Essex Street; afternoons except Sundays, Mondays, and holidays; 25 cents; Board of Trustees of Ropes Memorial.

This began as one of Salem's most important pre-Georgian houses, and in spite of alterations, its proud distinction is still strongly in evidence. In 1804 it acquired its extremely handsome fence in McIntire's best manner, even if not by the hand of the master. Filled with handsome mementos of many Salem generations.

HOUSE OF SEVEN GABLES *(1668)*
54 Turner Street; daily, 10 to 5, except Thanksgiving and Christmas; 75 cents and 30 cents to settlement work; House of Seven Gables Association.

It takes its name from Hawthorne's 1852 novel, having previously been the Turner House for almost two hundred years. It started off with four gables—two end ones and two cross ones in front. Then seafaring prosperity brought about additions that made the seven. For a while there were eight. It was in the year of the witchcraft delusions that the secret staircase was installed within the original chimney, which is now a feature of interest. It is a fascinating old house, weather-darkened and rambling, and picturesque—one of the most extensive and important of the country's Early Gothic constructional types.

RETIRE BECKETT HOUSE *(1655)*
54 Turner Street near House of Seven Gables; weekdays, 10 to 6; House of Seven Gables Settlement Association.

HATHAWAY HOUSE *(1682)*
54 Turner Street; July 1 through Labor Day (two exhibition rooms open); 15 cents; House of Seven Gables Settlement Association.

The Retire Beckett and Hathaway Houses contribute their own ancient charms to the beautiful group they now form with the House of Seven Gables.

JOHN WARD HOUSE *(1684)*
132 Essex Street; weekdays 9 to 4:15, May 1 through October 31; 25 cents; Essex Institute.

One of the same vintage, featuring the same bold cross gables and overhangs, which added much light and space to the second-floor rooms. It was moved to the Essex Institute Garden in 1909.

The House of Seven Gables will deservedly always be one of the greatest of Salem's ancient attractions.

The Derby house represents Salem's middle period at its best, a choice piece of New England Georgian.

WITCH HOUSE (*a restoration*) (*1692*)
Daily 10 to 6, June 15 to October 12; 30 cents; city of Salem.

Another one of those seventeenth-century rarities that help to put Salem in a class by itself as a storehouse of treasures, early and late alike. This is the house in which Jonathan Corwin, a judge in the witchcraft court, lived and held preliminary examinations of the accused. Now restored and furnished as it was in that fateful year.

PEIRCE-NICHOLS HOUSE (*1782*)
80 Federal Street; daily, 2 to 5, except Sundays and Mondays; 50 cents; Essex Institute.

Samuel McIntire's first enduring triumph. Probably the greatest and most elegant of the country's early wooden houses; big, white, beautiful, and bold. An incomparable craftsman, McIntire brought to his architectural conceptions a quality of naïveté which accounts for their non-academic manner—wonderfully illustrated here in this house's exterior. The wood-carving within is among McIntire's most brilliant. The furnishings do full justice to the house—which couldn't be higher praise.

DERBY HOUSE (*1762*)
168 Derby Street; daily, 10 to 5; 25 cents; National Park Service.

The Georgian gem that the great Salem maritime merchant built for his son Elias across from the long Derby wharf, was once the center of colonial seafaring trade. The oldest fine brick house in Salem, it has been faithfully restored and related to its surroundings—the RUM SHOP, the HAWKES HOUSE (a much-remodeled McIntire house that Derby didn't finish), and the CUSTOMS HOUSE, beautiful, stylish, and famous for the fact that Hawthorne worked in it for three years as surveyor of the port.

PINGREE HOUSE (*1804*)
128 Essex Street; daily; 50 cents and 25 cents; Essex Institute.

This great house came along in the latter part of McIntire's career, and here in the fine pale brick façade, set with a lovely semicircular entrance porch, the symmetry is expert in its rhythm and restraint. The carving inside is indescribably exquisite, and the rooms are among the most beautifully furnished in America, thanks to Mrs. Frances Crowninshield.

ANDREW SAFFORD HOUSE (*1818*)
13 Washington Square; to be open soon; Essex Institute.

One of Salem's largest and costliest Late Federal brick mansions. High, wide, and handsome, it has a double balustrade whose decorative purpose was to minimize the roof—it being a foible of the Federal style

Considered by many to be McIntire's masterpiece, the Peirce-Nichols house is naturally one of the wonders of Salem.

that roofs, like petticoats, should not show. Now in process of restoration, its garden is connected with that of the Pingree House, around the corner.

THOMAS WOODBRIDGE HOUSE (*1810*)

48 Bridge Street; not always open; occupied by a dealer in antiques.

The Woodbridge House has some McIntire paneling, as has the earlier DEAN HOUSE— now the EAST INDIA, operated as an inn. The very early and picturesque DANIELS HOUSE is also an inn, while the PIONEERS' VILLAGE represents Salem at its very earliest and bitterest—an expert piece of reconstruction demonstrating the indomitable fiber of the first settlers hereabouts.

¶ *Saugus* (*between Boston and Lynn*)

OLD IRON WORKS HOUSE (*1636–1642*)

237 Central Street; daily, 10 to 5, except Thanksgiving, Christmas, and New Year's; 50 cents and 25 cents; First Iron Works Association, Inc.

An Elizabethan beauty, now restored with great skill and understanding as part of the restoration here of the first ironworks in America. It was really the ironmaster's house, furnished in true seventeenth-cen-

tury fashion—the whole instructive enterprise subsidized by the American Iron & Steel Institute, with no effort or expense spared to achieve authenticity, in a project of which the house itself is only a part.

SCOTCH BOARDMAN HOUSE (*1651*)

From Newburyport Turnpike at crossing of Saugus and Melrose Street railway, following tracks toward Melrose, Howard Street; June through September (apply to custodian); 15 cents; S.P.N.E.A.

A survival from the seventeenth century, more nearly intact than any other New England dwelling of its age. It has the overhang, the narrow, weather-darkened siding, the central immense medieval chimney, and carries lightly, movingly, its more than two and a half centuries. Someday to be fittingly restored and furnished.

¶ *Topsfield* (*off Route 1 near intersection of 97*)

PARSON CAPEN HOUSE (*1683*)

Just off village common on Howlett Street; weekdays 10 to 4:30, except Mondays, Sundays 12 to 5, May 15 to October 15, other times by appointment; 25 cents; Topsfield Historical Society.

One of the most famous, it answers closely the Scotch Boardman House description, though containing more sophisticated

touches on its exterior. It has the advantage of a more suitable setting, and is furnished in full conformity with what might be expected of a seventeenth-century parsonage. To have such a house the Capens could only have been people of dignity and distinction.

¶ *Wakefield (near Reading, just north of Boston)*

COL. JAMES HARTSHORNE HOUSE
(west end 1681, east end late 1700s)
Church Street, on Lake Quannapowitt; by appointment, at all times; voluntary contribution; Hartshorne House Association and town of Wakefield.

The Colonel Hartshorne House is a good example of a local preservation project. The home for many years of an officer in Washington's Rifle Greens, it has an unpretentious charm and a heart-warming neighborhood interest.

¶ *Wenham (off 128 above North Beverly)*

WHITEGATES *(c. 1646)*
162 Cherry Street; by written appointment only; Henry A. Erhard.

Clearly a seventeenth-century house built by a man of moderate means with neigh-

borly assistance, all of it quite amateur and "without benefit of ruler," as its present owner testifies. Of special interest as a personal restoration.

CLAFLIN-RICHARDS HOUSE *(1664)*
Opposite the village green on Main Street; Monday to Friday, 1 to 4 (closed February and legal holidays); Wenham Historical Association and Museum, Inc.

An early cross-gabled house with later alterations, and with its weathered siding now painted. Good rooms with curved-brace framing and nice paneling, and a remarkable collection of dolls and figurines.

¶ *Woburn (just north of Boston on Route 38)*

RUMFORD HOUSE *(early 1700s)*
80 Elm Street, 2 miles east of town center; daily, 2 to 5, except in winter; Rumford Historical Association.

Count Rumford's birthplace happens to be an attractive early country house, made famous by the remarkable man born here as "Benjamin Thompson," knighted by George III and made a Count of the Holy Roman Empire. He was a scientist, philanthropist, and inventor of the Rumford Roasting Oven, the last word in cooking convenience for our grandmothers.

At the left the keeping room of the Ironmaster's house at Saugus contains a mouth-watering array of Early American articles and furnishings.

When you come upon the Parson Capen house you immediately feel yourself to be in the presence of a house with an almost human personality.

SOUTH OF BOSTON

Assinippi; Attleboro; Dedham; Duxbury; South Duxbury;
Hanover Center; Hingham; Kingston; Mansfield; Medfield;
Millis; Milton; Marshfield; North Swansea; Plymouth;
Quincy; Scituate

¶ *Assinippi (at intersection of Routes 3 and 123)*

JACOBS FARMHOUSE
(1726 and 1839)
Main Street and Jacobs Lane; Mondays, Tuesdays, and Fridays 2 to 5 June to October, and by appointment with caretakers; S.P.N.E.A.

This typical early farmstead is another good demonstration of well-organized domestic arrangements in the eighteenth century. In the barns is a collection of fire apparatus of 1760 to 1900.

¶ *Attleboro (on Route 123 almost to Providence)*

OLD PECK HOUSE (*early 1700*)
North Main and Elizabeth Streets; daily by arrangement with custodian, Mrs. Myra Hoxie; Attleboro Chapter, D.A.R.

A delightful and diminutive gambrel-roof cottage, important for the motive that inspired its preservation: "Acquired as an ancient landmark . . . for keeping ancient relics and curios."

¶ *Dedham (on outskirts of Boston)*

FAIRBANKS HOUSE (*1636*)
Eastern Avenue and East Street; daily 9 to 5, May 1 to November 1; 35 cents and 15 cents; Fairbanks Family in America, Inc.

This has been called the oldest frame dwelling still standing in this country, a title very difficult to establish. Its numerous very early additions make it not only picturesque but an extraordinary document. It was lived in by one family for nearly three centuries.

DEXTER HOUSE (*1761–1763*)
699 High Street; by appointment; George C. Seybolt.

A full, foursquare Newbury-type mansion, built by a distinguished colonial merchant, this house is rich in Revolutionary lore. It has paneled rooms and a carved staircase. Very worthwhile.

The ancient Fairbanks house at Dedham makes an interesting study of a domestic establishment that has been actively lived in for more than three centuries, and for the most part by one family.

Altogether appealing in many ways, the Jabez Wilder house at Hingham is famous for its bowed roof, obviously the work of ship carpenters turned housebuilders.

¶ *Duxbury & South Duxbury*
(*off Route 3 down by Plymouth Bay*)

JOHN ALDEN HOUSE (*1653*)
> *Alden Street, near the station; daily, April 15 to November 15; 35 cents; Alden Kindred in America, Inc.*

The Alden House has always been occupied by Aldens (including John and Priscilla) and still is today. Naturally, the ancient cottage and its colonial furnishings, which housed one of America's first families, have romantic as well as eye appeal.

ALEXANDER STANDISH HOUSE
(*1666, remodeled 1946*)
> *Standish Street, South Duxbury; will show when at home; David L. Patten.*

A remarkably well-preserved shingled house with gambrel roof and central chimney, built by the eldest son of Miles Standish, who married John Alden's daughter, you will recall. Captain Standish's own house once stood nearby, but was destroyed by fire.

KING CAESAR HOUSE (*c. 1798*)
> *King Caesar Road, Powder Point; by appointment, through the summer season; Miss Alice Moran and Mr. and Mrs. Weber-Fulop.*

This great imposing white house was built by Ezra Weston, Jr., known as "King Caesar II," his father being "King Caesar I." They were shipbuilders and bankers, and practically owned Powder Point. There is a slave house in the rear, and there goes with the house the story of a secret passage leading from the slave house to the bay.

There is also a monument to Honest Dick, the horse who died at thirty-nine after serving both Caesars. Scenic papers; fine furnishings.

FOUR CORNERS (*1780*)
> *Washington Street; by appointment; 50 cents for Winslow House Fund; Mr. and Mrs. Harold E. Fitzgibbons.*

A typical Duxbury Colonial, i.e., square, with a great central chimney, "Four Corners" is of the period just preceding the more ostentatious ship captains' houses of the turn of the century.

¶ *Hanover Center*

SAMUEL STETSON HOUSE
(*1694, enlarged 1716*)
> *Near Village Green, off Route 3; 10 to 5 daily except Mondays June through October, other times by appointment; 25 cents; S.P.N.E.A.*

Portions of the original chamfered frame are still visible, though the present trim is largely of the second, or "Drummer" Stetson, period. The house has been restored, with one room serving as a memorial to the Briggs family who gave the house to the Society. Another room contains local collections.

¶ *Hingham (beyond Quincy on Hingham Bay)*

JABEZ WILDER HOUSE (*1690–1790*)
> *557 Main Street (Route 128); by appointment; Lois Williams.*

Known locally as the "Rainbow Roof House," this is sparkling white and ship-shape. It is remarkable for its bowed, convex roof, the rafters for which were bent for strength by local shipbuilders, as were the ribs of ships. The corners of the clapboard walls are neatly trimmed with wooden quoins. The original pine floor contains boards as wide as twenty-seven inches; the steep divided staircase has a shiplike look, too, and three of the rooms retain their original paneling. Built by Jabez Wilder, the house remained in the family until 1950.

THE OLD ORDINARY (*1650*)
> *19 Lincoln Street; weekdays 2 to 5, April to November; 25 cents; Hingham Historical Society.*

One of the old New England roadside inns. Well preserved, with most of the country-tavern features still intact, it is fitted out and furnished as it should be.

The OLD SHIP MEETINGHOUSE is another feature of the town.

SAMUEL LINCOLN HOUSE (*1741*)
> *182 North Street; Mondays, 2 to 5 (two rooms open); S.P.N.E.A.*

The oldest house in town, with two rooms open as a Lincoln family memorial.

¶ Kingston
> (*on Routes 3 and 3A, 4 miles above Plymouth*)

SQUIRE WILLIAM SEVER HOUSE (*1760*)
> *2 Lindent Street; by appointment several days in advance; $2.00 per person for Historic Winslow House Association; Mr. and Mrs. Arthur E. Beane, Jr.*

This is a beautifully preserved house, simple, fine, and foursquare, with a handsome doorway, all lovingly restored and most appropriately furnished.

OLD BREWSTER HOUSE (*1690*)
> *Brewster Road (intersection of 3 and 3A, about 150 yards south of sign); weekdays 10 to 5, June to October; 30 cents and 15 cents; Edward L. Singsen.*

Built by Joseph Holmes, stepson of Maj. William Bradford, who married Mary, daughter of Love and Wrestling Brewster. Now occupied by the sixth generation of Brewsters, it contains period furnishings and relics of the Brewsters from the time of the landing of the *Mayflower*.

MAJ. JOHN BRADFORD HOUSE
(*1674 and 1720*)
> *Landing Road; daily 10 to 5:30 and Sunday afternoons, July 1 to Labor Day; 35 cents and 10 cents; Jones River Village Club.*

Built when Kingston was part of Plymouth by a grandson of Governor Bradford, who chose a lovely knoll overlooking the landing on the Jones River. He moved into it as a honeymoon house with his bride Mercy Warren. Later additions were made as the family grew to nine, and the house shows the transition from leaded casements to sliding sash. There are furniture, household utensils, and tools of the period, and the looms are in operation daily.

¶ Mansfield (*on Route 140 about 30 miles south of Boston*)

FISHER-RICHARDSON HOUSE
(*built 1704, enlarged 1800*)
> *Willow Street; Saturdays and Sundays 2 to 5 and by appointment, June 15 to October 1; town of Mansfield.*

This is an interesting primitive, with a wide gambrel, and a well sweep in the yard. A good restoration, it is furnished in its period and contains exhibits of early industries.

¶ Medfield (*on 109, 7 miles below Dedham*)

PEAK HOUSE (*rebuilt 1680*)
> *Main Street; by appointment; town of Medfield.*

So called because of the sharp pitch to its once thatched roof, this little house is unfurnished, but it is an interesting and nicely restored relic, with its leaded diamond-paned windows, said to be the originals. It is the immediate successor to the similar house destroyed when King Philip's Indians burned the town of Medford in 1676.

¶ Millis (*3 miles beyond Medfield*)

BASIL GAVIN HOUSE (*c. 1740*)
> *Millis State Road; by appointment; Basil Gavin.*

A fine Colonial house built by a member of the Adams family on land deeded to him by the King, it is notable for its woodwork. The moldings and doors of the master bedroom are very good examples of early work, and a duplicate of the mantel here is in the Boston Art Museum. An annual tour has been started here which takes in seven or eight houses dating from 1691 to 1810, all of interest. Mr. Gavin will give you more information about it on request.

¶ Milton (southern environs of Boston via Route 28)

GOVERNOR BELCHER PLACE (1777)
401 Adams Street; on application to custodians, Mr. and Mrs. Nathaniel Lord; Milton Historical Society.

This is an interesting Revolutionary house, built by the widow of Governor Belcher after fire destroyed a previous house on the same spot. Not a manor house, but distinctly more than a farmhouse. Interior restoration in progress.

SUFFOLK RESOLVES HOUSE (1765 and 1780)
1350 Canton Avenue; on request to owner; Mrs. James B. Ayer.

This is where the Suffolk Resolves of 1774, one of the major acts leading to the Revolution, were signed. Built by Capt. Daniel Vose, it was brought here from Milton Lower Mills Village and completely restored.

¶ Marshfield (on 3A above Duxbury)

WINSLOW HOUSE (1699)
Careswell and Webster Streets; July 1 to September 15; 30 cents; Historic Winslow House Association.

Built by Isaac Winslow, the son and grandson of two Massachusetts governors, it was later owned by Daniel Webster, a Duxbury man. Framed with "gunstock" timbers, it has a massive chimney, wide windows, and steep stairs adorned with acorn drops that give it a Jacobean look. Some Georgian remodeling was done in 1756 by the Gen. John Winslow who had just driven the Acadians from Grand Pré, but there is also evidence of Georgian detailing in the original structure, which would make this one of the earliest examples of Georgian work in New England, if not the first.

¶ North Swansea

MARTIN HOUSE (1728)
Fall River Avenue (highway between Providence and Fall River); daily 10 to 6, May 15 to November 1; 25 cents and 15 cents; National Society of Colonial Dames of Massachusetts.

A most attractive gambrel-roof farmhouse with silvery shingles and with one of those collections of local interest inside which always manage to strike a spark.

¶ Plymouth
(36 miles south of Boston on Plymouth Bay)

There is a good deal to see here which is of a historical nature not directly connected with the houses themselves, and individuals and groups who wish to arrange for a guided tour should write for detailed information to Arthur G. Pyle, Box 1620, Plymouth. Out of season individual houses may be visited by special arrangement with their custodians.

THE WINSLOW HOUSE (1754)
Winslow and North Streets; daily 10 to 5 except Mondays, June until it gets too cold in October; donation; General Society of Mayflower Descendants.

A large white frame Georgian house with balustraded roof, very handsome and distinguished, built by Edward Winslow, grandson of Governor Winslow of the Mayflower. It is furnished in Queen Anne and early Chippendale. It was in this house that Ralph Waldo Emerson was married.

ANTIQUARIAN HOUSE (1809)
126 Water Street; daily 10 to 5, June 14 to September 11; 50 cents and 15 cents.

This mansion of the Federal period is historically a far cry from the dwellings erected here by the early arrivals. It contains collections of dolls, costumes, toys, fans, lace, and books.

PILGRIM JOHN HOWLAND HOUSE (1666 and 1750)
Sandwich Street; daily 9 to 5, May 15 to November 1; 25 cents and 15 cents.

The only house still standing in Plymouth

which was occupied by actual Pilgrims, it was the home of Jabez, son of John, who came over on the *Mayflower*. The original paint is still on the walls of the 1750 living room, and the furnishings are mostly family heirlooms. Howland descendants meet here every year to keep alive the family traditions.

OLD FORT HARLOW HOUSE (*1677*)

119 Sandwich Street; daily 10 to 5, May 30 to September 15; 30 cents and 15 cents.

A museum of life as it was lived in seventeenth-century Plymouth, and furnished in the period. There are collections of early utensils, and demonstrations are given of spinning, weaving, candlemaking, dyeing, and fireside cookery.

RICHARD SPARROW HOUSE (*1636–1640*)

42 Summer Street; daily, 10 to 5, except Sundays; 20 cents and 10 cents; Miss Katharine Alden (custodian) 42 Summer Street (phone: Plymouth 1024–M).

This restored red clapboard house is probably the oldest in Plymouth. It serves as a home and as the headquarters of a co-operative guild known as the "Plymouth Potters," and several rooms are furnished with early things.

HARLOW-HOLMES HOUSE (*1649*)

8 Winter Street; open all year; 30 cents; Harlow Family Association, Mr. and Mrs. Knowlton B. Holmes.

This ancient gambrel-roof house is now lived in by the ninth generation of the Holmes family. It is completely furnished with family pieces left by previous generations, including the captain's table from the *Mayflower* itself. Every effort has been made to preserve the house in its original form.

PLIMOUTH PLANTATION

(*a reproduction*)

On waterfront adjacent to Plymouth Rock; First House 9 to 7 May 30 to Labor Day and weekends through Thanksgiving, First Fort 9 to 7; May 30 to Labor Day and weekends through Thanksgiving; 10 cents; Mrs. Deane Eldridge (custodian).

This is an interesting reproduction project in the process of development, containing among other exhibits a typical permanent Pilgrim dwelling of the period of 1623, complete with appropriate furnishings. Plans are under way for a reconstruction of the first fort and meetinghouse of the Pilgrims; and a full-size replica of the *Mayflower* is, or will be, a feature of great interest.

This is the fascinating old home of the famous Adams family at Quincy.

Speaking of family houses, this one at Plymouth is presently sheltering its ninth generation of Holmeses.

¶ Quincy
(virtually now the southeastern section of city of Boston)

ADAMS MANSION *or* THE OLD HOUSE (*1731*)

135 Adams Street; daily 9:30 to 4:45, May 10 to November 10; 30 cents; National Park Service.

This is one of the most remarkable American family mansions of one of America's most remarkable families, and constitutes, for all to see, a document of their lives through four generations of Presidents, great statesmen, and historians. In an intimate way, it tells the story of how the Adamses lived from 1787 to 1927—from the year John Adams bought it from a grandson of wealthy Maj. Leonard Vassall, who had built it fifty-six years before, to the year Brooks Adams, the last of the family to occupy it, died. The house contains the family furnishings as they came down from generation to generation, and with them it contains some of the character and culture that made the name of this family one of our greatest.

BIRTHPLACE OF PRESIDENT JOHN ADAMS (*1663*)

129 Franklin Street; daily 10 to 5 except Mondays, April 19 to November 1; 30 cents or 50 cents; city of Quincy and Quincy Historical Society.

BIRTHPLACE OF JOHN QUINCY ADAMS (*1675*)

131 Franklin Street; same.

These two old neighboring houses of the salt-box persuasion, clapboarded and each with its great central chimney, are as simple and unpretentious as most of their contemporaries. Neither President—father or son—was born in luxury, though the family had solid standing and belonged to the only aristocracy that existed then—that of brains. Both houses are attractive in their sturdy plainness. In the later house was also born the constitution of Massachusetts.

QUINCY HOMESTEAD *or* DOROTHY Q HOUSE (*1706*)

34 Butler Road, at Hancock Avenue; daily 10 to 5, April 19 to November 1; 25 cents and 15 cents; Commonwealth of Massachusetts; Massachusetts Society of Colonial Dames.

This Early Colonial mansion, with its inklings of the Queen Anne style—hip on gambrel, the hip hidden by balustrading— has great architectural charm. Within a very feminine feeling prevails. Fine paneling and the very French wedding wallpaper that was imported for the marriage of "Dorothy Q" and John Hancock.

COL. JOSIAH QUINCY HOUSE (*1770*)

20 Muirhead Street, Wollaston; Tuesday through Friday and Sunday 11 to 5 May to October 13, other times by appointment; S.P.N.E.A.

Imagine this fine foursquare white and yellow house as a gentleman's country seat,

as it was before the encroachments of Quincy Town. This former home of a prominent patriot, wealthy merchant, and shipbuilder has a pleasant portico with columns, and the corners of the clapboard walls are trimmed with imitation stone-block quoins, typical of the times.

¶ *Scituate (on Route 3A halfway between Quincy and Plymouth)*

CUDWORTH HOUSE (*1723*)

Opposite schoolhouse; daily 1 to 6, July 1 to Labor Day; contribution; Scituate Historical Society.

This is the kind of house that twentieth-century Americans hanker for: shingled walls neatly trimmed in white, gambrel roof, king-size central chimney. No matter how many of these modest eighteenth-century dwellings Massachusetts may have to offer, each one has its unique character. The barn of this one contains interesting collections of carriages and farm implements.

WEST OF BOSTON

Concord; Harvard; Lexington; South Sudbury; Sturbridge;

Templeton; Newton Lower Falls; Shrewsbury

¶ Concord

The houses here make vivid the events and personalities for which the town is famous, from Revolutionary heroes and happenings to the literary circles, figures, and families that lived here through the later years.

ANTIQUARIAN HOUSE

(a museum)

Daily and holidays 10 to 5 and Sundays 2 to 5, April 19 to November 11; 50 cents and 20 cents (plus tax); Concord Antiquarian Society.

The building was carefully designed to reflect the fine middle ground of early domestic architecture in New England. Incorporated in the museum as a wing, is the seventeenth-century house that was rebuilt here to contain some of the early collections. This has the true medieval look,

from diamond-paned casements and clamshell plastered walls down to the wooden latches and locks. The transitions of styles through which you pass—from the seventeenth-century-house wing to the Victorian room on the third floor of the museum proper—make an illuminating journey through time and taste. In addition, two "personality rooms" are placed as cul-de-sacs en route: a little Thoreau room, and an Emerson study.

EMERSON HOUSE (*1828*)

Cambridge Turnpike, opposite Antiquarian House; daily 10 to 11:30 and 1:30 to 5:30 except Mondays, Sundays 2:30 to 5:30, April 19 to November 15 (large groups by appointment); 35 cents and 15 cents; Emerson Memorial Association.

Having "dodged the doom of building," to quote the great man himself, Emerson purchased this house in 1835 and lived here the rest of his life. A large white house of quiet dignity and no stylistic pretentions, it reflects the cultivated American who was more interested in essence than appearance.

THE WAYSIDE (*1717*)

Lexington Road, near Hawthorne Road; weekends and most other days except Monday; daily except Monday, June 16 to September 30; 40 cents and 20 cents; Miss Margaret Lathrop.

Associated primarily with Nathaniel Hawthorne, the house was occupied first by the Alcotts as "Hillside." Later it was inhabited by Margaret Sidney, author of the popular series *The Five Little Peppers.* An early house to begin with, it shows plainly its later additions. The ungainly tower room was built by Hawthorne to avoid visitors while he was writing two of his masterpieces, *The Marble Faun* and *Tanglewood Tales.*

THE OLD MANSE (*1769*)

Weekends and by appointment 2 to 5 April 19 to June 1, daily 10:30 to 5 and Sundays 2 to 5 June to October, weekends October to November 11; 35 cents and 10 cents; Trustees of Public Reservations.

Built by Emerson's grandfather, the Reverend William Emerson, chaplain at Ticonderoga, it was here that Ralph Waldo began the writing of his famous essay *Nature.* Here, too, Hawthorne lived the first three idyllic years of his marriage and wrote many of the *Mosses from an Old Manse,* in the first of which there is a description of the house. A plain but well-built gambrel-roofed house, with an odd double dormer probably added by one of its later occupants, it had a front-row seat for the Battle of Concord. Right here, at the nearby river, was fired the shot that was to be "heard around the world."

ORCHARD HOUSE (*1650 and 1730*)

Lexington Road; daily 10 to 5 except Mondays, Sundays 2 to 6, April 19 to November 1; 35 cents and 20 cents; Louisa May Alcott Memorial Association.

Bronson Alcott brought two old houses together here and made them into one, in which his daughter Louisa May was to write *Little Women,* a classic book for girls as well as the tale of the delightful and improvident family who lived here. Bronson Alcott, a remarkable man and a domestic disaster, called by Emerson in his Journal "a tedious archangel," encouraged imagination and the creative urge in his daughters. But it is Louisa May's personality which predominates here, just as it must have during her lifetime. It is a house in which the emphasis on "simple living" is still evident, for little has been changed inside since the Alcotts' day.

There are three colonial inns on Lexington Road, all still operating: THE WRIGHT TAVERN (1747), HARTWELL FARM (pre-Revolutionary), and the REUBEN BROWN HOUSE (before 1775), which was the home of the colonial saddler who carried to Concord the news that hostilities had occurred, and is now a tearoom.

¶ *Harvard (12 miles beyond Concord via Route 111)*

FRUITLANDS (*early eighteenth century*) and the WAYSIDE MUSEUMS, INC.

On Prospect Hill; daily 1 to 5:30, May 30 to September 30; founded by Miss Clara Endicott Sears.

This is a fascinating cluster of various restorations, including an old Shaker house, an Indian mansion, a picture gallery, and a library, among which you will be amused to find to what lengths the Transcendentalists attempted to carry their experiments—this one a way of life which would not exploit man, beast, or even insect. It lasted only four months. There are fine collections of Shaker furniture and household ware and of Indian relics. House interest and human interest both.

¶ *Lexington (in northwest suburban area of Boston)*

HANCOCK-CLARK HOUSE

(*1698, enlarged 1734*)

35 Hancock Street; weekdays 10 to 5 and Sundays 2 to 5, May 30 to October 12; 35 cents; Lexington Historical Society, 1774 Massachusetts Avenue.

The typical unpretentious house of a substantial eighteenth-century citizen. One occupant here (for seven years) was John Hancock. Samuel Adams was here with him the night Paul Revere came by.

MUNROE TAVERN (*1695*)

*1332 Massachusetts Avenue; weekdays 9:30
to 5 and Sundays 2 to 5, April 19 to
November 11; 35 cents.*

This tavern was eighty years old and a going concern the day in April, 1775, when
Earl Percy took it over as his headquarters
and as a hospital for his wounded redcoats.
A sturdy, attractive two-story frame house,
with a very pleasantly pedimented doorway, it contains fine early furnishings and
fascinating mementos.

BUCKMAN TAVERN (*1712*)

*Facing Battle Green; weekdays 10 to 5 and
Sundays 2 to 5, Memorial Day to Columbus
Day; 35 cents; Lexington Historical
Society.*

The Minute Men assembled here in this
good-looking inn on the morning of that
famous April 19. Its fine façade looks out
over the village green, where they subsequently fought. Its well-maintained interior
contains an abundance of Revolutionary
household and tavern paraphernalia.

¶ *South Sudbury* (*20 miles beyond
Waltham on Route 20*)

LEONARD P. GOULDING HOUSE

(antique shop on premises) (*built
1700 in Wayland, Massachusetts,
moved 1925*)

Daily; Mr. and Mrs. Leonard P. Goulding.
This old, deeply weathered dwelling, two
stories and an attic, is a first-rate restoration with its diamond-paned casements and
its almost Tudor chimney. The great living
room in the lean-to is paneled even to the
summer beams, and the whole house is
furnished with the skill of veteran collectors. Don't miss it for anything.

¶ *Sturbridge* (*on Route 20 between
Worcester and Springfield where
Route 15 from Hartford intersects*)

OLD STURBRIDGE VILLAGE

(*re-creation of a New England
village of 1790*)

*At junction of Routes 15 and 20; April 1
to November 11; May 16 to November 11
$1.75, November 12 to May 15 $1.00
(groups of 20 or over $1.25 each).*

This is a three-hundred-acre community
created to represent, in effect, a far-flung
New England village, with homes, church,
store, farm, sawmill, gristmill, tavern, and
all the various shops that supplied the
household and business needs of an early
Yankee rural community. There are thirty-
five or more buildings, bridges, and other
installations, dating from 1704 to 1840,
which have been brought together here

from various parts of New England, properly placed, expertly restored, and appropriately furnished and equipped. Incidentally, it has been made into an entertaining place to visit. It is essentially a performance, painstakingly prepared and presented. You can learn a great deal about our past that you never knew before and have a lot of fun doing it. Complete information on travel and accommodations will be furnished by the director's office.

¶ *Templeton (on Route 2, 4 miles beyond Gardner)*

NARRAGANSETT HISTORICAL SOCIETY (*c. 1810*)

Saturday afternoons, June until October; Tuesdays and Saturdays 2 to 5, July 1 to September 15; Narragansett Historical Society.

Built by a man of obvious taste and talent named John Stiles, this is a very stylish foursquare brick dwelling in the prim, Late Georgian, symmetrical manner. Stiles had the store and post office occupying a portion of the house, and these now form part of the present display. The residential rooms are furnished with appropriate early pieces, mostly from hereabouts, and there are exhibits and collections of early local objects.

¶ *Newton Lower Falls (the Newtons form the western part of metropolitan Boston)*

JOHN PARKER HOUSE (*1750*)

2349 Washington Street; first Thursday in month all year and second Monday in month October through May; Lucy Jackson Chapter, D.A.R.

A foursquare Colonial with some Federal remodeling, this is a town house of considerable style, with a fine recessed doorway decorated with a fleur-de-lis and with many well-restored rooms of interesting furniture, china, glass, toys, and costumes. It was once the parsonage of the charming white church next door.

¶ *Shrewsbury (35 miles out on Route 9 and 1 mile off to the right on 140)*

ARTEMUS WARD HOUSE (*before 1775*)

May 15 to October 1; Harvard University, Mrs. Busbey (custodian).

An unusually handsome pre-Revolutionary house in unusually good condition, certainly very much worthwhile turning off to see. The home of Gen. Artemus Ward of Revolutionary fame, it was always lived in by the family, many of whose things are still there.

Across the page in this winter glimpse of Old Sturbridge Village, the Fitch house lies off to the left of the country store, and above it rises the steeple of the Greek Revival meetinghouse.

This very trim, attractive house that was built by John Stiles in Templeton is now the interestingly furnished headquarters of the Narragansett Historical Society.

THE CONNECTICUT RIVER VALLEY

Amherst; Bernardston; Deerfield; Hadley; Holyoke;

Longmeadow; Northampton; Springfield; West Hatfield;

West Springfield

¶ *Amherst*

NEHEMIAH STRONG HOUSE (*1744*)

> *67 Amith Street; Tuesdays and Fridays 2 to 5, June 1 to October 1; 25 cents; Amherst Historical Society.*

This is the oldest house in town. Three and a half stories, with a gambrel roof and the well-known weathered hue, it is fascinatingly constructed, of course, and contains fine collections of local early objects and furnishings.

¶ *Bernardston* (*a few miles below the Vermont line on Route 5*)

RYTHER HOUSE (*1745*)

> *Daily when convenient, on special request; Fred A. and Grace M. Donaldson.*

An interesting house in which all of the old features have been preserved, including a painting of a British spy on the plaster wall over the mantel (c. 1812) and, next to it, a wall of early stenciling. There are fourteen rooms, all furnished with American antiques, and original Indian shutters, made in one piece to slide over the window in case of attack.

¶ *Deerfield*

The ancient elms of Old Deerfield Street arch over one of the most homogeneous avenues of eighteenth-century buildings in America. At least twenty of the houses here were built before the Revolution, and Mr. Henry N. Flynt, the good angel of these precincts, numbers more than thirty from that century alone. The fact that almost every house is being used and that even the museum houses are occupied by their devoted custodians brings a town of museum quality to life.

Deerfield was a byword for Indian savagery long before the Revolution. Actually there were three major massacres and countless minor raids, beginning with the attack in 1675 that wiped out the first little colony and continuing on, even after the friendship pledge had been signed in 1735. But in time safety was assured and Deerfield was free to develop its prosperous agricultural economy. Its citizens had the courage and finally the means to build themselves comfortably fine homes, so many of which, by great good fortune and great good construction as well, have survived—to embark on a new lease of life in the twentieth century.

Certainly no one should attempt to see Deerfield without securing a booklet at the information center in the Hall Tavern, with a map of streets and houses. Another word of advice: winter may be flattering to the houses, but few of the buildings can be seen during the school months, when the town is more or less concentrated on its academic life, centering on Deerfield Academy for Boys.

PARSON ASHLEY HOUSE

> (*1726 to 1733*)
>
> *Weekdays 10 to 12 and 2 to 4:30 except Mondays, Sundays 2 to 5; 60 cents.*

Perhaps you will begin at the north end of the wide avenue with the Parson Ashley House, one of the pick of the crop. The narrow weatherboarding, a feature of these houses, is dark with age and the tall narrow windows give the house an almost fortresslike appearance. Its walls were, in fact, bulletproof. Its magnificent broken-arch pediment over the doorway, and the door itself, tell that it was made in the Connecticut Valley. When you see the

The doorway of the Parson Ashley house is one of the finest in Deerfield, the house one of the most colorfully furnished and decorated.

beautiful interior, you will find it hard to believe that it was rescued, back in 1869, from service as a tobacco barn. Its present perfection is the work of the Flynts, as they conceive it was lived in by the prosperous parson. It can be seen that in Deerfield a parson was not lacking in the blessings of this world, as well as the next.

INDIAN HOUSE (*1698 reconstruction*) and BLOODY BROOK TAVERN (*c. 1785*)

Old Deerfield Street; weekdays 9 to 12 and 1 to 5 except Tuesdays, Sundays 1 to 5; both buildings 30 cents.

You cannot mistake the Indian House, a darkly brooding reconstruction of a typical late seventeenth-century dwelling with second- and third-story overhangs, built on the site of a 1698 house built by Ens. John Sheldon within the stockade which was the scene of the 1704 Massacre—the one which resulted in the prisoners' being marched off in the dead of winter to Canada. Back of it stands old Bloody Brook Tavern (1675 to 1700), moved here from South Deerfield, where it had stood by the brook of evil memory.

As you pass, look at the JOSEPH STEBBINS HOUSE, a great gambrel-roof mansion of considerable style built for the hero of Bunker Hill in about 1772, his townsmen having helped him to become a tycoon by granting him perpetual tax freedom for his gristmill in appreciation of his war record. The rooftree easily accommodated his family of thirteen children. Corner quoins

and fine doorways distinguish it, the ornamentation hinting at the first advance of the Federal influences.

EPHRAIM WILLIAMS HOUSE (*1760*)

Upon application at Deerfield Academy office.

Now the home of the headmaster of the academy, it was built in 1760 and enlarged in 1794. Its rear wing, Greek Revival in character, seems to have been added still later.

MEMORIAL HALL (*1797*)

Deerfield Academy; weekdays except Tuesday 9:30 to 12 and 2 to 5, Tuesdays 10 to 12 and 2 to 4, Sundays 2 to 5; 50 cents and 15 cents.

This place has several rooms furnished in old Deerfield relics.

NIMMS HOUSE (*1710*)

The Nimms House can probably be visited upon request to the academy.

JONATHAN WILLIAMS HOUSE (*1707*)

Campus of Deerfield Academy; perhaps upon application at the Deerfield Academy office.

Worth a good look is the Reverend Jonathan Williams House, whose owner was the first preacher to the people of Deerfield, for its doorway is admittedly the finest in a town which does not lack for them. From it, he and his five children were dragged captive to be marched in bondage three hundred miles to Canada, while his wife and two other children were murdered. Williams lived to return to Deerfield, when he was given this home by his thankful congregation, to write his account of those harrowing times in a locally famous source book, *The Redeemed Captive*.

FRARY HOUSE (*1683–1763*)

Weekdays 9 to 12 and 1:30 to 5 except Mondays, Sundays 2 to 5, April 1 to November; 50 cents and 15 cents.

The only house in Deerfield that escaped in large part the disaster of 1704. Not so its owner and his wife, however, who were massacred. Today the staunch, rambling house, deeply weathered, is an almost perfect example of its times, both inside and out. The doorway of its north and earliest end has the kind of rich austerity so typical of Deerfield craftsmanship. In 1763 Selah Bernard added the south part and made it a tavern. Twelve years later it was the place Benedict Arnold chose to stop in on his way to Ticonderoga, and to feed his army he ordered a collection of fifteen hundred pounds of beef from the local farmers. One of the features of this U-shaped structure is the yellow ballroom, a room almost as necessary as a taproom in those times.

THE OLD MANSE *or* WILLARD HOUSE (*1694–1768*)

Upon application at Deerfield Academy office.

This place has one of the prettiest façades in town. It is a charming square house painted yellow, an unusual note in Deerfield, and the detail of its corner quoins and delicate cornice, and its window lintels and doorway (another fine one) are brought out in white. The handsome hip roof, broken by close-set dormers, completes a picture which is unmistakably Salem in character. It is told that Joseph Barnard took thirteen years to collect the pine for it, so that no panel should show a knot.

HALL TAVERN AND STORE (*1765*)

Weekdays 9:30 to 12 and 1:30 to 5, Sundays 1 to 5; 50 cents.

The Hall Tavern and Deerfield Store, the former moved here from nearby Charlemont on the Old Post Road, was the focal point of entertainment for the whole neighborhood and typical of the best New England hostels of the day. Spacious and clean, such inns as this one were a boon to travelers who had been in the saddle or

Among the extraordinary collection of early houses which forms Old Deerfield Village, the Frary house is outstanding, its yellow ballroom a special feature.

The main body of the Old Manse is one of the more formal of Deerfield houses. Note the older gambrel-roof section at the right rear.

jolting over the rough roads from dawn to dark. Lucretia Hall, the hostess here during much of its history, was a notable cook and provider of cheer. Her Thanksgiving pies, whose upper crusts were enlivened by a flight of pastry doves, are legendary. The seven fireplaces in the inn kept out the long winter chill. The ballroom on the second floor, with its narrow benches built in all the way round the walls, has a vaulted ceiling, and the brilliant stencil pattern that covers the wall with a special overmantel picture is something not to be missed. Several of the best of the old papers and stencils in the various homes, as

discovered by Mrs. Henry Flynt, have been well reproduced and are on sale here.

ASA STEBBINS HOUSE (*1799*)
Weekdays 10 to 12 and 2 to 4:30 except Wednesdays, Sundays 2 to 5; 50 cents.

The only two brick houses in town were both built by the wealthy Stebbins brothers. This one has the early rear wing attached, in which the father, Joseph, raised the family. The two sons, Asa and Joseph, were shrewd businessmen as well as patriots, and to this fact we owe the beauty of this little brick Federal mansion and the equally fine mansion which Joseph erected near the end of the avenue. Asher Benjamin, an unknown lad of twenty, was working on the academy at this time, and his influence is plain to be seen here. The Asa Stebbins House is as delicate as a shell inside and its lightness is in striking contrast to the houses already described. Its interior must have seemed a miracle of elegance when the Federal style was only just beginning to be seen. The pink walls of the drawing room (brick dust mixed with the plaster), its pargeted ceiling and elaborately decorated cornice, the brilliant freehand designs painted gaily on the dining-room walls (possibly by Jared Jessup), the graceful curved staircase—all these delicate innovations must have seemed almost frivolous to the townsfolk. If the house were half as finely furnished as it is today (thanks to the Flynts), they could not have failed to admire it.

Upstairs in the old Hall Tavern, which served as inn and village store, is one of the most interesting ballrooms in New England.

A glimpse of the restoration village of Storrowton with its interesting collection of early New England homes and other structures.

¶ Hadley (*on Route 9, 3 miles east of Northampton*)

PORTER-PHELPS-HUNTINGTON HOUSE (*1752 and 1799*)

Saturdays and Sundays 10 to 6, May to October; by appointment; 50 cents.

This is a delightful old family establishment—a large, ingratiating three-story gambrel-roof house, with kitchen ell, woodshed, and carriage house in a long low line connecting it with a later and smaller house of simple Colonial design. Surrounded by a split-rail fence, it is set in a grove of elms, maples, and hemlocks. Household articles include pieces brought to Dorchester from England in 1631 and items from every generation who lived in the house for the next one hundred and seventy-five years.

¶ Holyoke (*on Route 5 between Springfield and Northampton*)

THE TAVERN (*1785*)

Halfway between Springfield and Northampton; Eunice Day Chapter, D.A.R.

When this town was on the old coach line from Springfield to Boston, this old hostelry was known as "The Miller's Inn," and later became famous as "Craft's Tavern." Furnished in keeping.

¶ Longmeadow (*just above the Connecticut line on Route 5*)

COLTON HOUSE (*1734*)

Longmeadow Street; Mondays and Wednesdays 3 to 5 mid-June to mid-October, other times by appointment; 25 cents; S.P.N.E.A.

STORRS PARSONAGE (*1786*)

697 Longmeadow Street; Thursdays 2 to 5, August and September; Longmeadow Historical Society.

These two houses of considerable distinction grace an old street of noble beauty.

¶ Northampton

ISAAC DAMON HOUSE (*1812, remodeled 1825*)

46 Bridge Street; summer, by appointment, (phone: 990); contribution; Northampton Historical Society.

Damon was an early New England architect and bridge builder. Here are his drafting instruments, models of bridges, and other memorabilia; also a collection of Jenny Lind articles.

CORNET JOSEPH PARSONS HOUSE (*1658, remodeled about 1806*)

58 Bridge Street; Wednesdays, Fridays, and Sundays, 2 to 5; contribution; Northampton Historical Society.

This is the oldest house in the town; built by the first settler, it is furnished with a variety of pieces presented mostly by Northampton people. The list of its possessions is endless, and a matter of considerable local pride and general interest.

THE CAPEN HOUSE (1825), THE DEWEY HOUSE (1827), and THE SESSIONS HOUSE (1700) (now dormitories)

> On request, at reasonable hours; Smith College.

The Capen and Dewey Houses are Greek Revival.

¶ Springfield

ALEXANDER HOUSE (1811)

> 284 State Street; weekdays by application to caretaker; S.P.N.E.A.

Designed by Asher Benjamin, which gives it special interest.

CONNECTICUT VALLEY HISTORICAL MUSEUM or WILLIAM PYNCHON MEMORIAL BUIDING

(a reproduction of a Colonial mansion)

> Tuesday through Saturday 1 to 5, Sundays 2 to 5; City Library Association.

In the museum there are two interesting early rooms taken from the Chapin Tavern, which stood in Chicopee, Massachusetts, and some reproduction rooms furnished with excellent antiques.

¶ West Hatfield (on Route 5, 4 miles north of Northampton)

SOPHIA SMITH HOMESTEAD (1796)

> By application to college.

This home of the founder of Smith College has been very well restored and becomingly furnished by the alumnae.

¶ West Springfield (across river from Springfield)

STORROWTON VILLAGE

> Daily 9 to 5, May 1 to November 1; 75 cents; Rampagne Historical Society.

An assembled and re-created village consisting of early New England houses and miscellaneous buildings. Many of the installations are actively in use for the convenience and entertainment of visitors, including the tavern. Among the buildings brought here from various New England sites are the ATKINSON TAVERN (1789), the CHESTERFIELD BLACKSMITH SHOP (1850), the EDDY LAW OFFICE (1806), the GILBERT HOMESTEAD (1794), the LITTLE RED SCHOOLHOUSE (1810), the PHILLIPS HOUSE (1767), the POTTER HOUSE (1777), the SALISBURY MEETING HOUSE (1834), and the TOWN HOUSE (1822).

JOSIAH DAY HOUSE (1754)

> Town green, corner of Hanover and Park Streets; Tuesdays, Thursdays, and Saturday 9 to 6, May 1 to November 1.

This is one of the extremely rare early salt boxes to be made of brick. It is very stylish with its broad chimney, and has never been lived in by any but the original Days and their descendants.

THE WESTERN HILLS

Great Barrington; Richmond; Sheffield; South Egremont;

Stockbridge; South Lee

¶ Great Barrington (near junction of Routes 7 and 23)

WILLIAM CULLEN BRYANT HOUSE (1739)

> Berkshire Inn.

Now part of the inn. Bryant was married here when he was serving as town clerk in 1815. The handsomely paneled wedding room has been carefully preserved.

¶ Richmond (on Route 41 halfway between Lenox and Pittsfield)

SHAKER FARM

(early nineteenth century)

> 5 miles from Tanglewood; by written or phone appointment; August; Dr. and Mrs. Edward D. Andrews.

This is a rare opportunity to see some of the finest Shaker interiors in the country, in the house occupied by the two outstand-

The kitchen of the Shaker Farm at Richmond is filled with the kind of household wares and furnishings for which the sect was famous.

ing Shaker authorities. The utilitarian perfection which makes Shaker craftsmanship a uniquely American contribution to the art of cabinetry can be seen here in its purest form. To see the house and all that it contains is one of the rarest privileges offered to readers of this *Guide*.

¶ *Sheffield (on Route 7 in southwest corner of state near Connecticut line)*

COLONEL ASHLEY HOUSE (*c. 1735*)
Southern end of town off Cooper Road; open on request to interested visitors during 6 summer months; Mr. and Mrs. E. A. Brewer.

This is probably the oldest house in this part of the state, and a choice one beautifully restored and furnished by connoisseurs of the period. The high spot is the upstairs study, with impressive paneling and shell cupboard, and a raised hearth with fine original molding. Here Sheffield's

declaration of independence is supposed to have been written. The living hall in the southwest corner was willed by Col. John Ashley to his housekeeper for "her use and improvement during her natural life," having its own outside door.

¶ *South Egremont (on Route 23 in southwest corner of state near the New York line)*

EGREMONT TAVERN (*1730s*), **MOUNT EVERETT INN** (*1780*) *and the* **OLD GRIST MILL** (*1790*) (*still being operated as inns*)
All three together in center of town; daily; James Adie.

It was at the tavern here that Sir William Johnson stopped on his trips from New York to Connecticut on the King's business. Plans for Shays' Rebellion were laid here. Also used for barracks in the Civil War.

¶ *Stockbridge (on Route 7 between Great Barrington and Lenox)*

MISSION HOUSE (*1739*)

Main Street; weekdays 10 to 12:30 and 2 to 6 April 1 to November 1, Sundays 2:30 to 6 during summer months, during winter admittance by ringing bell of Cobbler's Shop; 35 cents; Trustees of Public Reservations.

The outstanding architectural feature of this fine old house is the often-photographed double-pediment doorway, beautifully carved and paneled. The house was built by John Sargeant, first missionary to the Housatonic Indians, and some of his furniture is still here, along with the Indian exhibits.

¶ *South Lee (just east of Stockbridge)*

MERRELL TAVERN (*1760*)

Main Street; Saturday and Sunday afternoons, July 14 to September 2; contribution.

When the ballroom was added to this atmospheric old brick inn, it was superimposed as a third story in frame, giving the building considerable distinction.

The stove, the cabinet, the chairs, are rare examples of Shaker craftsmanship in this rare example of a lived-in Shaker house.

CAPE COD & THE ISLANDS

Barnstable; Chatham; Edgartown; Falmouth; Nantucket; Sandwich; North Falmouth; Woods Hole; Yarmouthport

¶ *Barnstable (on Route 6A, 15 miles past Cape Cod Canal)*

CROCKER TAVERN (*c. 1754*)

Main Street; Mondays, Thursdays, and Saturdays 10 to 5, June 1 to October 13; 25 cents; S.P.N.E.A.

This old inn is being carefully preserved as an example of the simplicity and honesty of our early building manners.

¶ *Chatham (on southeastern tip of Cape)*

OLD ATWOOD HOUSE (*1752*)

Stage Harbor Road, off Route 28; Wednesdays and Fridays 2 to 5 July and August, and by appointment; contribution; Chatham Historical Society.

Capt. Joseph Atwood, noted navigator, built it the year he stayed home because the pirates were so bad. The building tim-

The Thomas Cooke house points up the early attractiveness of charming Edgartown on Martha's Vineyard.

bers were cut and rough-hewn right here. It is the oldest and by far the loveliest house in town, now a veritable Cape Cod museum.

¶ *Edgartown* (*Martha's Vineyard*)

This is a charming old whaling village, now a most attractive resort in summer, with many a fine early house along its old streets. Over at Oak Bluffs is a picturesque cluster of tiny ornate Victorian cottages surrounding an old camp-meeting site.

THOMAS COOKE HOUSE (*special exhibits in summer*) (*1765*)
> *Cooke and School Streets; weekdays 10 to 12 and 2 to 4:30 and Sundays 2 to 4:30 June to October, winter hours on request; Dukes County Historical Society.*

This trim, silvery-shingled salt-water house was built by ships' carpenters. Unaltered, its original fireplaces and paneling are still intact. Reflecting the life of the once great whaling port, the house contains furniture, china, and portraits by Vineyard primitives, ship models and gear, Indian relics, and special exhibits in summer.

¶ *Falmouth* (*in southwestern corner of Cape*)

WICKS HOUSE (*1790*)
> *Opposite green on Palmer Avenue; Tuesday, Wednesday, Thursday, and Friday afternoons 2 to 5, Saturday mornings 10 to 12; Falmouth Historical Society.*

Recently restored, this old house has French eighteenth-century wallpaper, fine portraits, furniture of the period from Falmouth homes, and a fine whaling collection. The captain's walk, the two-story porch, and the restoration of the garden are special attractions.

JOHN JENKINS HOMESTEAD (*1820*)
> *20 Hewins Street on Green; on written request to Mr. and Mrs. Edward Richardson, 120 East 31st Street, New York City; 25 cents for Falmouth Historical Society.*

A stately, small-scale house with some unusual features, including its lunette windows and staircase. It is furnished well with late-eighteenth- and early-nineteenth-century pieces and a number of good paintings. As the owner suggests, it has "a thin-lipped suggestion of Southern grace in a small Cape Cod seaport," inspired, she believes, by the old-time trade with Charleston, South Carolina. Other Falmouth houses around the green here seem to bear this out.

¶ *Nantucket*

There is nothing else like it in America. Twenty miles out in the sea from Cape Cod lies the "faraway" island whose town is a clustered harmony of old gray houses. The old section still contains four hundred houses antedating the great fire of 1846, which largely burned out the dwellings of the central district, most of which were immediately replaced by new ones that looked just like the old. That is the great thing about Nantucket —even the houses built today conform, and it is hard to tell them from the old gray-shingled or clapboarded dwellings. It is this homogeneous quality that makes the island unique, and the inhabitants intend to keep it that way. The good gray cottages, of which there is a preponderance, are the oldest type on the island, while the imposing Federal and Greek Revival façades lining both sides of Main Street are the results of the great whaling prosperity which hit its peak during the first decade of the nineteenth century. To see the interiors of some of these mansions you should be here in August when the annual tour takes place and several of them are on view. Contact The Hospital Thrift Shop for information on it.

JETHRO COFFIN HOUSE (*1686*)
Sunset Hill Road; weekdays, June 15 to October 1; 50 cents; Nantucket Historical Society.

The oldest house in Nantucket, of the medieval Ipswich type, its small, infrequent diamond-paned casements are among the many marks of its long-ago era. Inside it has been little changed, and much of the crude original construction remains to tell its story. It is furnished with fitting simplicity, mostly with island pieces.

MARIA MITCHELL MEMORIAL HOUSE (*1790*)
1 Vestal Street; daily 10 to 5 except Sundays, June 15 to September 15; Maria Mitchell Association.

The island woman of this name was born here in August, 1818, and here, when she had reached the age of twenty-nine, she awoke one morning to find herself famous —a fame which was to take her name not only to the mainland, but to many other lands as well. For she was the discoverer of a new comet. Descended from the same Folger ancestor as Benjamin Franklin, her father, called "William the Teacher," was among other things astronomical observer for the Coast Survey. When she was a small girl, she helped her father make observations from the captain's walk which perched steeply atop their house. In fact, the plain gray house is almost indistinguishable from many another plain gray house along these quiet streets, and is as simple within as without.

LYDIA S. HINCHMAN HOUSE
7 Milk Street; daily except Sundays, June 15 to September 15; Nantucket Historical Society.

This was one of the fine brick mansions whose exteriors remain much as they were; but inside the walls of most of the rooms have been removed to accommodate the exhibits. They are unusually interesting, devoted for the most part to whaling in all its aspects. One room contains some good portraits of a number of the first settlers. Observe family resemblances in the faces.

1800 HOUSE (*1800*)
Mill Street; daily 10 to 5, June 15 to September 15; 50 cents; Nantucket Historical Society.

Assembled in this house that once belonged to the high sheriff of the county are the

One of the famous and handsome sights on Nantucket's Main Street, lined with beautiful private homes, is the row of brick Starbuck houses.

furniture and possessions of former generations of islanders, covering a period of about seventy-five years, some of it made by local artisans. The interior has been restored with discretion.

DELL HOUSE (*c. 1800*)

> *Academy Hill; by written appointment, open afternoons August and September; Mr. and Mrs. Burnam Dell.*

On a hilltop overlooking the sea, this captain's house, faced with narrow clapboards, is painted yellow with white trim. Its corner quoins and fine porticoed doorway are sparkling Federal details. The small captain's walk is perched as if on stilts over the roof ridge, as it is on so many of these houses, almost crowding the chimneys. They were meant for business, and not for decoration, so they aren't fancy. From this one the captain or his lady could have seen a sail for twenty miles.

BROOKS HOUSE or JOSIAH COFFIN HOUSE (*1723*)

> *60 Cliff Street; by written request well in advance, June 15 through Labor Day; Mr. and Mrs. Emerson Tuttle.*

Mrs. Tuttle is the sister of Mrs. Frost of Sherburne (column 2), and her well-preserved house is one of the most unspoiled examples on the island. Tucked in behind tall hedges, its weather-frosted exterior, deceptively small in scale, hardly prepares you for the space you find within. Woodwork richly mellowed by time and attention has never been altered. In fact, the fine, heavy structural elements are everywhere in evidence. The house is furnished with simplicity and great taste.

SHERBURNE or ELIHU COLEMAN HOUSE (*1722*)

> *Hawthorne Lane, on the moors; upon request, Tuesday, Thursday, and Saturday mornings July and August; Mrs. Elizabeth Hollister Frost.*

Perhaps no book could be a better introduction to the island and its people, or to Mrs. Frost's home, than her epic novel *This Side of Land*. This weathered grayshingled house nestles into the moor, its long sweep of roof almost touching the earth on the far side. A garden of heather suits the landscape to perfection. Everything about the house has been done with thoughtful understanding of its quality and the kind of life that went on in it through the earliest years.

¶ Sandwich

OLD DANIEL WEBSTER INN (*1694*)

Open as an inn and not much altered downstairs. The food is good, and it is a pleasant

High on its hill overlooking the ocean, the Dell house is filled with true Nantucket character.

The Josiah Coffin house at the right is one of the more distinguished and venerable houses on the island.

place to stay. Daniel Webster often stayed here. It was originally the home of the Reverend Ferrenden, the greatest of all missionaries to the Indians.

HOXIE HOUSE (*1637*)
> *Grove and Canal Streets; apply for information to Sandwich Historical Society, Main Street.*

¶ *North Falmouth*

MALONE HOUSE (*c. 1775*)
> *Old Main Road; on request, weekends in July, August, and April to December; Mrs. Joseph A. Malone.*

A good early Cape Cod cottage, close to the ground and covered with hand-split shingles, it has a six-panel entrance door and a simplified Adam-style mantel typical of Falmouth. Nicely furnished with antiques of its period.

¶ *Woods Hole (on southwestern tip of Cape)*

TO WINDWARD (*1775*)
> *North Street; by appointment during summer months with owners; 75 cents for Falmouth Historical Society; Mr. and Mrs. Lawrence Saunders.*

This large, handsome house, typical of its time, was built far away in East Bridgewater, thirty miles south of Boston, and a likely legend is that the day the roof was shingled the workmen felt the reverberations of the cannon at the Battle of Bunker Hill. Anyhow, it was moved here by the man responsible for Storrowtown, and has made itself very much at home.

¶ *Yarmouthport (on Route 28 past Hyannis)*

COL. JOHN THATCHER HOUSE (*1680*) or 1680 HOUSE
> *King's Highway and Thatcher Lane; daily 10 to 5, June to October 15; 25 cents; S.P.N.E.A.*

This place has the atmosphere of a prosperous Cape Cod home of the early eighteenth century. In the later paneled rooms a fine collection of old silver is effectively displayed. The furnishings are charming throughout.

WINSLOW CROCKER HOUSE (*1780*)
> *Next to Thatcher House; by appointment; contribution; S.P.N.E.A.*

A handsome house of sizable dimensions which was built two miles away at West Barnstable and moved here in 1934. Like the Thatcher House, it is appropriately furnished, and the two houses make an excellent pair to see.

*Captain Moffatt had his ship room on the second floor of his stately Ports-
mouth mansion, where he could look down upon his wharves below the bluff
in front of the house and watch his ships sail out the Piscataqua. The low
building beyond the house was his office. There is an old-fashioned garden
behind that goes with the house, and within the house there is great elegance
of furnishing and décor, one of the most impressive interiors being the entrance hall opposite with its grand staircase all paneled and carved.*

NEW HAMPSHIRE

*P*EOPLE have said that after the fine great Portsmouth houses, all other New Hampshire houses are an anticlimax. This canard, of course, is folderol, as town after town throughout the state will testify, and as house after house among the hills of this handsome countryside will bear witness. Still, we will say for Portsmouth that the stateliness of its outstanding old homes, along with their number and variety, leaves it few rivals among early American cities of its size. We would call it the New England counterpart of Charleston, South Carolina; and as for the rest of New Hampshire, we would say that only two other states could touch it for the number and attractiveness of its towns with unspoiled early architectural charm; those two states are Vermont and Connecticut.

As for the lover of early American homes, New Hampshire is particularly rich in two most ingratiating kinds—distinguished frame houses in the Federal style and white well-to-do frame farmhouses in the colonial tradition, both kinds dating from the early 1800s and indicating the prosperity of that period here.

A word as to the regional arrangement above. Portsmouth and vicinity

47

seemed the obvious area in which to start our listings and descriptions. Geographically, historically, and architecturally important, it is, furthermore, practically the main entrance to the state. Since Concord is not only the capital of the state but the virtual center of a region that is rather rich in good early houses, at least of good old houses that can be visited, it is a convenient focal point for the section, even though it is not especially house-rich itself. And, of course, there is the Connecticut River Valley (right bank), a valley that is ever a rich region for the best in early domestic architecture, no matter whether the state is New Hampshire, Vermont, Massachusetts, or Connecticut.

By no means are all the good house towns listed, only those in which there are houses that can be visited, but you can be pretty sure that the best remaining possibilities will be found in the vicinity of the towns named. For example, anyone passing through Hanover, on the way to or from Orford, will want to pause for a look in the neighborhood of the Dartmouth College campus. And anyone who fails to look

into little Bath Village, about eighteen miles above Haverhill, will have missed one of the most delectable early architectural treats in New Hampshire.

¶ Portsmouth

Above all, the thing that marks the houses of Portsmouth and gives them the unmistakable flavor of an English ancestry is style. They are not "great" houses, perhaps, in the sense of the mansions of Virginia or Maryland, but they are the *splendid* homes of wealthy merchants and sea captains who had pride in how they built and lived. Here balance and proportion are more important than ornament, though detail was by no means neglected either outside or within. With a history dating back over three hundred years, the town retains an eighteenth-century flavor, although you will find a range which extends from the earliest salt boxes, protected from the sea gales of winter by roofs that touch the ground, to houses of the Federal period. It was the eighteenth-century trade with the West Indies which brought the prosperity that built the houses. Mid-

The richly detailed façade of the Wentworth-Gardner house is a memorable sight down by the water.

dle Street, with its high, square, delicate white abodes is virtually unspoiled; flat hipped roofs and captain's walks, fine doorways, and beautiful fences are the rule rather than the exception.

The older stretches of Middle Street and vicinity will lead you directly into the most flavorsome period of the fine old Portsmouth houses; for while the highest architectural distinction of the town must be reserved for the best Georgian houses—the Moffatt-Ladd, the Warner, the Wentworth-Gardner, and the Governor Langdon—it is the big foursquare Federal houses which play such a powerful part in the personality of the place. Ironically, none of these can, at this time, be listed for visiting, but you can enjoy to your heart's content their highly pleasing façades, which indeed constitute one of their chiefest charms.

The Warner is one of the great early brick houses of America, containing endless features of interest from top to bottom.

WARNER HOUSE (1716)

Daniels and Chapel Streets; daily 10 to 5, June 15 to September 15; 50 cents.

This belongs to the nobility of early American brick homes. Built by Capt. Archibald Macpheadris, a Scotsman, whose daughter married Jonathan Warner, it housed their descendants until 1930, when the Warner House Association took over its care and security. It couldn't be in better hands. The astonishing staircase murals, accidentally discovered in the 1840s under many layers of wallpaper, the balustraded gambrel roof, which began as rare double gables with a valley between, and the lightning rod installed in 1762 under the personal supervision of Benjamin Franklin, are merely a few of its many arresting features. It is, of course, fitted out and furnished to perfection.

WENTWORTH-GARDNER HOUSE (1760)

Gardner and Mechanics Streets; daily 10 to 5 July 1 to September 15; 50 cents; Wentworth-Gardner and Tobias Lear Houses Association.

Still another famous beauty. Down by the river, it has a waterside setting worthy of its white and yellow stateliness, with a wonderful doorway crowned with a broken scroll pediment, which in turn is placed against the wooden yellow-block front façade, framed in by white contrasting quoins and cornice. Within, the carved woodwork is superb, including the black-cherry staircase; brilliant scenic wallpapers and beautiful furnishings. The mansion has had many owners, among them the Metropolitan Museum, which at one time had in mind moving it to New York and putting it up in Central Park.

MOFFATT-LADD HOUSE (1763)

154 Market Street; daily 10 to 5, June 15 to September 15; 50 cents; Colonial Dames of America in New Hampshire.

The fine great gray and white foursquare mansion from which Captain Moffatt could look down upon his ships sailing out the Piscataqua to all parts of the world makes a pretty exciting spectacle itself. Within, the paneled entrance hall and staircase bowl you over with the beauty of their design and workmanship. The Colonial Dames have made the appearance of the whole house one of their superlative performances. The terraced garden is a colonial delight, and the little counting house, all in keeping, in the side yard, is a

The carved woodwork of the north parlor in the Gov. John Langdon house called forth a pretty compliment from President Washington.

reminder of the money that must have gone, first and last, into the making of the proud Captain's establishment. One of the finest of the great New England four-squares; handsomely fenced, quoined, windowed, and balustraded.

GOV. JOHN LANGDON MANSION (*1784*)

143 Pleasant Street; daily 1 to 5, June 1 to September 15; 50 cents; S.P.N.E.A.

If you feel that "this is the handsomest house in Portsmouth," you will be glad to know that this was just what Washington said about it in 1789. It is without question one of the handsomest. Slightly more florid in effect than the three earlier homes mentioned above, it has a Chinese Chippendale balustrade crowning the roof, ornately pedimented dormers, Corinthian fluted pilasters up the corners, and a porch that is perhaps rather playful for the house. Within, the woodwork is richly and luxuriantly carved, and the furnishings are of a very high order indeed.

JOHN PAUL JONES HOUSE (*1758*)

Home of Portsmouth Historical Society, State Street; daily 10 to 5, June 15 to September 15; 50 cents; Portsmouth Historical Society.

This is the typically Portsmouth house with a fine big gambrel roof, that Capt. Gregory Purcell built when he was about to marry Governor Benning Wentworth's daughter Sarah—she who was destined to conduct here a genteel boarding house after her husband's death in 1776 and to attract

as a boarder a dashing young Captain Jones who had come to Portsmouth to get the U.S.S. *Ranger* outfitted for action, the same young man whose name the house bears today. Some of the rooms are furnished, and there are, of course, many fascinating collections of Portsmouthiana.

RICHARD JACKSON HOUSE (*1664*)

Jackson Hill Street; daily 11 to 5, June 1 to November 1; 25 cents; S.P.N.E.A.

The oldest house in Portsmouth; picturesque as only seventeenth-century houses can be, in a medieval way, with long sweeping rooflines and many details to delight the antiquarian, such as leaded glass, mammoth oversize framing, and furnishings to fit.

THOMAS BAILEY ALDRICH MEMORIAL (*1790*)

386 Court Street; daily 10 to 5, June 15 to October 15; 50 cents and 25 cents.

There is an intimate description of this house in *The Story of a Bad Boy*, whose author lived here in the Victorian period, in keeping with which the house is furnished today. However, the house itself, built by Aldrich's grandfather, is a good example of a simple white clapboard in the early Portsmouth tradition.

TOBIAS LEAR HOUSE (*before 1760*)

Hunking Street; not officially open or presently furnished; Charles M. Dale.

A Georgian dwelling with a steep hipped roof, nicely dormered, a real Portsmouth air, and considerable style. It stands near the Wentworth-Gardner House and was occupied by George Washington's secretary, Tobias Lear, who also tutored the general's two stepchildren.

GOV. BENNING WENTWORTH HOUSE (*1695 and later*)

On Little Harbor, out past the Hotel Wentworth-by-the-Sea, 2 miles south via Route 1A from the center of city; will be open daily; State Recreation Division.

This uncommonly impressive mansion of some thirty rooms, with a cellar in which a small troop of horses was kept stabled whenever there was need for cavalry protection, bids fair to be one of the more spectacular historical sights of Portsmouth when the restoration now under way is completed. It was the home of the Wentworth who became Royal Governor of the province at the time of New Hampshire's separation from Massachusetts—the same Wentworth who on the occasion of his sixtieth birthday banquet here, in the presence of many guests of high degree, called in his housekeeper, Martha Hilton, announced their intention to marry, and forthwith requested a clergyman present to perform the ceremony. Longfellow describes the house in his poem *Lady Wentworth*:

It was a pleasant mansion, an abode
Near and yet hidden from the great
  highroad,
Sequestered among trees, a noble pile,
Baronial and colonial in its style.

It was Benning who made it baronial, having inherited it as a much more modest house from his grandfather. In the dining room are three small ovens, which were used to heat the rum for toddies.

¶ Exeter

WELLS KERR HOUSE (*1783*)

Open on special request; house of the dean, Phillips Exeter Academy.

Built by John Phillips, founder of Phillips Exeter, as the first academy building, it served as the school for the original fifty-six students and *one* preceptor. It was moved in the early nineteenth century and then in 1917, relocated near its original site. It is a pretty, trim white house, now the dean's dwelling.

GARRISON HOUSE (*1650–1658*)

Water and Clifford Streets; by appointment; William Perry Dudley.

So fine is the woodwork in this house that one room went to the Metropolitan Museum. The oldest house in New Hampshire, the main part was built to meet Indian attacks. For this purpose, the upper story projected a foot or more over the lower and the windows were narrow. The door actually had a portcullis. The front wing was added in 1772 by Gen. Peter Gilman to provide a proper place to entertain Governor Wentworth, who was about to pay a visit. Later, while a student at Exeter, Daniel Webster boarded here with Mr. Clifford, a noted woodworker. The paneled rooms are very chaste and elegant, the furniture sparse but excellent. William Perry Dudley, the owner, has restored it with skill and devotion.

A dwelling of earlier distinction than the Georgian and Federal mansions of Portsmouth is the ancient Jackson house here.

CINCINNATI HALL, *formerly* LADD-GILMAN HOUSE (*1721*)

Governor's Lane; Thursdays 2 to 4, and by application to caretaker at any time.

The lengthy façade, seven windows across, is not symmetrical, the windows in the later part being longer. There is some impressive paneling within, fluted pilasters, and a fluted summer beam. Purchased by the Society of Cincinnati in 1903, the house was the birthplace of Nicholas Gilman, delegate to the Constitutional Convention, and was used as the state treasury during the Revolution. It is furnished with some appropriate pieces and interesting portraits and engravings. A private meeting place of distinction, not a home.

GIDDINGS TAVERN (*1723 or 1728*)

Park and Summer Streets; on request; Mr. and Mrs. F. E. Kusiak.

Built by Noah Webster for his daughter Debrah, who married Zebulon Giddings, it was in the family until 1884. Fortunately, the present owners have done little to modernize it; the old paneling is unchanged. They keep it painted and in repair, but it serves as a home for their seven children.

FULSOM TAVERN

1770 Spring Street.

Washington had breakfast here.

Also worth noting are the GILMAN HOUSE (1736), at 46 Front Street, and the GILLEY HOUSE (1745), at 77 Park Street—the former used by Phillips Exeter Academy, the latter owned by the Colonial Dames.

¶ Dover

ANNIE E. WOODMAN INSTITUTE (*a museum*)

182 Central Avenue, owns the following group of houses at this address: JOHN PARKER HALE HOUSE (*1813*), WOODMAN HOUSE (*1818*), *and* WILLIAM DAMM HOUSE (*1675*); *daily, 2 to 5, except Monday; Harry O. Berry (custodian).*

The Hale and the Woodman are large foursquare houses in the style of early nineteenth-century Portsmouth, and contain interesting collections of everything from china and furniture to birds and minerals. The William Damm House was built to withstand Indian attacks, of massive hewn timbers more than twenty feet long. It is one of the last of the old garrison houses.

¶ Concord

FRANKLIN PIERCE HOUSE

52 South Main Street; April 1 to December 25, by request; contribution.

Although this later house is the last one Pierce lived in, and the one least associated with him, it is the only one which may be seen. It has furnishings of the 1850

What could be more attractively typical of New Hampshire village architecture than the foursquare Pierce homestead in Hillsboro?

period. At 18 Montgomery Street is the only house he owned here, and the one he lived in from 1842 to 1847, when he also served in the Mexican War. When he was elected President, the Pierces were living at 60 South Main Street. He boarded for two years at 52 South Main Street and died there in 1869.

¶ North of Concord

Boscawen

FORT ACRES (c. 1760)

On Daniel Webster Highway (King Street); daily, May through October; Mr. and Mrs. Omar T. Lassonde.

First came the fort and then the salt box house and barn a few rods away from it. The old house has outlasted the fort and commands a magnificent view of the Merrimack. Mrs. Lassonde is a direct descendant of the Reverend Robie Morril, who built it, which fact she discovered only by chance, after living in the house ten years. Mr. Lassonde, an artist, has converted the barn into a small art gallery. Both buildings are well preserved; on one of the beamed ceilings the date 1769 is clearly discernible.

¶ Franklin

THE PINE CUPBOARD (1790)

925 Central Street; by appointment; Mr. and Mrs. Raymond G. Clifton.

Once owned by Daniel Webster and moved to its present location in 1808. It is furnished with pine and maple antiques and collections of pewter and toleware.

DANIEL WEBSTER MEMORIAL

Off Route 127 between Franklin and Salisbury; daily May 15 to October 15; with guide 25 cents; State Parks and Historical Sites, Recreation Division; Mr. and Mrs. Orr (caretakers).

A miniscule house where Webster was born in 1782 on a hardscrabble farm, furnished sparsely with originals of the period and Webster belongings. The MANSION (1790) next door was occupied by Webster's father and family for many years; has authentic Webster relics. ABIGAIL WEBSTER HOUSE is also next door. Both private.

¶ Canterbury

SHAKER SETTLEMENT

(main dwellings 1793; white meeting-house 1792)
Off Boscawen Road. New Hampshire Historical Society.

It consisted originally of thirty buildings nestling among huge maples. Men and women lived apart. In 1949 there were still sixteen Shaker women living there; *no* men. In summer, now, they live scattered one or two in a house. The meeting-house (1792) dominates the compact group. The Community was formed in 1792 on the farm of Benjamin Whicher. He became Elder in 1794 and remained so until his death.

The parlor of the Hillsboro Pierce house in which the President lived for a while is papered in French scenics.

¶ *Bridgewater*

ELM LAWN INN, *formerly* **HOYT'S TAVERN** (*c. 1800*)

Newfound Lake; Robert E. Erickson.

A stagecoach stop, the original section was built by Hoyt, the first proprietor. Still used as an inn.

¶ *Wolfeboro*

CLARK HOUSE (*1778*)

South Main Street on Route 28; July and August, on varying days; headquarters of Wolfeboro Historical Society.

Fully furnished with early nineteenth-century pieces, including a display of rare pewter. Tea and punch served in old-fashioned garden without charge.

¶ *Laconia*

SHELTERFIELD

(lunch or dinner by reservation) *(1760)*

Off Parade Road; daily, May to November; Mr. and Mrs. William Allen Camp.

New Hampshire houses have their own distinction and character. This one, with its huge central chimney, double oak sills, wide floorboards, petticoat molding on staircase, original hardwood, and excellent paneling is in the tradition. It is furnished with some old pieces; the other furnishings are harmonious. A collection of blackberry milk glass.

¶ *Center Sandwich*

ELISHA MARSTON HOUSE (*c. 1847*)

Headquarters of Sandwich Historical Society.

The house is filled with the Society's collections of furniture, books, records, and mementos of early times. There is also a fine collection of early tools used in farming and industry on display, and the bar houses a replica of an old country store, cracker barrel and all. Elisha Marston was a shoemaker and tanner by trade who made copper-toed boots. The building is one and a half stories with barn attached, typical of Sandwich.

Other notable old houses in Sandwich are the SHERMAN HOIT HOUSE, built in 1810 by Gen. Daniel Hoit; the JERE-

Many of the early houses all through New England were specially built to serve as places of refuge in emergencies: log-built, heavily boarded, and so on. It was from such a house that Fort Acres at Boscawen got its start.

Ocean-born-Mary house does not need a colorful legend to give it real distinction, but a colorful legend it has, as you will see, along with its real distinction of design.

MIAH SMITH HOUSE, next to the above and built before 1810; the old BLANCHARD HOMESTEAD, built in 1822 by Augustus Blanchard and maintained in its original state by its owner, Miss Jessy Flanigen; the STEPHEN FELLOWS place, built in 1806 and now the summer home of Professor Cornelius Weygandt of the University of Pennsylvania, who takes such delight in the "survivals of yesterday"; and the THOMAS BURLEIGH PLACE, used as an inn in its early days (1806), recently restored and now called the VILLAGE INN.

¶ *West of Concord*

¶ *Hopkinton (the first town below Concord)*

THE TOWNE HOUSE (*c. 1790*)
June and October, Mondays, Wednesdays, and Fridays 10 to 4; $1.00; Mabel K. Lomas.

An unusually imposing square white house with large fanlights in the gable ends. The hall, forty by twenty, gives an idea of its spaciousness; the hall, incidentally, is hung with its original French wallpaper. It was built by Joseph Towne, leading merchant banker, on what was then the Boston-Montreal Highway. Furnished with fine eighteenth-century American pieces.

¶ *Henniker*

OCEAN-BORN-MARY HOUSE (*1760*)
About 3 miles from town, well marked; May to December, afternoons only; 25 cents; L. M. A. Roy.

This isolated house on a hill has a romantic history without parallel in New England. Why such a fine house with so many unusual features was built in this out-of-the-way spot is a part of the story. In 1720 a party of Scotch-Irish immigrants were on their way from Londonderry to New Hampshire when pirates boarded the ship. At this inauspicious moment, Mrs. James Wilson, recently widowed, gave birth to a girl. The pirate captain was moved to spare the ship provided the baby was named for his mother Mary. Boarding the ship again, he brought gifts to the infant, among them a fine piece of blue silk for her future wedding gown. His command was carried out. After doing service for the weddings of Mary and many of her descendants, a piece of the silk still survives, now in a frame in the house. There is some difference of opinion as to the builder of the house. But the present owner states that it was the pirate himself, who retired with his crew, which included ship's carpenters and Negro slaves, and built it so that in time Mary might live here with her sons. The pirate met with a violent death near the house, but Ocean-born Mary lived to be ninety-four years old and died in what is now called the eagle room, in 1814. The room was hers and the blue eagle with its *sixteen* stars painted over the mantel was her work, the stars representing the number of states then in the Union. The beautiful paneling in this room is unsurpassed in this section of the country. Deep cornices, large twenty-four-pane windows, wainscoting two feet wide, and six-panel doors fitted with box locks and H and L hinges; many of the doors have the Crusader cross. The front door has crane hinges. A door on the stair landing leads into the massive chimney, which was used to smoke hams. The house contains six fireplaces, two of which contain brick cooking ovens. The weather-beaten exterior, with its hip roof and two dormers, has unusually fine fenestration. Mr. Roy and his mother took the beautiful old house some years ago, after it had stood empty a long time, and rehabilitated it—for the most part with their own hands. Both of them are skilled in crafts, and they have treated it with an inspired affection and understanding. Mrs. Roy revived the old arts of spinning and baking here, and her spirit lives on in the house with that of its first occupant, Ocean-born Mary.

¶ *Hillsboro*

PIERCE HOMESTEAD (*1804*)
Near junction of Routes 9 and 31; daily 1 to 5, May 15 to October 15; State Recreation Division.

Square and simple, with a fine doorway, this handsome house was the home of Franklin Pierce's father, who was twice Governor of the state. The parlor contains noteworthy French wallpaper, still in fine condition. Another room has a fine stencil by an early itinerant painter, well preserved. The grandnieces Misses Mary and Susan Pierce act as hostesses here, and are as interesting as the house.

¶ *Hancock*

HANCOCK HISTORICAL SOCIETY HOUSE (*c. 1809*)
Wednesdays, Saturdays, and holidays 3 to 5, May 30 to October 12; Hancock Historical Society.

On one of the finest typically New England main streets in the state stands this simple, handsome brick building with flat hipped roof, tall end chimneys, and twenty-four-pane windows, widely spaced. Within, there are simple mantels, lovely dado paneling, and appropriately simple furnishing; also exhibits of all types of utensils, clocks, tools, and band instruments.

JOHN HANCOCK HOUSE (*an inn*) (*c. 1793*)
In town on Route 123 just off Route 202; Mr. and Mrs. William D. Roche.

A drovers' inn at the turn of the nineteenth century, it is one of the prettiest places to stop in New England. Both spacious and gracious, the interior preserves the best of the old-time atmosphere, with modern conveniences added. The frescoed walls of one bedroom were painted by an itinerant at that time, and there is evidence that he may have done other rooms during his stay. Pay for these beautiful murals was often taken in board and lodging.

HISTORICAL HOUSE (*1809*)
Main Street; Memorial Day to October 12, Wednesday, Saturday, and holidays 2 to 5; donation; Hancock Historical Society.

Built as a tavern by Charles Symonds on a farm that adjoined the property of Governor Hancock, this strikingly fine brick building, with its twenty-four-pane windows spaciously separated and its tall chimneys soaring above the hipped roof, is another demonstration of the pride and skill of the country craftsmen in the days when these far Northern states were almost wilderness. Tavernkeeper Symonds introduced an innovation in 1835—the first cookstove. Before that there was only the fireplace, of course. Later the building became the home of Albert Anthony, the town harness-maker. Today it is cherished by the residents of Hancock, who have donated many of the furnishings, most of which are of local interest and origin.

¶ Sharon

LAWS HOUSE (c. 1800)
New Ipswich Road (Route 123); by appointment; S.P.N.E.A.

This interesting old house is part of the Sharon Art Center.

¶ New Ipswich

BARRETT HOUSE (1800) or
FOREST HALL
Main Street (Route 123); daily 11 to 5 except Wednesdays and Saturdays 11 to 1, mid-June to mid-October; 25 cents; S.P.N.E.A.

An impressive three-story white clapboard mansion of the Federal period, it is surrounded by a beautiful iron fence. The grounds were landscaped in the early 1800s; ancient maples, fourteen all told, line the ascending terraces leading up to an old summer house. Within there are portraits, early wallpaper, delft tiles on eight of the fireplaces, Waterford and lusterware—a housefull of treasures. Across the front of the third floor is the "grand" ballroom, unspoiled. The musical glasses are still here.

South of Concord
Manchester

CURRIER GALLERY OF ART
129 Orange Street; daily 10 to 5 except holidays, Sundays 2 to 5.

Large collections of American furniture, silver, pewter, and textiles, of the seventeenth and eighteenth centuries; some rooms completely furnished.

STARK HOMESTEAD (1736)
1070 Canal Street; shown any time by occupant or member of Molly Stark Chapter, D.A.R.

Built by the father of General Stark, it remained in the family until 1821. Given to the D.A.R. by the Amoskeag Industries, it was restored as nearly as possible to its original state. A typical New England farmhouse, painted red with white trim, it has some fine paneled walls and high oak mantels, but only a few rooms are furnished in period. Three rooms are used for museum exhibits.

¶ Derry

PINKERTON HOUSE (1735–1816)
On request; Mr. and Mrs. Ralph A. Smith.

Fortunately, the fine paneling, said to have been brought from England, and the beautiful stairway, were not too badly damaged by a fire here in 1952. The house was built by Maj. John Pinkerton, one of the founders of the Pinkerton Academy, who operated a store in it. The scale of the woodwork is manorial, but why and how such a house happens to be here is not known.

¶ Up the Connecticut River Valley

¶ Walpole

HARMONY HILL (1818)
On written request, June 15 to October 15; 50 cents for Walpole Historical Society; Mrs. Robert A. Hubbard.

Built by Ephraim Holland, whose descendants still occupy it, it is in the clear-cut, appealing Colonial tradition of these parts, but with ornaments here and there on doorways and mantels which betoken the advent of the Classical Revival. Family furnishings of many generations back are here, along with old pewter and silver. In the kitchen many fascinating old household things are now on display.

¶ Charlestown

SAWYER HOUSE (c. 1804)
By appointment; Mrs. Eleanor Sawyer; antiques.

A very fine Federal house with unusual details. The furniture and furnishings couldn't be better for the house.

¶ Claremont (12 miles below Hanover)

RIVERFIELDS (early 1800s)
Route 12A, 20 miles south of Hanover, at D.A.R. marker; on written request, June 1 to September 15; Mr. and Mrs. Charles B. Officer (address other times: 810 2d Place, Plainfield, N.J.).

In 1825, when Lafayette visited Dartmouth College, some of the students pulled him to "Riverfields" in a wicker carriage. If he expected to see a farmhouse, he must have

This is one of a notable "row" of Federal houses set far back from the highway at Orford, of which the Capt. Samuel Morey house is another. The arched recesses that occur in some of them, as here, have given rise to the supposition that Bulfinch may have worked on them, this being a familiar device of his.

been quite astonished; for here is a façade full of hand-carved detail of a most unusual nature. The fluted pilasters, ornate Palladian window over a still more ornate entrance, and carved and dentiled cornice all go to make up one of the most charming exteriors in the state. It was built by Godfrey Cooke, whose father was said to have paid for the land with a bushel basket full of Continental money. A few pieces of his furniture have been purchased by the present owners and have been supplemented with Chippendale, Sheraton, and Hepplewhite. Two rooms have their original hand-blocked paper.

¶ Cornish

AUGUSTUS ST. GAUDENS MEMORIAL, *formerly* HUGGINS TAVERN (*1800*)

> *Route 12A, 2 miles north of covered bridge on Connecticut River at Windsor; daily*

> *10 to 6, May 30 to October 15; 25 cents; Augustus St. Gaudens Board of Trustees.*

The well-known sculptor lived in this large two-story brick house with its two fine chimneys and stepped gable ends, and it was remodeled for his greater convenience in the 1880s. The studio, reached through a lovely garden, was once the stable for the inn. Later a larger studio had to be built for his monument of General Sherman, which now stands at Fifth Avenue and 59th Street in New York City. The marble Ionic temple in the meadow is the tomb of the sculptor and his wife.

¶ Orford

CAPT. SAMUEL MOREY HOUSE (*1793–1798*)

> *May to October, written request; Mrs. Lyman Tiffany Dyer.*

This is one of a remarkable row of seven

elegant houses of the Federal period, set well back from the road and all different— one of the rare collections of the state. The Captain Morey who built this house built a little steamboat at about the same time and ran it on the Connecticut River here some years before Fulton's more famous trip on the Hudson. The houses are all Federal in feeling. One *may* have been designed by Bulfinch.

¶ Haverhill

THE 1812 HOUSE (*an inn*)
(*1808 or 1809*)
Dartmouth College Highway; daily, June 15 to Labor Day; Miss Sue Ralston.

Charmingly small and personal. Miss Ralston, who is glad to show anyone around, has furnished it with assorted antiques and chosen appropriate wallpapers and wall colors. A good place to stop over, for Miss Ralston will arrange to show, or direct you to, other houses that may perhaps be visited.

THE MAINSTAY, *formerly* BLISS TAVERN
By appointment, July, August, and September; 50 cents; Mrs. Howard W. Sullivan.

This is a stately square white frame structure with identical doorway front and side and eight-paneled doors capped by fanlights and a broken pediment. Bliss was the first postmaster, commissioned by George Washington in 1790; he was probably also the innkeeper, and obviously a man of substance to be able to build such a fine house. It was later a station on the Underground Railway.

GEN. JOHN MONTGOMERY HOUSE
(*1785*)
June to October; Cecil and Grace Wilson-Lavery.

Now an antique shop, it is another charming house whose beautiful proportions and fine simple lines are typical of the abundant good architecture in this town, which represents New Hampshire unspoiled.

This little gem stands at the northerly end of the famous Orford "row."

The delicacy, fantasy, and naïveté which went into the design and execution of this mantel and chimney piece in the Ruggles house at Columbia Falls are rare qualities to encounter in such a faraway spot. This parlor is the prize room of the house, but on page 71 you will see the staircase which is equally fine. Across the page is the Hamilton house, standing in great style near South Berwick.

MAINE

¶ Kittery Point ¶ York Village ¶ In & out of South Berwick:
Alfred; The Kennebunks ¶ In & out of Portland
¶ In & out of Brunswick ¶ The back country from Brunswick:
Winthrop; Hallowell ¶ Augusta ¶ Back to the coast and
continuing down east: Pittston; Wiscasset; Thomaston; Belfast;
Castine; Ellsworth; Columbia Falls; Machias; Dennysville

IN THE *WPA American Guide Series,* Maine architecture is characterized as "eminently suited to its time and place" and as belonging "to its particular background and landscape." This pretty well describes the early houses in all the states, but especially so the early houses of Maine. The long cold winters of this coastal country were responsible for the evolution of the typical long, rambling farmhouse in which every outbuilding is connected to the main one, so that in bad weather one could keep under cover. Rooflines step pleasantly up and down, and woodshed openings often form a flat arch. The effect is not only trim and attractive, but gives the farmsteads a homey look of self-sufficiency much like the character of the people who live in them. The houses, like the famous Maine fishing boats, are built for practicability first of all rather than for mere attractiveness, but like the boats they manage beautifully to achieve both. This is a common characteristic throughout northern New England, but it seems to be most in evidence in Maine. Right here let it be said, however, that when Maine houses decided to be elegant, they did so with the best of them—as will be noted.

In such towns as York, Kittery, Saco, and Kennebunk you will see a number of eighteenth-century homes, and even a few dating back to the late seventeenth. But of the first French and British settlements along the coast few if any traces remain, except blockhouses or forts. Life in the territories granted by the Crown to the proprietors was unstable in the extreme. The bitter fighting, between the French and English, both sides enlisting the Indians when they could, or between red men and white, lasted a long time. It wiped out the early settlements on Monhegan Island, where Capt. John Smith made a landing in 1614; on Mt. Desert Island, where Champlain landed in 1604; and on the mainland as well, populated sparsely with adventurers and fur traders who were tough enough to brave the hard life.

With its long, deeply indented coastline strewn with islands, Maine has always been married to the sea, and whatever wealth it has accrued has come from the sea. This is why so many of the choice early houses here are to be found in the towns and villages that lie in close communication with the coast, all the way from Kittery to Canada. Some of the houses, especially near Kittery, reflect the tastes of the British aristocrats who built them in the early days, but they are the exception in Maine and not the rule. Their elegance may be found in similar modes of building in other parts of New England. But as time went on, the lords and ladies disappeared, and sea captains and merchants took their places. This later breed built houses with an eye toward comfort and durability—which is still the way many Maine houses are being built, so that sometimes you can hardly tell the new from the old.

From the latter part of June to the end of August there are ample opportunities

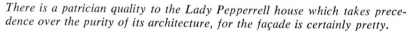

There is a patrician quality to the Lady Pepperrell house which takes precedence over the purity of its architecture, for the façade is certainly pretty.

for visiting some of Maine's more distinguished early houses which happen to be private homes. At least a dozen towns hold house-and-garden tours, but not all make yearly events of them. Some celebrate bi- and tricentennials; that's how old many Maine towns are getting to be.

To be absolutely sure when and where house-and-garden tours and open-house days are going to be held, write to the Maine Publicity Bureau, Gateway Circle, Portland, for its calendar of events for the summer, and also for a list of its information centers, which you will find to be extraordinarily helpful institutions.

The towns which follow are arranged as you would come upon them entering the state at Portsmouth, New Hampshire, and working your way "down East," with occasional forays inland as indicated.

¶ *Kittery Point*
  (on Route 103, 4 miles from Portsmouth)

On November 4, 1789, Washington landed here briefly from a barge while exploring Portsmouth Harbor—the farthest north he ever went.

LADY PEPPERRELL MANSION (*1760*)
  Daily 10 to 12 and 2 to 4, mid-June to mid-September; 50 cents; maintained by S.P.N.E.A.

This house, built for Lord Pepperrell's widow by British workmen brought over by her ladyship, is one of the great ones of New England. It is striking in appearance, with its Georgian façade of snow-white shiplap styled with unusual sophistication and strength of character. It is as elegant within as without, and beautifully finished. Even after the Revolution had rendered its owner's title null and void by transforming her into an American citizen, Lady Pepperrell still insisted that she be addressed with the deference she fancied to be her due. There was never any question about the nobility of the house itself.

SIR WILLIAM PEPPERRELL MANSION (*1682*)
  On request in advance; Mr. Joseph W. P. Frost.

Still occupied by a direct descendant of Sir William's, this two-and-a-half-story gambrel built of wood stands firm and unaltered, much of its interior paneled from floor to ceiling. The furniture is Queen Anne and Chippendale; the rugs, silver, and pewter are all handed down from the Pepperrells, the Brays, the Frosts, and the Goodwins. A complete eighteenth-century library contains, among other choice items, the diary of Chief Justice Samuel Sewall, who was the judge at the Salem witchcraft trials and a grandfather of Lady Pepperrell.

BRAY HOUSE (*1662*)
  By appointment in advance; Mrs. David A. Wasson and Mrs. N. C. Ayer.

Even older than Sir William's, the Bray House retains many of its medieval features, but the owners have made certain concessions to comfortable living which add greatly to its charm and interest—for there are plenty of early museum houses in which no such concessions are made. Maintained and furnished with feeling, its sunny windows open on a beautiful, boat-filled bay.

SPARHAWK HALL (*c. 1740*)
  Not open, but can be seen from the road.

CHAMPERNOWNE FARM (*1680–1880*)
  By appointment only; Miss Rosamond Thaxter.

This was the home of the Maine poet Celia Thaxter, grandmother of the present owner. It is the third of three houses built on the foundations laid by Capt. Francis Champernowne, who back in the seventeenth century planted the English elm that still stands on the lawn, a flourishing giant that people come from far to enjoy.

¶ *York Village*

Take your time here—lots to see. York celebrated its three hundredth anniversary in 1952, and though several other Maine towns have done the same, York can claim to be the oldest permanent settlement in the state.

Whoever has been enchanted by the writings of Sarah Orne Jewett will appreciate the personality that shines forth from her house, and nowhere so much as from her bedroom.

COVENTRY HALL (*c. 1790*)

By appointment, first and third Fridays of July and August; Mr. and Mrs. John Jacob Gunther (other address: Twilight Point, South Norwalk, Connecticut).

The mansion that Judge Sewall erected for himself here, and in which he entertained President Monroe, is still one of the finest in Maine. The wonderfully carved woodwork is much in the style of McIntire. It is fortunate for readers of the *Guide* that a connoisseur of Americana now owns the house and has agreed to let it be seen, even if only at limited times.

MOODY HOMESTEAD (*c. 1800*)

Moody Lane; by appointment, May 15 to early October (if owner there, may be seen also in winter); Mrs. William J. Neal.

The beauty of this house lies in its simplicity and directness. Its functional qualities mark it as the true Maine farmstead in which house, barn, and outbuildings join to form a harmonious whole. The owner is a descendant of the builder, which is part of the harmony.

ELIZABETH PERKINS HOUSE (*1686–1730*)

At Seawall's Bridge; daily, 11 to 4; 30 cents; York Society for Preservation of Historic Landmarks.

This was also a Sewall house and was the gift to the society of Miss Perkins, its recent owner. She left it furnished as she had lived in it, partly in antiques, both Victorian and earlier.

WILCOX HOUSE (*1740*)

In center of village; daily 10:30 to 5:30, Sundays 1:30 to 5:30; 50 cents; owned by Old Gaol Committee.

This had been a post office and tavern before it became first a private residence and then a museum house; its interior is now thoughtfully restored and furnished.

There are many other old houses of great interest in York: the SAYWARD MANSION, the JEREMIAH MOULTON HOUSE, the PATCH, the THOMAS CROCKETT, and WOODBRIDGE TAVERN. Mrs. Lucien Horton, an officer of The Antiquarian Society, will be glad to answer your questions about them. If you have a particular house you want to see that is not on our list, she may be able to arrange it for you. While you are there, don't miss the OLD GAOL, one of the town's most attractive possessions, with its bedroom for the gaoler, whose bed has the finest of crewelwork furnishings; JEFFERD'S TAVERN, brought here from Wells with some remarkable wall paintings intact (tea served from four to six); and the SCHOOLHOUSE, with its old school furniture (key at the Gaol).

¶ *In & out of South Berwick*

SARAH ORNE JEWETT HOUSE
(*1774*)
101 Portland Street; Wednesday through Saturday 12 to 5, late June to mid-September; 25 cents; S.P.N.E.A.

From the street this is a good example of a Maine town house of more than ordinary importance. Within it reflects the very special personality of a delightful and cultivated woman. The author was born here, and the fine furnishings are all hers. One of the lovely wallpapers was intended for a French colonial governor down Portsmouth way, but somehow the paper got here instead. The hall, with its charming wide arch and paneled dado, prepares you for the elegance of the little drawing room, with its delicate carved cornice and fluted corner posts. Built by Miss Jewett's grandfather, a wealthy shipowner, it was passed on to her father, a cultivated country doctor; but it is Sarah's own personality which is most clearly stamped on these rooms. Although some of the family furniture is here, much of it was of Sarah's own choosing and communicates an unmistakable fineness of feeling. The unassuming person who wrote that minor masterpiece *The Country of the Pointed Firs* and most of whose quiet life was spent here has left the imprint of a rare personality on the whole house.

HAMILTON HOUSE (*c. 1770*)
Ask at Jewett House for directions; Wednesday through Saturday 12 to 5 and Sunday 2 to 5, late June to mid-September; 50 cents; S.P.N.E.A.

This stately Georgian country seat reminiscent of Portsmouth grandeur has a beautiful riverbank setting above the Piscataqua, lovely to enjoy while relaxing on the terraced lawns. John Paul Jones was a frequent visitor. The accent inside is on color, and again feminine charm is in evidence, but of a less sensitive variety.

GEN. ICHABOD GOODWIN HOUSE
(*1797*)
Route 103, ½ mile from village square; on request to Miss Elizabeth Goodwin (phone: South Berwick 4362).

Across the field from the Hamilton House and in sharp contrast to it is this very attractive early country dwelling, now sheltering its fifth generation of Goodwins—namely, Miss Elizabeth, who is the hostess at the Hamilton House. Her own home is pleasantly furnished, and has a stenciled room of particular interest.

¶ *Alfred*

You can reach this nice little inland col-

The Jewett house is a simpler version of the Hamilton house just out of town and a relative of the Georgian mansions of Portsmouth not far away.

lege town from South Berwick via Route 4; then return to the coast at Kennebunk.

HOLMES HOUSE (*1802*)

Opposite village green; open upon request when owner is at home; Mrs. Elizabeth Marshall.

A remarkable house, with tall, slender two-story columns which support a roof whose balustrade is broken by square panels containing a delicate pattern of bows and arrows. Among other odd and charming features of this house is the vestibule room behind the porch columns, with its solid fan and shutters, whose roof forms a small square second balcony with colonnettes at its corners and a French window repeating the fanlight. John Holmes was one of the first two United States senators from Maine and chairman of the committee that drafted the state constitution. He employed a master builder with a mind of his own, for the house takes a lot of liberties with local traditions—with delightful results. There are many stories about the bow-and-arrow pattern of the roof balustrade, among them one that it was meant as a reply to those who said that Holmes was part Indian.

¶ *The Kennebunks*

THE BRICK STORE (*1825*)

117 Main Street.

A museum at which it is possible to obtain a map that points out the best early houses in town, dating from 1752 to 1826. None of these are open to the public except on special occasions, but they can be enjoyed from the street. Notable are the LORD MANSION, the BOURNE HOUSE, and the WEDDING CAKE HOUSE, the last a delightful fantasia of superimposed romanticism.

¶ *In & out of Portland*

The four houses below are the most entertaining in town, but three blocks of State Street from York to Congress Streets and a quick turn through High and Danforth Streets will give you a bittersweet glimpse of what it must have been like around here in the early 1800s. Keep imagining, and note especially 116 High and Number 51, Number 106, and Number 162 State.

TATE HOUSE (*1755*)

Just off highway leading from turnpike entrance to Portland, in Stroudwater; daily 2 to 5 except Mondays, July to mid-September; 35 cents; Maine Society of Colonial Dames.

The Colonial Dames have restored this remarkable old house with sparkle, taste, and skill, with the old exterior siding left to weather as they believe it has been doing

In noting the slender colonnade that so effectively surrounds the Holmes house, do not fail to take in the bow-and-arrow panels of the roof railing.

since the day the house was built. Note especially the recessed continuous dormer that lights the attic rooms where the house slaves were quartered; and for a neat decorating idea note the black strip painted above the bolection molding of the dining room. This was the strategically located home of the King's agent, whose responsibility it was to provide masts for the British Navy from Maine forests.

WADSWORTH-LONGFELLOW HOUSE (*1785–1786*)

485 Congress Street; daily 9:30 to 4:30 except Sundays, June 19 to September 18; 40 cents and 30 cents.

This is very pleasant Late Georgian. Filled with Longfellow memories and much personalia, it was built by the poet's grandfather Peleg Wadsworth, who later moved to the home in Hiram.

SWEAT MANSION (*1800*)

Spring and High Streets; daily 10 to 4:30 and Sundays 2 to 4:30, except July and August; Portland Society of Art.

Reached through the Sweat Museum, this is one of several fine Federal houses here in Portland by Alexander Parris, an architect from Boston at a time when professional architects were still few and far between. The detailing inside is just as delicately academic as the outside, and the furnishings exactly as the last owner willed them to remain forever.

VICTORIA MANSION (*1859*)

Park and Danforth Streets; daily 11 to 4:30 except Mondays, June 13 to October 1; 60 cents; city of Portland.

Perhaps the most remarkable Victorian mansion in America, it is the work of Henry Austin, an outstanding eclectic architect of the period. The general stylistic scheme is Louis XV, and splendor is really laid on with a lavish hand. No expense was spared to put into play the finest of rare woods and imported marble. Anyone with a weakness for Victorian in its more monumental mood will find this rewarding.

WADSWORTH HALL (*1787*)

40 miles out on Route 25, 1 mile from Hiram; daily; 25 cents.

The Hiram house that Longfellow's grandfather came here from Portland to build after the Revolution. During the war he was captured by the British at Thomaston and imprisoned at Castine, but promptly escaped. The place has furnishings of both personal and historical interest.

BAXTER HOUSE (*a museum*) (*1808*)

15 miles out on Route 25, on South Street in Gorham; Wednesday and Saturday afternoons 2:30 to 5, July and August.

Now a local museum with collections of early and late military relics, Indian artifacts, and rare coins.

The Tate house has one of the most aristocratically turned-out interiors of any small house in the country. Take, for example, the dining room here.

¶ *In & out of Brunswick*

In addition to the houses below, Nathaniel Hawthorne roomed at 76 Federal. The CHANDLER HOUSE at 75, and the DUNLAP HOUSE at 27, are the work of Samuel Melchers III, a master builder of Brunswick, who also did the GILMAN HOUSE at Oak and Union Streets; all of these were built around 1800. Melchers also erected the ALDRICH and other interesting houses just across the river at Topsham. After seeing them, you may agree that his was an unusually attractive talent.

HARRIET BEECHER STOWE HOUSE
   (an inn) *(1804)*
   63 Federal Street; open all year; Mary Baxter White.

Uncle Tom's Cabin was written here, and Longfellow lived here while a student at Bowdoin. It retains much of the original interior and considerable Stowe-period charm. A very good inn as well.

GILMAN MANSION *(1799)*
   Union and Oak Streets; open by special permission; small fee; Mr. George Foster.

The great white Colonial Gilman House sits in its own small park with a long view down the Androscoggin River, protected by its fountainlike elms. Melchers designed the twenty-four-room mansion, with its balustraded roof and arched dormers, for a sea captain, John Dunlap, whose great-grandchildren are living in it today. The principal rooms are paneled in Brunswick white pine. The drawing rooms run the fifty-foot length of the house, and are papered with gilded wallpaper and lit by crystal chandeliers, all from France. The heirlooms and mementos are in themselves a history of Maine notables. The century-old garden should not be overlooked.

PENNELL MANSION *(1837)*
   Out of Brunswick between Harpswell and Merepoint on Pennellville Road midway down peninsula; by appointment in advance; Mr. and Mrs. Andrew Pennell.

Master builder James Pennell's house looks out upon the Atlantic. He was one of seven Pennells who came here, built their homes, and set up their shipyards nearby. His great map of the coast of China is unfurled on a wall with his sea chest beneath, and his spyglass is right where he left it. From the octagonal cupola there are sweeping views of the sea. The great white house has never been altered, and little has been added to the original old family furnishings. There are six or more Pennell houses here —all fascinating.

¶ *The back country from Brunswick*

¶ *Winthrop (15 miles west of Augusta on Route 202)*

METCALF HOUSE *(1790)*
   Occupied summers only, visitors welcome any time on request; Mrs. Guy E. Healey.

Deacon Metcalf, a cabinet and furniture maker who came to this section from Franklin, Massachusetts, in 1789, built his house of hewn native-oak timbers fastened with wooden pins, and two-inch elm planks. The interior, with its six brick fireplaces, has extensive native-pine paneling. There is a FAIRBANKS HOUSE here where Deacon Metcalf stayed when he arrived (see Dedham, Massachusetts), and there are the WILLIAMS and LONGFELLOW HOUSES nearby, both built in 1766, as well as the BISHOP TAVERN *(1790)*. All are sturdy and simple dwellings, well worth a look. Mrs. Healey, a hospitable person, will help you to identify them, and you can probably get in to see the others if you ask.

¶ *Hallowell (just south of Augusta)*

PRECEPTOR MOODY HOUSE
   (eighteenth century)
   Recently remodeled but not now occupied; Mr. and Mrs. Gilbert W. Maxwell, 14 Middle Street, will show it as long as it belongs to them.

THE BIRD CAGE
   (nineteenth century)
   159 2d Street; by appointment at owners' convenience; Mr. and Mrs. Charles Gatchell.

Known to local people as the "Bird Cage" partly because of its small size and partly because of its extraordinary iron balconies. Architecturally speaking, it is unique for the downstairs is made up of two twelve-sided rooms. The façade of this amazing villa, whose inspiration is Italian, has two windows and a door whose immense openings cover virtually the entire front wall. Tall chimneys, rising at the one-story level of these two rooms, bracket a pediment supported by Ionic columns. The proportions are odd but pleasing.

VAUGHAN HOMESTEAD (*1794*)
June to October, by written appointment with Mrs. Langdon Marvin; the Vaughan family.

Benjamin Vaughan came to the new country a man of parts, for he had been secretary to the English Prime Minister and a member of Parliament. Naturally he came to know all the important Americans of his time, and letters from Jefferson, Adams, Bowditch, Rush, and many others are part of the family possessions here. For his spacious home he could not have chosen a lovelier location: on a curve of the Kennebec River, with a section of virgin pine and spruce still covering the steep banks of a nearby ravine whose waterfalls cascade down to a swift stream. The house itself is in the foursquare Maine tradition, with hip roof, tall chimneys, and considerable elegance of country-seat quality. Ample to begin with, it has been augmented in the spirit of the original by the family who have always lived in it and still do. The original furniture, brought from England by Benjamin Vaughan, is for the most part still here.

¶ Augusta

BLAINE HOUSE (*1830s*)
Daily, 2 to 4, except Saturdays and Sundays; state of Maine.

The Blaine House, on the capitol grounds, built in the Classical Revival vein, is pleasantly impressive rather than picturesque or stylistic. It is now the residence of Maine governors. There are things to see inside if you have the time. It was once the home of James G. Blaine.

STATE HOUSE (*1829*)
Any time.

This place still has most of its Bulfinch exterior.

FORT WESTERN (*1754*)
Daily, May to October; 25 cents.

A very interesting example of the fortified communities in which Maine settlers sought refuge in wilderness days. As close as anything you will see to early provincial architecture here.

¶ *Back to the coast and continuing down east*

¶ Pittston (*10 miles from Fort Western toward Wiscasset*)

MAJ. REUBEN COLBURN HOUSE (*1765*)
Less than 1 mile from village; open by appointment in advance (phone: Gardiner 248); Mr. and Mrs. Paul S. Plumer, Sr.

Like the old houses in the little roadside town nearby, the Major Colburn House is a plain white frame country house with green shutters. It has twelve rooms, and was built by the four Colburn brothers, who came here with their four sisters from Dunstable, Massachusetts, in 1761. The Colburns built the two hundred and twenty boats that carried Col. Benedict Arnold's little army of eleven hundred soldiers on the Quebec expedition. Arnold and his officers lodged here; their men lived in crude shelters on the grounds.

¶ Wiscasset

Note the LEE-PAYSON-SMITH HOUSE on High Street opposite the library, and the ABIEL WOOD HOUSE on the corner of High and Lee Streets—both lovely. For that matter, there is a lot more that is lovely along the unspoiled streets of this notable old town.

TUCKER CASTLE (*1807*)
East End of High Street; by advance appointment; Miss Jane Tucker.

A sea captain's copy of a castle in Dunbar, Scotland, it is an unusual and fascinating house, full of the character of the family that lived in it for more than a hundred and fifty years. Miss Jane Tucker will show the house when she is able. She evokes the memories of this house so vividly that everything in it comes to life again.

NICKELS-SORTWELL HOUSE
(1807–1808)

Main and Fort Streets; by written or phoned appointment; $1.00; Miss Frances A. Sortwell.

A tall and most attractive town house with a fine entrance portico, Corinthian pilasters, and a central Palladian window. You enter through one of the loveliest doorways in Maine. The interior is correspondingly interesting and fine in detail, furnished with many old family pieces.

¶ *Thomaston*

MONTPELIER (*reconstruction of Henry Knox House of 1795*)

Route 1 1 mile north of town; daily 10 to 6, May 30 to October 31; 50 cents.

This gleaming mansion which dominates the landscape celebrates the hero of the Battle of Bunker Hill and the Secretary of

Still pretty fine in spite of the traffic, Wiscasset has been one of the wonder towns of Maine, and the Nickels-Sortwell house is a prize possession.

War in Washington's first Cabinet. The façade is elaborate, the central section elliptical and ornamented by four engaged columns. The low roof is surrounded by a balustrade. Its eighteen rooms are furnished with antiques, many of them saved when the original house burned down.

¶ *Belfast*

FIELD HOUSE (*1807*)

139 High Street; on written or phone request; Mrs. John R. Dunton.

An imposing square hip-roofed house, typically Maine, with the barn snugged in close. It overlooks the whole city and the Penobscot, and what a sight that is! Built by the present owner's grandfather for his bride, it has been occupied continuously and lovingly by members of the family. Well kept up and full of gracious family atmosphere. Fine cornice carving both inside and out.

¶ *Castine*

As you approach Castine on either 166 or 166A, there are many fine Maine houses to be seen, and plenty of them in Castine itself, hanging over its harbor. On Perkins Street the BARTLETT HOUSE is known for its interesting fireplaces and staircase. Opposite is the WHEELER HOUSE (1810), of brick covered with clapboard. FORT MADISON, on the same street, was built before the War of 1812. The ABBOT, DYER, WHITNEY, and PARSON-MASON HOUSES all date from 1765 to 1805. Most of these are shown in the annual tour, which usually takes place the last week in July and includes twelve houses. It is sponsored by the Castine Women's Club.

JOHNSTON HOUSE (*1805*)

Main Street; by appointment; reasonable fee; Col. and Mrs. E. C. Gillette, Jr.

The Johnston House has a lovely doorway and a Palladian window. It is a sophisticated town house, with fine Adam detailing inside and a flying staircase. Good furniture.

The flying divided staircase of the Ruggles house shares the honors there with the mantelpiece in the parlor shown on page 60.

¶ Ellsworth

COLONEL BLACK MANSION (*1802*)
Main Street on Route 1; daily 10 to 5, July to November; small charge for guide service; Hancock County.

This handsome house was designed by Asher Benjamin for the Blacks, who filled their big home with the fascinating things that go with affluence and fashionable taste; fortunately it is all still here. Little was added after the 1860s. It is a great period piece, a little on the cluttered side within, which we happen to like once in a while—especially when the house is an Asher Benjamin.

¶ Columbia Falls

RUGGLES HOUSE (*1818*)
Daily; contribution; Ruggles House Society; Mary Ruggles Chandler (custodian).

You are really "down East" now and will be delighted to find this exquisite and un-expected piece of country Adam, with a divided flying staircase, a drawing-room chimney piece of superb cabinetry, and re-markable carving. This is one worth com-

ing many miles to see, which is what you'll have to do. Its custodian, Mary Ruggles Chandler, is the granddaughter of the builder. A house close to our hearts.

¶ Machias

BURNHAM TAVERN (*1770*)
Saturday afternoons June to October, or inquire.

This old tavern, with its continuous dormer on the order of the Tate House, is full of relics. The first owner placed slips of paper beneath each of the four cornerstones reading "Hospitality," "Cheer," "Hope" and "Courage." They are still here.

¶ Dennysville

LINCOLN HOME
(guest house) (*c. 1787*)
Mrs. Lois M. Styles.

This is a sturdy, eye-catching country homestead on a green slope overlooking the Dennys River docks and sailing vessels, and the bay. It is now a guest house, and there couldn't be a better place to break your trip. Breakfast is served. It passed from the Lincoln family only recently. General Lincoln, who was Secretary of War and Lieutenant Governor of Massachusetts, came here with Gen. Henry Knox right after the Revolution on a scouting trip through the wilderness. Later on Audubon spent some time here while Tom Lincoln, who accompanied the famous naturalist on his Labrador expedition in 1833, fitted out the schooner in which the trip was made.

The Field house in Belfast is a picture of prim Maine proportions—simple, four-square, and forthright.

Vermont is by no means a state of white clapboard cottages alone, as evocative as they are. The early houses here have great variety and a lot of individualism, the Langdon-Cole house in Castleton being an outstanding example of the latter, with its two-story bays and the attenuated columns of its entrance porch, the work of one of the rare early local architects. On the opposite page is the Dutton house at Shelburne Village, more typical of the early farmhouses, yet full of its own very personal character.

VERMONT

¶ *Up the western border: Bennington; Shaftsbury Center;*
Manchester; East Poultney; Castleton; Brandon; Middlebury;
West Addison; North Ferrisburg; Vergennes; Shelburne;
Burlington; St. Albans ¶ *More or less down the center:*
Brownington; Calais; Morrisville; Brookfield; South Randolph;
South Royalton; Woodstock; South Reading; Weston; Newfane
¶ *Up the Connecticut River Valley: Vernon; Brattleboro;*
Putney; Weathersfield Center; Windsor; Hartland; Norwich;
Newbury-on-the-Bow

*S*ETTLERS were getting established in the rigorous Vermont wilderness at about the same time that pioneers were striking out into the Middle West. The earliest frame dwelling still standing in the state, said to be the Parson Dewey House in Bennington, was built well after 1750, when the earliest houses you can see today in Salem, Ipswich, and elsewhere were already a hundred years old.

Vermont has always been famous for frugality, so it may come as a surprise to find here so many stylish and handsome houses. It is surprising too that the granite and marble so plentiful here rarely found their way above the foundations and doorsteps. Wood and, later, brick were far and away the favorite materials, as they were elsewhere throughout New England. And Vermont styles are pretty much an extension of New England styles that prevailed from 1750 on. Still, as in every other state, you feel a special regional quality which you soon begin to recognize.

Every year the Federated Garden Clubs of Vermont hold a State Garden Tour in early August (exact dates can be obtained from Walter R. Hard, Jr., Vermont Development Commission, or from Miss Shoemaker, Greater Vermont Association—both in Montpelier). These tours cover the towns of Bennington, Newfane, Manchester, Brownsville, Rutland, Middlebury, Barre, and Burlington, and while they are more concerned with gardens, they "try to have one or two old houses on display in each community as they are popular always."

The following arrangement of towns in Vermont is a regional one, and should work very well hand in hand with a good road map.

¶ Up the western border

¶ Bennington

There is nothing "open" here except the OLD FIRST CHURCH and the BENNINGTON HISTORICAL SOCIETY BUILDING down the hill on the way to Bennington, but both of these are beauties, and the village itself is very well worth a long, lingering look.

¶ Shaftsbury Center

GOVERNOR GALUSHA HOUSE
(*1804*)
On request; Mr. and Mrs. D. Henry Werblow.

A white Colonial frame house with a Palladian window over the front porch, whose fine qualities have caused authorities to attribute it to Lavius Fillmore, noted architect of the Middlebury and Bennington churches. Built for a Revolutionary hero who was nine times Governor, the house has always been so well cared for that everything is still intact, even the windowpanes and hardware. The present owners say that some of the Governor's own shirts, woven from flax grown on the farm, with even their buttons made of linen thread, are still preserved by his descendants. The house is furnished mostly with antiques. The southeast "best" bedroom has wall paintings done in 1810 by an itinerant French artisan.

MUNRO-HAWKINS HOUSE (*1820*)
Vacant at time of publication; apply for information to Herbert H. Leonard, Marhawlen Farm.

This is one of the gems of Vermont, and it is hoped that a local group led by Mr. Leonard will succeed in their desire to preserve it and allow it to be seen. The house was probably designed by Lavius Fillmore

The house that Joshua Munro built for himself at Shaftsbury Center when the price of wheat went sky-high during the Napoleonic Wars has been rightly called "an aristocrat among farmhouses."

Also in Shaftsbury Center is the Governor Galusha house with its remarkably sophisticated detailing; a house that is even more fascinating within.

of Bennington fame, but Joshua Munro, who built it, probably did a great deal of the work himself and with the help available in the neighborhood. Munro's story is of the rags-to-riches variety. Having been left an orphan in Bennington when he was a child, bound out to a shoemaker, he became wealthy by trading wheat when the Napoleonic Wars inflated the price. He built himself an "aristocrat among farmhouses," as Herbert Congdon has remarked. There is no doubt of it, for the restrained but elegant detail of the façade, with its Palladian window and perfect proportions, can hold its own in the society of more sophisticated mansions. As you might expect, the woodwork of the mantels, cornices, and doorways within is carefully contrived to please without ostentation. However, there is a surprise in store on the second floor, for here the broad hallway, beautifully lit by a Palladian window,

has a vaulted ceiling; and naturally the hall is flanked on either side by quite impressive bedrooms. For Mr. Munro's guests— only the best!

¶ *Manchester*

THE OLD TAVERN (*an antique shop*)
   (*1790*)
There are two rooms here well worth seeing, with finely carved woodwork in both mantels and chair rails.

¶ *East Poultney*

"When I entered Poultney, an aspirant to apprenticeship in her printing office, I knew no one of her citizens . . . I have never since known a community so generally moral, intelligent, industrious and friendly—never one where so much good was known and so little evil said, of neighbor by neighbor." When Horace Greeley wrote that over a hundred years ago, the harmonious atmosphere that pervades the town must already have been in evidence. The meetinghouse and the Eagle Inn, on the green, will make you stop your car even if you had not intended to, and there are many others that are worth your attention as well. The RISING SUN TAVERN, built in 1790, would have been one of these; owned by Mr. and Mrs. Richard Davis, it burned to the ground soon after they had given the *Guide* their consent to allow visitors. As you can see, compiling a book like this is not without its sad occurrences. However, look at the RANSOM-LOVERIDGE HOUSE next to St. John's Church, with its beautiful fanlight and lunettes, built in 1800 and unchanged throughout. Mr. and Mrs. Gilbert Loveridge are

the owners. There is another equally fine doorway at the HOWE-DEWEY HOUSE (1813) with a triplicate window above and pilasters framing both door and windows, which are repeated full length on the façade. It is owned by Miss Lottie Dewey.

On the annual tour in the middle of August these homes and several more are thrown open to the public under the auspices of The East Poultney Historical Society, whose president, Miss Agnes Haynes, may be able to help you see some of the houses if you write or phone her in advance.

EAGLE TAVERN (*c. 1785*)
> *Route 30A and Horace Greeley Memorial Highway; always open; 50 cents; Walter E. Johnson.*

Surely one of the loveliest and least typical buildings in Vermont, its parlor window looks out across the triangular green at the meetinghouse. Now a private home whose

The columns of the old Eagle Tavern at East Poultney, now a private home, were originally cut as masts for the British navy, but never managed to fulfill that purpose, creating instead the only colonnade of its kind hereabouts in its day.

hospitality is still in the tavern tradition, it is painted yellow, with twelve slender Doric columns supporting its hip roof on two sides. The columns were originally cut as masts for the British Navy, and for some reason are rather irregularly spaced. The interior, now furnished with antiques, has many fine features, but most interesting is the great vaulted room on the second floor, which served as a Masonic meeting place as early as 1791 and later was, of course, the scene of balls and entertainments for the whole countryside. Horace Greeley boarded here for two years, and much earlier Ethan Allen was a frequent guest. The rooms must have echoed to many a Revolutionary toast when the Green Mountain Boys passed this way.

GRANT-PEVERELLY HOUSE
(c. 1780)
April to January, by written appointment; Mr. and Mrs. A. O. Peverelly.

Built by John Grant, who was a cousin of Ethan Allen and father of Gen. U. S. Grant, this is one of the most interesting and oldest homes in town. The living-room woodwork is curious and beautiful, with wrought-iron medallions set into the window frames. Very little altered and furnished with heirlooms, it also contains a good collection of Currier and Ives. The key to the melodeon factory next door may be obtained here. The Historical Society is restoring the factory now.

THE OLD MELODEON FACTORY
(1808)
Key at Grant-Peverelly House; Poultney Historical Society.

THE OLD CHEESE FACTORY
(an antique shop)
Mrs. Arthur Williams.

THE BLACKSMITH SHOP
(an antique shop)
Mrs. Florence D. Clark.

¶ Castleton

Strung out along its wide country street, Castleton presents a rare opportunity to examine the work of a remarkable architectural craftsman who made this village his career. He was Thomas R. Dake

(1785–1852), and while there is no evidence that he was ever a pupil of Asher Benjamin's, his houses here show that he was familiar with Benjamin's books, though too much of an individualist to be a mere imitator. His Castleton houses have features you don't encounter anywhere else.

The first Wednesday in every August Castleton holds its Colonial Day, sponsored by the Castleton Women's Club. You can spend the night comfortably at CASTLETON INN (the ARMSTRONG HOUSE), which is really three houses joined together, the oldest dating from 1835. However, it is not essential to be there on that particular day to see most of the homes on the tour, for Castleton people are usually pleased to show their homes to visitors who are genuinely interested. A walk through Castleton, with pauses to see some of the unusual exteriors, will hardly consume a half hour. Be sure to see the MEACHAM-AINSWORTH HOUSE, with Dake's exquisite little portico carved, as is the frieze above it, in delicate, garlandlike traceries. The MALLORY JONES HOUSE has Dake's fine exterior detail—a paneled frieze with dentiled cornice. The RANSOM HOUSE is ambitiously Greek Revival (possibly not by Dake). Do not fail to see the staircase and paneling in the OLD DAKE HOMESTEAD; the fluted carving of the stringer is a delight. Another stairway which demonstrates Dake's great ability is that in the GRANGER-RANSOM HOUSE. The MALLORY-JONES HOUSE has a beautifully proportioned triple arch in the hallway, although the scale of the house is modest —as are, in fact, all the Dake houses (even the Langdon-Cole, in which he outdid himself.)

ST. JOHN-COLE HOUSE (1806)
On request.

Family heirlooms, Chippendale, and Hepplewhite.

LANGDON-COLE HOUSE (1823)

Summer and fall; owner's convenience; Mr. and Mrs. French Campbell.

This is Dake's masterpiece. No other house in the state has this scheme of two-story bays flanking recessed porticoes. Built for a popular gentleman named "B. F." Langdon, it was designed to suit his personality, it is claimed. From the free-wheeling style of the house, both odd and harmonious, we may gather that "B. F." went all the way with the gifted and original builder. The house is fittingly furnished with antiques.

HENSE HOUSE (early 1800s)

On request.

This place has hand-hewn beams and floors made of boards which are tapered like the trunks of the trees they were made from.

DEACON MERRILL'S COBBLER SHOP (c. 1785)

On request; Historical Society.

Being restored by the Historical Society, this is the oldest brick house in the state.

THE MAPLES (1811)

On request; Mr. and Mrs. Harold Brown.

Higley pewter and six ample fireplaces.

WOOLDRIDGE HOUSE (1850)

On request; Mr. and Mrs. Reginald Wooldridge.

Built for the owner's grandfather and left unchanged in memory of his good taste, this house has a Victorian parlor.

¶ *Brandon*

STEPHEN A. DOUGLAS BIRTHPLACE (before 1813)

4 Grove Street facing Conant Square; by appointment; Lake Dunmore Chapter, D.A.R.

In the room where the "Little Giant of Illinois" was born are his cradle and a table he made, for he was a cabinetmaker by trade before he became a debater. The simplicity of the house is its primary distinction.

¶ *Middlebury*

The Congregational church in this lovely old college town is one of the prettiest in New England. There are several houses of real distinction, and many of great charm. On the first Wednesday in August about ten of them are opened for the tour day; for further information write to Mrs. Chester M. Way, 1 Court Street.

MIDDLEBURY INN, THE ANNEX (1801)

Remainder modern.

SHELDON MUSEUM (1829)

May 31 to September 15 Monday through Saturday 10 to 5, September 16 to May 30 Tuesday through Friday 1 to 5; 50 cents and 25 cents; Board of Trustees.

In this three-story brick mansion each one of the dozen or more rooms represents a different phase of the early life of the community here and, in fact, of all Vermont. There is the comfortable, family-size kitchen with its huge fireplace; the schoolroom of 1810, complete with rum bottle; the country store, properly stocked; and the Victorian parlor, properly horsehaired. And in a building nearby there is a fine collection of early Vermont tools and vehicles.

COURT SQUARE (1802)

1 Court Street; first week in August; $1.00 for Veterans' Hospital; Mr. and Mrs. Chester M. Way.

Mrs. Way's own home is also permanently a part of the tour. This splendid Federal mansion with its double crown of balustrades on the hipped roof, looks as though it might have been brought here from Portsmouth, New Hampshire. If you are here when the house is open, there is much within to make a visit well worthwhile.

BATTELL HOUSE or COMMUNITY HOUSE (1814)

Main Street next to post office; daily September 25 to June 25 except Mondays; Middlebury.

This rates as one of Vermont's best "big" houses. Of yellow-painted brick, it is beautifully fenced along its sidewalk wall, and above a balustrade connects the two great gable ends. At the main entrance is a hood, oddly graceful, with its elaborate carved brackets resting on curved pilasters. The main entrance hall has a charming spiral staircase, overarched at its base. There are twelve mantels in the house, all well designed. The house is furnished with some antiques and some reproductions.

THE PRESIDENT'S HOUSE (*1840*)

3 South Street; any time on request by appointment; Mrs. Samuel S. Stratton.

This spacious residence has been very becomingly enlarged from what was originally a farmhouse. Now the home of Middlebury College presidents, it is furnished with some fine antiques and interesting pictures.

¶ *West Addison*

GEN. JOHN STRONG MANSION (*1796*)

Inquire at Vermont end of Lake Champlain Bridge; July and August, 10 to 5; 30 cents; Miss Erminie Pollard in charge; Vermont D.A.R.

Strong brought his family here in 1768 from Salisbury, Connecticut, traveling in winter because it was easier to make the trip by sleigh. Their first house was burned down in the border fighting, and Strong, who was away from home, lost track of his family. Finally one night at an inn one of his children heard his voice; his wife had taken a job in the kitchen there. Reunited, they returned to their land, and in the course of time were able to build this little mansion—an aristocrat among Vermont homes. The brick is laid in Flemish bond, and its Georgian elegance must have been something of an anomaly in its wilderness surroundings. Its perfect little portico, with delicate fluted colonnettes, is surmounted by a Palladian window, and that in turn by a fanlight in the low gable, giving it quite an air of sophistication. The lives of this courageous pioneer family, strong and simple, are reflected in the interior, with whose plainness the exterior seems to be delightfully at variance. The house was a station on the Underground Railway in slavery days, when the design of the brickwork provided a handy identification for the

A glimpse into the colorful old kitchen of the Langdon-Cole house at Castleton.

refugees. The false ceilings in the closets were installed as places of concealment, with secret access from the attic. The house, well cared for by the D.A.R., is furnished with Vermont antiques.

¶ *North Ferrisburg*

ROKEBY (*before 1792*)
> One mile north of Ferrisburg Center; daily, May to October; 25 cents; Mrs. Rowland T. Robinson.

Set high on a hill, this typical Vermont farmhouse was the home of Rowland Evans Robinson, famous and most loved Vermont author of nature and dialect stories. It was also a station on the Underground Railway. It has antique furniture and many of the author's possessions.

¶ *Vergennes*

GEN. SAMUEL STRONG HOUSE
(*an antique shop*) (*1793*)
> Southwest of Vergennes on Route 17, 1½ miles northeast of Lake Champlain Bridge; Mr. and Mrs. Samuel Wagstaff.

This house would be notable anywhere for its fine proportions and its masterly use of ornament on the façade. The handsome, unprotected doorway has successfully withstood the weather all this time, and its dignified and nicely executed entablature is repeated in small scale over the lower windows. The roof pitch is beautifully broken by a broad pediment with an oval window. The leaded glass in this window and in the fanlight over the doorway is particularly graceful in design, the latter centering on a gilt eagle.

¶ *Shelburne*

VERMONT VILLAGE
> 6 miles south of Burlington on Route 7; daily 9 to 3, May 15 to October 15; $1.75 and 50 cents (also group rates); Mr. and Mrs. J. Watson Webb (owner), Mr. Sterling D. Emerson (director).

A remarkable gathering of old buildings and one of the best collections of American folk art and early furniture and implements in the whole country. The project reflects the enterprise and taste of the owner, Mrs. J. Watson Webb, a collector of rare ability and discrimination, whose life has been devoted to bringing these things together. The Village and its collec-

The interiors of the Dutton house at Shelburne Village, whose exterior was shown on page 73, are masterly restorations, along with all the fascinating preservations of this museum village.

tions, which include the great old lake side-wheeler *Ticonderoga,* are constantly increasing. The VERMONT HOUSE, of gray stone, an austere building outside, has an extremely elegant interior both as to furnishing and woodwork, while the DUTTON HOUSE, an early red salt box from Cavendish, home of Gov. Redfield Proctor's mother, has a typical country-farmhouse interior of the early period, furnished to perfection. The STAGE COACH INN, a spacious building which dates from the wilderness period when Vermont was a republic, contains a ballroom extending across the whole east side. It houses what is probably one of the finest collections of folk art in the country. The QUILT ROOM contains over one hundred quilts and woven coverlets. The HAT SHOP contains half a hundred hat boxes covered with early decorative papers. The collections, including the early tools and the country-store items, constitute a complete education in each field. The STORE, by the way, with its cracker barrel and jiggle chair, dispensed men's corsets, shoes with copper toes, painkillers, and blood purifiers. Every detail is carried out by Mrs. Webb and her advisers with a human as well as a scholarly approach. Few restored villages in the country can compare with this one when it comes to making history colorful, entertaining, and human.

¶ Burlington

GRASSEMOUNT (*1804*)
> *Public rooms may be seen on request to University of Vermont.*

Regarded as the best example of Georgian in the state, this is now being used as a dormitory by the University of Vermont.

¶ St. Albans

HOUGHTON HOUSE (*1800*)
> *86 South Main Street; any time; Theodore S. Houghton.*

The exterior of this frame house, in spite of its fine doorway beneath a Palladian window, hardly prepares you for the beauty of the woodwork and wall painting within, most of which was done in 1828 by the first Houghtons to occupy the house when they decided to remodel the interior. The

Houghton daughter's diary, which has been preserved, tells of living at the hotel while the work was being done; it also describes the wall painting of birds and flowers in one of the bedrooms which had to be papered over on account of plaster damage. The decoration on the raised center panel of the parlor mantel may be the work of the same hand. This mantel, flanked by richly carved recessed arches which in turn frame a recessed doorway, is a beauty. The south parlor is equally ornate though less formal, with rope moldings on chair rails and baseboards, and a cornice to match the one in the hall. The dainty colonnettes which support the mantel taper to the bottom in true country Adam style. The present owners of the house, direct descendants, are happy to show it to those who will appreciate its unusual features.

¶ *More or less down the center*

¶ *Brownington (near Orleans in the extreme north center on Route 5)*

OLD STONE HOUSE (*1836*)
> *Orleans; daily, May 1 to October 31; 50 cents; Orleans County Historical Society.*

It was Rev. Alexander Twilight's idea to build this four-story granite dormitory for the academy which he founded. It took six years to complete. The exterior is plain, the low fourth story being a continuous six-window dormer. Twenty-six rooms are filled with antiques, furniture, clothing, home appliances, farm implements, and a library of historical documents.

¶ *Calais (10 miles north of Montpelier on Route 12)*

KENT TAVERN *or* FARMERS MUSEUM AND COUNTRY STORE (*1835*)
> *10 miles north of Montpelier; daily by appointment, admission by card from Vermont Historical Society, Montpelier, or from Mrs. Louise R. Kent, next door; Museum of Vermont Historical Society.*

Now used as a historical museum, this foursquare substantial brick-and-granite building has been preserved through the generosity of Atwater Kent, a Vermonter, who as a boy visited his grandfather Remember Kent here.

¶ *Morrisville (intersection of Routes 15 and 100, a little north of Stowe)*

NOYES HOUSE (c. 1820)

1 West High Street; daily in summer and any time by appointment; contribution; village of Morrisville, leased to Morrisville Historical Society.

This is set up as a local historical museum, one exhibit being a collection of 2,000 pitchers and Toby jugs and another a collection of clothing and household articles used by the first family of white settlers in the vicinity.

¶ *Brookfield (south from Barre on Route 14)*

MARVIN NEWTON HOUSE (c. 1831)

On request to custodian, Mrs. Ellen Bigelow; Brookfield Historical Society.

Partially furnished with belongings of its early residents, this house of primarily local interest was presented to the society by a descendant of the first owner. It has never been altered.

¶ *South Randolph (south of Brookfield on Route 14)*

THE ANTIQUE SHOP (1781)

Built by Experience Davis, this old house is said to contain one of the best collections of historic china in New England.

¶ *South Royalton (still farther down Route 15)*

FOX STAND (1818)

On written request; Mrs. Natalie Mickelson (usual address: 32 Adams Street, Oyster Bay, Long Island, New York).

Another impressive square red-brick house, with immense gabled ends, it was originally built as a hostelry, or "stand." Its doorways, both front and end, are amusingly off center. Neglected for some time, its present owner recognized its unusual distinction and is restoring it slowly. The simply paneled doors and wide fireplaces are in keeping with its impression as an inn of some substance, as is its grand ballroom on the second floor extending the whole length of the place. The owner plans to furnish it appropriately and to create an old-fashioned garden around it.

¶ *Woodstock (14 miles west of White River Junction on Route 4)*

This is one of the prettiest and most unspoiled towns in New England. It has become famous as both a summer and winter resort, partly because of its lovely situation on the Ottauquechee River, surrounded by mountains, and partly because so many of its old streets preserve the flavor of an early, prosperous rural village. The Woodstock Tour takes you into most of the fine old houses here. It takes place annually during the first week in August as a rule and lasts two days; The Historical Society, whose secretary is Mrs. A. W. Fowler, can furnish full information.

The only house which is regularly open to visitors (June through October) is the society's headquarters, the DANA HOUSE (1807), a pleasant village home on Elm Street furnished with antiques; various exhibits are displayed there during the summer. The WHITE CUPBOARD INN dates back to 1794, the RICHARDSON HOUSE to 1787, and the BENJAMIN SWAN HOUSE to 1801. The imposing LYMAN MOWER HOUSE (1823), built of brick with massive, broad chimney ends, is pictured in the *First Treasury,* as are the attractive JOHNSON HOUSE façade (1809), the early CONVERSE HOUSE, and the WARREN-KIDDER HOUSE (1807). The dates are all a good indication that the town is a delight to the eye, and the Woodstock Inn is excellent.

¶ *South Reading (south on Route 106 from Woodstock)*

EBENEZER ROBINSON HOUSE (rear 1792, front 1824)

Thursday through Sunday 2 to 5, June through October, by written or phone request only (Reading 4332); $1.00; Albert L. Brooks.

The new owners of the house have said, "Come for sunset"; for it is situated over one of the most exciting views of mountains and valleys in the state. The house, however, deserves daylight. The fanlight which crowns the triplicate window duplicates exactly the one over the doorway. The windowpanes are twelve over twelve below and twelve over eight above. There is a ceiling-to-floor stencil in the hallway, and another was discovered in the parlor behind the wallpaper. The present kitchen has the original maple paneling around the fireplace, including a little rum-cup cupboard paneled in the same. The early part of the house, in the back, was little more than a cabin.

¶ *Weston (west to Route 8)*
ORTON-ROSS HOUSE (*1828*)

On the green; by written request in summer; Mr. Vrest Orton.

Mr. Orton is the moving spirit of this out-of-the-way restored village. It is fitting therefore, that his fine tapestried brick house, presenting its façade to the green, should be the one that catches your eye first when you drive in here—and drive you must if you wish to visit this town. The walls are four bricks thick; the color is warm, but the arched doorway and the detail are chaste. In fact, it might easily have

One of the best off-beat early brick houses in Vermont, this is the home of Vrest Orton, who operates his early American country store nearby.

stood in any New England seaport fifty years before it was built here. The elegance of brick came late to Vermont as a rule, which makes these Weston houses all the more interesting. The Orton family, which settled in Vermont in 1763, left their descendant many fine pieces of local fabrication, late-eighteenth-century pine for the most part. Mr. Orton operates an early American country store nearby which stocks many of the items that were sold long ago. He tells us that he has upwards of fifteen hundred visitors a day here during the summer season.

FARRAR MANSUR HOUSE, MUSEUM, AND COMMUNITY HOUSE (*1797*)

Weston-on-the-Common; Tuesday to Sunday 1 to 5, June 27 to September 1; Weston Community Club.

Although this is a community house and is used as such, it is also a museum. It has retained much of its original flavor of a country tavern in an out-of-the-way village, which in early days was also the main center of communal activities and pleasures.

The Captain Farrar who built it came from a family of innkeepers in New Hampshire, but he made his public rooms so big that there was hardly room for extra bedrooms beside those needed for the family. Thus the tavern was well suited to becoming a private home, which happened in 1857 when it passed to the wealthy Mansur family whose mills and shops still stand behind it. They must have enjoyed the huge fireplace in the old barroom, whose heavy beams are smoked from countless fires and the rich fumes emanating from many a spitted roast turning there while it browned. The so-called "council chamber" was probably the best parlor, and well suited for that function by its odd and yet dignified mantel and the sliding inside shutters that afforded warmth and protection on cold winter nights. On the second floor, running across the whole front, is the ballroom, which was and still is the place for big gatherings, either festive or solemn. Most of the furniture here today was donated by people of the town, and so has a distinctively local quality, pleasantly informal, as

As typical an early Vermont village inn as there is to be found in the state is this large and famous one at Newfane.

you would expect. Some good primitive paintings on the walls.

¶ *Newfane* (*south from Weston via Routes 8 and 30*)

NEWFANE INN (*1787*)

> *On the green; open June 10 to October 25; Mrs. Gus Pucillo (proprietor).*

A large, rambling white building with long porches situated on an historic green, and facing other buildings of antiquity, such as the renowned OLD WINDHAM COURT HOUSE. The inn preserves much of its atmosphere, with no sacrifice of the comfort of the guests. Antiques are featured throughout. The food is said to be the best.

¶ *Up the Connecticut River Valley*

¶ *Vernon* (*a few miles south of Brattleboro on Route 30*)

JONATHAN HUNT HOUSE *or* **MANOR HOUSE** (*1770–1779*)

> *Power Plant Road; by appointment with owner by letter or phone (Alpine 4–2808); $1.00 for Vernon Children's Special Service Center of Brattleboro; Miss Florence Stol.*

You will see how it came by its second name when you go inside, for, while this oversize farmhouse with its big central chimney may seem a little austere, many people consider the interior, with its four paneled rooms, the very finest in Vermont. The elegance of the workmanship at the chimney end of the drawing room is as astonishing as the pine used for its creation; hewn from the giant first growth that Hunt found here, it is completely clear, without a knot. It is used in the wainscoting on three sides of these rooms as well. The rest of the house is unadorned like the exterior. Hunt started building his home on his land grant of ten thousand acres while he was still fighting in the French and Indian Wars. It was finished in time for him to bring his Boston bride here, and since it constituted a midway stop between Boston and Albany, it soon became a social and cultural center. After Vermont entered the Union, Hunt became the first Lieutenant Governor. His daughter founded one of the earliest hospitals for the treatment of mental illness, and his grandson was William Morris Hunt, the well-known nineteenth-century painter. The house has had its vicissitudes. It was famous as a station on the Underground Railway, and it is now being beautifully restored by an owner who appreciates it fully.

¶ *Brattleboro*

CARUSO HOME (*1768*)

> *140 Western Avenue, West Brattleboro; by written or phone appointment; 50 cents and 35 cents for local music center; Mr. and Mrs. Joseph Caruso.*

A typical Vermont house, the oldest in the township. The central chimney is intact, with a smoke chimney on the reverse side. All the floors are of unusual hardwoods, hand-planed. The house is pleasantly furnished in Early American, with some Victorian.

¶ *Putney*

DUMMERSTON (*mid-1700s*)

> *By appointment; Mr. and Mrs. John Locke, R.F.D. 2.*

An unusual example of a weathered Vermont farmhouse with "broken" clearstory gable. Built by Samuel Loughton, Jr., it was sold way back in 1790 to ancestors of the present owner. There is some interesting paneling, and the house, now remodeled for comfortable living, is suitably furnished for its display.

¶ *Weathersfield Center*

REVEREND DAN FOSTER HOUSE
(*summer home of minister*)
(*rear 1785, front 1825*)

> *On Meeting House Green; open summer months most of the time; voluntary contribution; First Congregational Church of Weathersfield (owners), headquarters of Weathersfield Historical Society, Box 275, R.F.D. 2, Springfield.*

A plain, typical Vermont farmhouse, it is furnished with examples of Weathersfield furniture, crafts, and pictures. There are many interesting old implements in the workshop and the kitchen. It was the home of the first minister, and later Cook's Tavern.

¶ *Windsor*

OLD CONSTITUTION HOUSE
(*c. 1768*)
15 North Street; daily, April 15 to
December 1.

A long, narrow frame building with a
steeply pitched roof, built as a tavern, it is
one of the earliest in Vermont. The Vermont constitution was drawn up and signed
here in 1777, and the first session of the
legislature took place here as well. It is
furnished with antiques, and has many interesting documents and portraits.

¶ *Hartland*

SUMNER-STEELE HOME *or* HATCH'S ANTIQUE SHOP (*1804*)

This is an extraordinarily fine Adamesque
house with an Asher Benjamin look. The
white balustrade which surrounds the lawn
is a fitting ornament to a most ornamental
country residence. The interior may be
viewed only at the owner's convenience.
Antiques are in the barn.

¶ *Norwich*

HATCH-PEISCH HOUSE (*1771*)
By written appointment, June, July, and
August; Mr. and Mrs. Archibald M.
Peisch.

Outwardly another austere New England
farmhouse with a big central chimney, it
has a living room considered one of the
finest in the state. Built by Capt. Joseph
Hatch, it was the first two-story structure in
the area; the beams were cut from first-
growth pine, as was undoubtedly the
sheathing. The paneling in the living room
is of first-rate workmanship; but of even
greater interest are the walls of the hall and
a bedroom of beautifully smooth pine
planks with wide V joints. The staircase is
a masterpiece of the joiner's art in its
delicate simplicity. The owners had the delight of uncovering all this excellence,
which was buried under plaster and wallpaper when they bought the house.

Mrs. Peisch will be able to tell you
whether it is possible to see the OLCOTT-
JOHNSON HOUSE nearby. The chimney wall
in its dining room is pronounced the finest
in Vermont, and there is little doubt that

any better paneling will be found in the
state.

¶ *Newbury-on-the-Bow*

This is one of the earliest settlements in
the state, set in lush green pastures
formed by the double bends of the Connecticut River. It has a long rectangular
Common, and many of its dignified old
homes are still standing in the northern
and oldest section of the village, known
as the "Oxbow." Here some of the
descendants of the Johnson family are
still living in the homes that were built
by Col. Thomas Johnson, of Revolutionary fame, who came here as a young
man in 1760 and helped to establish the
settlement along with Isaac Bayley. One
of these descendants is the well-known
best-selling author, Frances Parkinson
Keyes. Mrs. Keyes and her cousins, who
live across the road, are the fifth generation of the Johnson family to live in both
homes. These houses and the Isaac Bayley House, along with a few others, are
also open during the Annual Cracker
Barrel Bazaar (week of August 1), sponsored by the D.A.R.

DAVID JOHNSON HOUSE (*1806*)
Open on request when owner is in
residence, with reasonable advance notice
(when not there, her cousins at guest house
across street have key and are authorized
to take people through at their discretion.
House dismantled and unheated in winter);
Mrs. Frances Parkinson Keyes.

As Mrs. Keyes wrote us, "The front part
is an extremely interesting example of early
American architecture . . . the ell is
wholly Victorian in style. When my mother
inherited the house, the ell was in a bad
state of disrepair and, though she employed
one of the leading architects of the day—
Bowditch of Boston—to advise her in its
reconstruction, he did so in accordance
with the then prevailing taste. The result
is extremely commodious and comfortable
to this day, and, as a matter of fact, the
ell, in its own way, is as much a period
piece as the six rooms comprising the main

part of the house and their exterior. It is furnished throughout with Victorian family pieces." The front hall and the brown sitting room in the 1806 part of the house still have the original wallpaper. In this older section are many early heirlooms of unusual interest.

OXBOW FARM (*c. 1820*)

By appointment in advance; Mr. and Mrs. William J. Taisey.

A handsome foursquare brick house with a long one-and-a-half-story wing. The fine fenestration, arched doorways, and four good chimneys give the house its forthright character. The interior of Oxbow Farm has lovely woodwork throughout, each room but one having its own fireplace. It is furnished with antiques—English, American, and French.

In back is the original JACOB BAYLEY HOUSE, a white frame structure of the late eighteenth century which has not been restored but will be shown on request.

ISAAC BAYLEY HOUSE (*c. 1786*)

Oxbow Road, left off Route 5; by written request; Mr. and Mrs. Frederick B. Cobb, Wells River.

A white frame house of ample proportions, with a balustraded hip roof. The present owner is the seventh generation to live in it, a descendant of Gen. Jacob Bayley, who founded the town, and of Isaac, who built this house. Originally six rooms, it has

been augmented by successive generations five times, so that there are today seventeen rooms. The interior presents a picture of the changing tastes of a family, as some of the earliest pieces, along with examples of all the subsequent ones, are still here. The parlor is the outstanding room, having alcoves on either side of the fireplace—the so-called "courting" and "marriage" alcoves. In this room the sliding interior shutters may still be seen.

JOHNSON'S-ON-THE-OXBOW *or* HAINES JOHNSON HOUSE (*1800*)

Guest house mid-May to mid-November, at other times by special arrangement; Mr. and Mrs. Haines Johnson.

Your host and hostess here in this ample square New England farmhouse are the Haines Johnsons, for one of whose forebears the house was built—one of the four homes that Colonel Johnson erected for his sons after the Revolution. To savor the early atmosphere in this village, you could not do better than spend the night here. Little has been changed, except for the comfort of guests. The house has dispensed hospitality to the public before during its long history; the arched ballroom, running right across the front of the second story (now divided), tells a tale of the festivities and dances that made many of the early inns the social gathering places for the whole countryside.

For many years after it was erected in 1687, this was known as the "splendid mansion of Eleazar Arnold," and is a rare example of early Rhode Island dwelling, with many curious characteristics of construction inside and out. The masonry ends and the pilastered chimney are distinctive of the state. On the opposite page is the very stylish dining room of the fine Georgian Hunter house in Newport.

RHODE ISLAND

As FAR as heritage homes are concerned, the two particular high spots of this tiny but historic state are, first, the early part of Newport, with its rare assortment of colonial buildings, and, second, the College Hill section of Providence, with its remarkable array of post-Revolutionary mansions and other fine older houses. There might even be a man who would put Providence first and Newport second. If so, it would not be the first time that Rhode Island, small as it is, made room for another way of thinking. For remember, the Colony of Rhode Island, as founded by Roger Williams, embraced all beliefs, quite in contrast to the one-way conservatism of neighboring Connecticut and Massachusetts; and there are architectural historians who suggest that the varieties of thought and opinion that found a haven here might have been reflected in the early building manners of the colony— in such a house, for instance, as the little Clemence-Irons House at Thornton (a very early survival if the date of 1680 is correct). It is a highly individual type, found only in the region fanning out north and west from Providence. Stone-ended, with the masonry gable end rising into a pilastered chimney, and heavily framed in medieval fashion, it has the air of a house built with the strength of its own convictions.

And look how different the Wanton-Lyman-Hazard House of an even slightly earlier date is in Newport. The latter's trimness, its stylishness for the time, are surely a reflection of the fact that Newport was being settled by people of wealth and social position (though they too came to Rhode Island as religious dissenters), who established in the town a tradition of aristocracy that is still very much in evidence.

It is then "out of Providence," as indicated in the headings above, that you will be most apt to find the early and more ruggedly individualistic houses of Rhode Island. It is in Newport that you will see the fine Georgian town houses of fashion and beauty, dating back to the period of the town's prosperity before the Revolution, when it was one of our five most important and populous colonial cities. And it is on College Hill that you will come face to face with the elegance that the merchant princes of Providence gave to their great houses on this eminence. These potentate owners of the time looked down from their doorways and windows onto a forest of masts in Providence River, where dockworkers in the early 1800s unloaded cargo after cargo of rum, tea, spices, and goodness knows what else from the Gold Coast, the Orient, the South Seas, the Indies. Unloaded too was a lot of lovely foreign miscellany for the adornment of these palatial establishments, adding to our delight as we look at them now.

Then you have still to take in the Rhode Island towns from Charlestown to East Greenwich that were served by the Old Post Road for two centuries before that ancient highway became known as "Route 1"—towns that are still made charming by choice examples of houses from both the earlier and later periods.

Warren and especially Bristol are both worthwhile for the fascinating Federal houses you can see there from the streets, on your way between the two high spots of Providence and Newport. And for another aspect of Newport we call your attention to the most spectacular sideshow of late-nineteenth-century houses in America—as instructive as it is entertaining. For here by the sea are the summer estates, staggering in size, conception, and maintenance, that provided a perfect setting for the fabulous fortunes of this country at a time, between the 1880s and the Crash, when no expense had to be spared for taxes. Not early houses, to be sure; yet they couldn't be a more irretrievable part of our past. A stroll along the Cliff Walk here and a visit to the vast Vanderbilt château, "The Breakers," make a fitting climax to your fling among the houses of old Rhode Island. They show that here a man was permitted to *build,* as well as believe, any way he wanted—just so he had enough money.

¶ *In & out of Providence*

The four "greats" of the College Hill houses are the JOHN BROWN and CARRINGTON HOUSES (both open and described below), THE NIGHTINGALE, and the IVES HOUSE (both private but viewable from the street). These comprise as splendid a quartet of post-Revolutionary town houses as you will find anywhere, all of them mansions in the true sense of the word. Between the owners and the builders there were wealth, taste, and skill to spare, all of which are good ingredients.

THE NIGHTINGALE (1792), at 357 Benefit Street, now occupied by John Nicholas Brown of the famous old Providence family, is probably the largest early frame house of distinction in the land, strikingly detailed in the good forth-right Georgian tradition, balustraded around the roof like its fellows, and the only frame house of the four—fine, white, and palatial. The big brick façade of the beautiful IVES HOUSE (1811), at 66 Power Street is decorated with a rounded and balustraded portico under a large, flat-arched window. Though it has a strong family resemblance to the John Brown House, Thomas Poynton Ives, who built it after marrying into the Brown family, is said to have sent to England for the plans which came labeled "for a Georgian Manor House." The JOHN BROWN HOUSE, on the other hand, was designed right here by Joseph Brown, the talented brother of the owner, who also designed his own house (1774) at 50 South Main Street—much altered now, but still outstanding for its bold, broad ogee-pedimented roof. What dominates the slope of College Hill, mansions and all, is not a house, but Joseph Brown's masterpiece, the stunning FIRST BAPTIST MEETING HOUSE (1775).

A few more unlisted houses to look at are the EDWARD DEXTER (1799), at 72 Waterman Street, very gaily adorned for its date; the TRUMAN BECKWITH (1826) (now the HANDICRAFTS CLUB), at Benefit and College Streets, Late Federal, trim and stylish, and the SULLIVAN DORR (1810), at 109 Benefit, modeled after Alexander Pope's house at Twickenham, with Roger Williams's grave behind it. At 159 Benefit the famous, bold GOLDEN BALL INN, now a rooming house, was once the social center of the town. The SARAH HELEN WHITMAN HOUSE (c. 1790), at 88 Benefit, was the home of the young widow to whom Edgar Allan Poe indited his poem *Annabel Lee*. Note finally at 9 Thomas Street the DEACON EDWARD TAYLOR HOUSE (1790), now occupied by a community

school of music and also by some particularly fine colonial carpentry.

PROVIDENCE ART CLUB (*brick portion 1793, wooden portion 1789*)
11 Thomas Street; 10 to 5 weekdays, 2 to 4 Sundays.

This is really two houses joined by an archway; the earlier one in particular, built by a silversmith named Cyril Dodge, has noteworthy woodwork.

STEPHEN HOPKINS HOUSE (*1743*)
Hopkins and Benefit Streets opposite courthouse; Wednesday and Saturday afternoons, year round; Colonial Dames.

The home of the man who was ten times Governor of Rhode Island, a member of the Continental Congress, a signer of the Declaration, and the first Chancellor of Brown University. When he signed the Declaration of Independence, he made the moving statement, "My hand trembles but my heart does not." A fine restoration of a choice small house, with many interesting details of woodwork, it is skillfully and suitably furnished. Like the Bishop Berkeley House it shows how unpretentiously some of the "great" men lived before the sea brought so much wealth to Rhode Island.

BETSEY WILLIAMS COTTAGE (*1773*)
Roger Williams Park; year round, from 9 to 5 daily, except Thursdays; city of Providence.

Once owned by a descendant of Roger Williams, who gave the land to the city to establish a museum of colonial furniture. An attractive gambrel-roofed cottage.

PENDLETON HOUSE (*a replica*)
224 Benefit Street; Monday through Saturday 10:30 to 5, Sundays and holidays 2 to 5, Wednesday nights until 10 (closed in August, except by appointment); Rhode Island School of Design.

A replica of a Georgian mansion of the Providence type, it was built to house the famous Leonard Pendleton Collection of English and American furniture and *objets d'art*.

SHAKESPEARE'S HEAD (*1763*)
21 Meeting Street; 9 to 5, Monday through Friday.

Once one of the most important buildings in the town, it is square, with a low hipped roof and central chimney. The home of John Carter, an apprentice of Benjamin Franklin's, it was used as a print shop for the first Providence newspaper. A colonial-style garden has been planted here.

JOHN BROWN HOUSE (*1786*)

52 Power Street; year round except holidays, 9 to 5 Monday through Friday (not open Sundays during June, July, and August, 3 to 5 other Sundays); headquarters of Rhode Island Historical Society.

John Quincy Adams wrote of it after visiting here, "The most magnificent and elegant private mansion that I have seen on the continent." And so it must have seemed, for the merchant princes of Providence were emerging from their period of Quaker sobriety and were having their fling. John Brown's brother Joseph was its enormously able designer. Its carved woodwork, ornate and forceful in character, its fine furniture of the same style, evoke, along with its distinguished neighbors, the heyday of Providence prosperity. The exterior is particularly striking and harmonious—built of red brick, trimmed with white wood and sandstone lintels and columns; the doorway is one of the best in town, and the balustraded parapet outstanding.

EDWARD CARRINGTON HOUSE (*1810–1811*)

66 William Street; daily, 1 to 5, except Mondays; Rhode Island School of Design.

When Capt. Edward Carrington bought this big brick house from John Corliss in 1812, it was only two years old. As new as it was, and already large, he set to work at once to add a third floor and to decorate it with a two-story porch and an all-round roof balustrade, both of brownstone. The house has the distinctive style of a period when money was pouring in faster than it could be spent. It has dignity of form, and the austerity of color you notice from the street does not continue indoors. Carrington, who was our consul in Canton as well as a shipowner and builder of means, filled his home with rare chinoiserie, furniture, and handmade scenic wallpapers from China, which are still wonderful today. The imposing mansion, presented to the city by the last member of the family, is preserved exactly as it was when the family lived in it, and looks as though they were still here. The first floor is the most resplendent in Providence; but don't by any means miss the rest—sitting rooms, sewing rooms, bedrooms, and baths.

¶ *Pawtucket* (*the adjoining city on the eastern side of Providence*)

DAGGETT HOUSE (*1685*)

Slater Park; by appointment with Mrs. Irving K. White (phone: Pawtucket 2-4917); Pawtucket Chapter, D.A.R.

Containing period furnishings and personalia of Samuel Slater and Nathaniel Greene, it was built to replace an earlier house erected in 1644 by John Daggett which had been burned during King Philip's War. This house, built in 1685, was remodeled in 1790. The Daggetts were slaveholders, and the rings from which Prince, one of the slaves, swung his hammock can still be seen in one of the center beams. In the attic is a secret closet where the family could hide from the Indians. On display in the house are many historical items, including a blanket woven by Samuel Slater, builder of the first cotton mill. Interesting antiques here.

¶ *Foster Center* (*near the Connecticut line on 101*)

PARDON WILLIAMS HOMESTEAD

(*antique shop and tearoom, 1796*)

On Dolly Cole Hill (Route 6).

¶ *Cumberland Hill* (*north of Pawtucket*)

ELDER BALLOU MEETING HOUSE

(*before 1749*)

Elder Ballou Meeting House Road; year round, by obtaining key from Adelbert H. Whipple, R.F.D. 1, Woonsocket.

Not a house, but extremely interesting to house lovers for its very early and fascinating structural features.

¶*Lincoln Woods* (*Saylesville Village*) (*5 miles north of Providence on 146*)

ELEAZAR ARNOLD HOUSE (*c. 1687*)

449 Great Road (leave Route 1 at Highland Avenue and follow "Lincoln Downs" signs); weekdays except Mondays 12 to 5, June 15 to October 15, other times upon application to custodian in adjacent house; 25 cents; S.P.N.E.A.

A remarkable example of an early Rhode Island stone-end dwelling, with a pilastered chimney. It was well restored in 1952 and fittingly furnished.

FIREPLACE HOUSE (*a restoration*)

(*1675–1710*)

Lincoln Woods; a state restoration; Division Parks and Recreation of Rhode Island; open when restored fully.

A small stone house with a supersize chim-

Left: From its balustraded terrace to its balustraded roof, the John Brown symbolizes the residential splendor of Providence in its prime. Beyond it can be seen part of its famous neighbor, the Nightingale house.

Rarely if ever in this country will you find a more richly decorated pair of rooms than the double drawing rooms of the Carrington house on the hill in Providence, done chiefly in Chinese.

ney and fireplace, as the name implies; restored by the state as representing an outstanding example of its early type.

¶ Anthony Village (a few miles west of 3 on 117)

GEN. NATHANIEL GREENE HOUSE
(1770)
20 Taft Street; Wednesdays, Saturdays, and Sundays, 2 to 5; Valley 1–8630; The General Nathaniel Greene Homestead Association, L. E. Wagner (caretaker) (phone: Valley 1–8360).

Designed and built by Nathaniel Greene in 1770, when he was manager of the Coventry Ironworks, and before he was second in command to Washington. He made the hand-wrought hardware himself. In 1774 he brought his bride to the house, and a year later a son was born here and christened George Washington. The house is simple in form and substantial in size, with six rooms in the attic for the slaves. The entrance doorway is the ornamental exterior touch—a beautifully chaste composition of pediment and pilasters, put on like appliqué. Nice interiors too.

¶ Coventry (5 miles west of Anthony Village on 117)

THE TREASURE CHEST
(early eighteenth century)
On Route 1; June 1 to October 1, daily 9 to 9; Virginia G. Salisbury (owner).

An early salt box, it has the original stairs, with a double Rhode Island rail. Almost everything is intact, including a very early mouse hole in a kitchen cupboard. If you stop by, ask to hear the fascinating history of the house. Filled with antiques for sale.

¶ Thornton (just west of Providence on 14)

CLEMENCE-IRONS HOUSE
(c. 1680)
38 George Waterman Road, Manton; open reasonable hours upon application; 25 cents; S.P.N.E.A.

Very small and very early, with diamond-paned windows and a primitive pilastered stone chimney; your attention was directed to it in the introduction to the state. It is another fine restoration of the S.P.N.E.A., whose houses are all worth seeing. It contains some interesting pieces of its period.

¶ On & off the Old Post Road

Now Route 1, this old highway has been in active service between New York and Boston since early colonial days. Every traveler of the time knew well its towns, taverns, and hospitable homes.

¶ Wakefield

COMMODORE PERRY FARM *(1750)*
Post Road; by appointment; $1.00 to charity; Wisner H. Townsend, care of John H. Lewis & Co., 63 Wall Street, New York City, N.Y.

A small, pleasing gambrel-roofed cottage, with only two windows in front and a small wing. It has the typical big central chim-

The Nathaniel Greene house at Anthony Village has been restored and furnished as becomes a home of its time, place, and importance.

ney but no dormers. In addition to its unusual charm, it was the birthplace of Oliver Hazard and Matthew C. Perry, and there is a Perry family burying ground on the place. The Japanese government planted a cherry tree here in 1937 in honor of the famous commodore.

¶ *Charlestown* (*halfway between Westerley and Wakefield*)

GENERAL STANTON INN
> (*before 1775*)
>> *May 30 through October; Mr. and Mrs. Grafton M. Wilson.*

OLD WILCOX TAVERN, *formerly*
MONUMENT HOUSE (*dining and overnight guests*) (*c. 1730*)
>> *Route 1, Bradford; April 1 to November 30; Joseph Szydlowski, Bradford.*

Gen. Joseph Stanton, a hero of the Revolutionary and French and Indian Wars, was born in the Wilcox Tavern. He later made the Stanton Inn his home, as did his descendants until recently. The former is now a private home, furnished throughout with antiques; the latter is still an inn. Both these eighteenth-century houses have been moderately modernized.

¶ *Kingston* (*few miles north of Wakefield on 138*)

HELME HOUSE
> (*pre-Revolutionary*)
>> *Main Street; summer 3 to 5:30, Thursday through Sunday; headquarters of South County Art Association.*

Benjamin Franklin was frequently entertained here as he traveled the Post Road between Boston and Philadelphia. From the roof during the Revolution it was possible to watch the British fleet blockading Newport. The house got its good name from its longest occupant, Chief Justice Helme. Previously it had been occupied for a short time by Samuel Casey, a counterfeiter.

KINGSTON INN (*1757*) *and* **ELISHA POTTER HOUSE** (*now part of inn*)
> (*1809*)
>> *Main Street; Dr. Frederic Benschoten.*

The inn has retained some of its eighteenth-century charm, and the house makes an interesting nineteenth-century addition.

¶ *Jamestown* (*138 halfway between Saunderstown and Wickford 5 miles from toll bridge*)

CARR HOMESTEAD (*late 1600s*)
>> *On Carr's Lane; open during August (and in July during tour) by written or phone appointment with Mrs. A. W. Bowser (Jamestown 191R); 25 cents toward upkeep of house; Carr family (owners).*

The house and farm still form an undivided estate, with twenty-six heirs scattered all over the world. Built by Nicholas Carr, oldest son of Gov. Caleb Carr, it passed from father to son for seven generations. Except for a small addition, it is as originally built—a simple, sturdy home, with a central chimney. Much of the early furniture and portraits are still here. This is a home that has been well lived in and cherished by its generations of owners.

MEADOWSWEET (*c. 1830*)
>> *131 Narragansett Avenue; on written request; Mr. and Mrs. J. N. Porter.*

An excellent example of a post-Revolutionary "town house," finely furnished and with several portraits by Sully.

¶ *Wickford* (*3 miles north of toll bridge*)

SMITH'S CASTLE (*1678*)
>> *2 miles north of Wickford on Route 1; open daily 11 to 5 except Mondays, Sundays 2 to 5, all year round; 25 cents; Cocumscussoc Association, Mrs. Elizabeth Warren Green (President), 126 West Main Street, Wickford (phone: 2–0232).*

A "castle" in the sense that Richard Smith built it in "the thickest of the barbarians" as a substantial fortified dwelling in the 1637 wilderness. When it burned in 1676, he rebuilt it in its own image within two years. In 1740 the interior was modishly remodeled. It is the only Rhode Island house left in which Roger Williams lived and wrote.

¶ *Saunderstown* (*between 1A and 138 just north of Kingston*)

BIRTHPLACE OF GILBERT STUART *and* **EIGHTEENTH-CENTURY SNUFF MILL** (*1751–1752*)
>> *Hammond Hill Road; year round; 25 cents and 10 cents; maintained by Gilbert Stuart Association.*

The birthplace and boyhood home of our best-known colonial artist and foremost

This attractive town house in East Greenwich was the home of General Varnum, the Revolutionary hero.

painter of George Washington portraits is a large gambrel-roofed dwelling, rather austere but full of character, with a gristmill adjoining that was operated for almost a hundred years after Stuart's day. Stuart's father operated a snuff mill in the present immense kitchen. Now that the house has been restored, the primitive manufacture of snuff is being demonstrated here today with an old water-driven snuff mill brought from England.

¶ *East Greenwich*

GEN. JAMES MITCHELL VARNUM HOUSE AND MUSEUM (*1773*)

> *57 Pierce Street; Wednesdays and Sundays 3 to 5, June 1 through November 1, also by appointment (phone: Turner 4–9260); maintained by General Varnum Association, Lt. Col. Howard V. Allen (Chairman).*

A stately white town house of noble proportions. Foursquare, clapboarded, and done with restrained Georgian elegance, it has thirteen rooms, eight fireplaces, and two central chimneys. Among its many fine features are a broken pediment mantelpiece, original paneling, and old tiles. It is furnished with real distinction. In the rear is a historical museum; also a coach-house museum covering early transportation.

THE WHITE SWAN (*1810–1820*)

> *4365 Post Road; appointment by letter or phone; Mrs. Arthur B. Lisle.*

Owned by the late Arthur B. Lisle, President of the Society for the Preservation of New England Antiquities for twelve years, it is another very fine house of the Federal period, full of rare and interesting Oriental things as well as American antiques.

This is one of the most attractive early towns in the state, with a half dozen private homes to look at as you stroll around such as the CAPTAIN JOHN CONGDON HOUSE (1711), Division and Pierce Streets; the ELDREDGE HOUSE (1757), Division and Pierce Streets; the WINDMILL COTTAGE (1818), Division and West Streets; the GOV. WILLIAM GREEN HOMESTEAD (1680), Division and West Streets (opposite Windmill Cottage); the DANIEL HOWLAND (1677), Howland Road; the CAPT. THOMAS ARNOLD (1735), 28 King Street; and the old picturesque ALBERT C. GREENE HOUSE (1724), at 86 Main Street.

¶In & out of Newport

There are certain early American communities of less than metropolitan vastness in which anyone with a passion for searching out vintage houses will find his heart's desire. Outstanding in this respect are Portsmouth, Salem, Annapolis, Charleston, and Newport. These aren't museum towns in any sense of the word; they're just fine old colonial cities, somewhat smitten in spots by modernity, but holding on to certain ancient streets, certain old sections, and single houses here and there hemmed in by nondescript modern surroundings.

It is possible that in the popular mind today Newport is chiefly notable as the summer resort of legendary nabobs—a place, now somewhat dated and on the decline, of shingled châteaux, palatial cottages, and monumental seaside mansions on esplanades of lawn heaped with hummocks of huge blue hydrangeas. Yet, of the five cities mentioned above, it is perhaps Newport which offers the greatest historic variety of treasures, both early and late, to people on a house-hunting spree.

By all means get in touch on arrival with the Preservation Society of Newport County, at 5 Charles Street, for maps, further information, and good local guidance. The Hunter house and "The Breakers" are at present their two particular showpieces (and what an odd pair of showpieces!); but everything architecturally worthwhile in town is under the wing of the Society. Don't miss any of it!

HUNTER HOUSE (*1740*)
> *Daily 10 to 5, July 1 to September;*
> *admission (see "The Breakers").*

It is an early eighteenth-century manor house which became the headquarters of Admiral de Terney during the Revolution. There is fine furniture made by Goddard and Townsend, the great eighteenth-century Newport craftsmen; Newport portraits; and silver. Restored with skill, expert knowledge, and taste, it is today the most important and beautiful eighteenth-century house in town, and has been called one of the best Georgian houses in the country. The interior colors are stunning.

One of the most distinguished houses of its day, the Hunter is now one of the showpieces of Newport not to miss by any means.

Second only to the Hunter house in Georgian distinction in Newport, the Vernon house has no rival here as far as historical fame is concerned. And while The Breakers is a very recent newcomer indeed by comparison, its palatial proportions and fabulous splendors make it a sightseers' paradise.

WANTON-LYMAN-HAZARD HOUSE AND GARDEN (*1675*)

82 Touro Street; daily 10 to 5, July 1 to September; admission (see "The Breakers").

This is the oldest house in town and one of the finest Jacobean houses in New England. It is furnished as an inn or tavern, and after the color and excitement of the Hunter house it may seem at first sight somewhat austere. However, it was built with a strength and solidity, and in a style which reflects the courage and culture of the early settlers here. Take note in the second-floor bedroom of the chimney end with its original and once colorful free-hand painting; but look too at the revealed structural features of this room, which gives it such a noble character.

VERNON HOUSE (*1708–1760*)

Clark and Mary Streets; Monday through Friday 9 to 5, by appointment, year round.

It was Rochambeau's headquarters, and here Washington planned his future campaign on March 6, 1781. It is not furnished. The mural paintings discovered behind the wall paneling, believed to be of eighteenth-century Chinese origin, are of considerable interest here.

THE BREAKERS (*1894*)

Ochre Point; daily 10 to 5, June 1 to September; adults $1.50 and children 60 cents, combination ticket (adults $2.00 and children $1.00) admits visitors to Wanton-Lyman-Hazard House, Hunter House, "Whitehall," and "The Breakers" stables (single admissions to each house may also be purchased).

Built for Cornelius Vanderbilt, modeled after north Italian palaces of the sixteenth century, furnished with the utmost luxury, and immensely ornate in every decorative detail, this is among the masterpieces of Richard M. Hunt, the great Beaux Arts architect of the 1890s. It was the pride of the Newport summer colony. To see it is an experience not to be missed.

MAWDSLEY-GARDNER-WATSON-PITMAN HOUSE (*center 1700, front 1747*)

228 Spring Street, corner John Street; at reasonable hours, by application to Mr. and Mrs. L. Feller, 18 John Street; S.P.N.E.A.

This is an interesting house with a paneled parlor and good staircase; but only the hall and parlor are shown.

¶ *Middletown (few miles north of Newport on 114)*

WHITEHALL (*1729*)

July 1 through Labor Day; 25 cents; Newport Society of Colonial Dames of Rhode Island (on 99-year lease from Yale University).

A beautiful restoration of the red frame house occupied by Bishop Berkeley during his three years' residence in the Colonies, during which time the famous British philosopher wrote the poem which contains the prophetic words "Westward the course of empire takes its way." It is sparsely furnished, as it would have been at the period, but with fine Jacobean pieces. The structural details are of great excellence. Original delft tiles in the study and some exceptional paneling in the northeast parlor.

The house called Bonnet Hill near Darien is a true collector's item, and fascinating for the reason that while the main body of the structure was brought from Stamford, various other parts were gathered from here and there in Connecticut, among them rare paneling of museum quality and this very appropriate mid-seventeenth-century doorway done in what might be called Connecticut Jacobean. On the opposite page is the ancient Glebe house on Hollow Road at Woodbury, one of the choice Connecticut towns.

CONNECTICUT

T IS hard at times to tell which plays a more important part in the landscape of Connecticut—her boulder-strewn fields or her lean-to houses, also called "salt boxes," but known locally as "leanters." One thing is certain, however: no other type of house today harmonizes so attractively with the historic countryside.

A thing to keep in mind is that, of the two thousand or more carpentered houses built in Connecticut before 1700, less than twenty remain, and of these, only a very few, such as the Whitman House in Farmington and the Buttolph-Williams House in Wethersfield, still stand in their original form. But you will see hundreds of simple Connecticut houses, at crossroads and in country towns, of vintages up to 1820 or so which emulate the earlier ones in both form and substance.

While the simple, utilitarian Connecticut salt box, of which many examples are actually quite large, with two full stories and an attic, and even often with wings, was always the basic house, you will discover from the dates that around the 1750s many houses began to be embellished with fashionable Georgian doorways, porches, cornices, pediments, and Palladian windows—for instance some of the more elegant houses in Litchfield. Yet underneath and through it all the conservative Connecticut character prevails, and along with it the scrupulous workmanship of the Connecticut carpenter. No builders in America had better woods to work with or were better able to work them; no builders in America left more enduring and delightful examples of colonial skill.

Connecticut house tours vary so much from year to year—listings would only mislead. For timely information write to Mr. Don Parry of the Development Commission, State Office Building, Hartford. The Connecticut Antiquarian and Landmarks Society (Mrs. Frank Cogan, Farmington) runs two tours each summer beautifully organized for members. Since membership includes free access to their several houses and covers a subscription to their excellent magazine, it is an antiquarian bargain at $3.50 a year.

ON & OFF THE SHORE ROAD

Greenwich; Darien; Fairfield; Stratford; Bridgeport;
Milford; New Haven; Guilford; Madison; Clinton; Old
Lyme; East Lyme; New London; Mystic; Stonington

¶ *Greenwich*

KNAPP TAVERN *or* PUTNAM COTTAGE (*1692–1729*)

243 East Putnam Avenue; Mondays, Thursdays, Fridays, and Saturdays, 10 to 5; Putnam Hill Chapter, D.A.R.

It was from this inviting early-eighteenth-century roadside inn, still faced today with round-ended shingles, that General Israel Putnam, surprised at his toilet, eluded the British by running from the house and plunging on horseback down a declivity which was steeper than his pursuers cared to tackle. It is part of the legend that he had seen the redcoats' arrival reflected in his mirror while shaving. The four rooms

Note as Connecticut characteristics the boldness of the window framing at Bonnet Hill, the great substantial central chimney around which the house was erected. On the opposite page, Churchside at Fairfield is charmingly restored.

open to view are fittingly furnished with antiques.

¶ *Darien*

BONNET HILL FARM *or* RICHARD WEBB HOUSE (*c. 1670*)

By written request; Monroe Dreher.

This delightfully restored Connecticut salt box was moved here in 1945 from Stamford, where Richard Webb had built it well over two centuries before, and where it had degenerated from being the nucleus of a prosperous colonial farmstead to being used as a glue factory. Its preserver has made it his home and an antiquarians' delight, furnished and finished to perfection. The exterior is pumpkin yellow trimmed with oyster white; the living room is one of the rare fully paneled rooms in Connecticut, and many of the furnishings are of museum rank.

¶ *Fairfield*

CHURCHSIDE (*1823*)

39 Meeting House Lane, Greenfield Hill, Fairfield; by appointment; Henry B. Spelman.

This is one of a cluster of charming old houses handsomely maintained for convenience and attractiveness. It was first occupied by the Reverend Richard Varick Day when he was called to the lovely old church here.

¶ *Stratford*

DAVID JUDSON HOUSE (*1723*)

967 Academy Hill; Fridays and Saturdays 2 to 5, May to October, and by appointment (Edison 7–0395); 25 cents and 10 cents; home of the Stratford Historical Society.

Overhanging gable ends, a monumental chimney, and a stunning entrance doorway with inch-thick panes of glass set in its paneling would make this an arresting house even apart from its fine interiors.

¶ *Bridgeport*

HARRAL HOUSE *or* WALNUT WOOD (*1846*)

350 Golden Hill Street; by written request to C. N. Gardner, c/o Archer C. Wheeler (owner).

This extraordinary Gothic mansion fills with joy all devotees of Alexander Jackson Davis, that most ardent of nineteenth-century American architects, who has been described with such enthusiasm by Wayne

Andrews in *Architecture, Ambition and Americans,* a book warmly recommended to readers of the *Guide.* "Preserved in all its original splendor by the present owner," Mr. Andrews writes, "Walnut Wood is one of our as yet unrecognized national monuments and it is difficult to know which to admire the more, the mirrored parlors or the intensely Gothic grand staircase, dining room and bedrooms. The complete convenience of the place is reflected in the brilliant asymmetry of the exterior."

¶ *Milford*

EELS-STOW HOUSE (*c. 1669*)

34 High Street; daily May to October, and by appointment; Milford Historical Society.

It is full of odd structural and historical items. For one thing, Capt. Stephen Stow's wife was named Freelove Baldwin. Also, there is a rare 1687 portrait of the Samuel Eels who built the house and willed one half of it to his daughter if his son should die—"Which halfe she pleaseth." For this eventuality two separate kitchens were provided. The gable overhangs, the coved cornice, and the dog-legged stairs are items to see. The furnishings and exhibits in this fine old salt box are mementos of all periods from Colonial to Victorian.

¶ *New Haven*

PARDEE-MORRIS HOUSE
(*1680–1685, 1780–1800*)

325 Lighthouse Road, 8 miles east of New Haven; weekdays 10 to 5 except Mondays, Sundays 2 to 5, May 1 to November 1; New Haven Colony Historical Society.

A great handsome ell of a house, with stone ends (unusual around here) laid up in mortar of oyster shells and lime. Its various roof levels are all composed with fine informality. The massive masonry end walls provide flues for eight fireplaces. There is a vaulted ballroom and a vast beamed basement kitchen. Not only is it finely furnished in character but attractively gardened in true colonial fashion. The original house was burned by the British in 1779, so that the rebuilding of 1780 had only a portion of the early house to start with; the ballroom part was added a little later. A house of great character has emerged as a result of the work done at

different dates. This fact together with its fine furnishings make it an instructive house to visit.

¶ *Guilford*

There may well be in the vicinity here more than a hundred houses from before the Revolution, putting Guilford almost on a par with Ipswich; and there is a Guilford style as clearly as there is an Ipswich style, with many characteristics in common. The great size of the village green gives a clue to the past importance of the place, and many of the best of the old houses can be covered in a brief stroll around it. Note in particular the tiny entrance-staircase hallways with their courting benches, the solid-paneled wall cupboards, and the general medieval manner of the houses as a whole.

PELATIAH LEETE HOUSE (*1730*)

Leete's Island, Guilford; by written request during summer months to resident, Mrs. Oliver Bowen; 75 cents for Dorothy Whitfield Society; Mrs. Harry E. Glen (owner).

The rosettes that decorate the doorway of this house were meant to ensure that no harm should come to the dwelling—and no harm ever has. It is one of the finest here of its time, with massive beams, lamb's-tongue-chamfered corner posts, a studded door with a wooden latch, and old cupboards and chests of Guilford cabinetry. Primitive interior woodwork was never in Connecticut finished with greater care and taste.

HYLAND HOUSE (*1660–1720*)

Boston Post Road; daily 11 to 5 except Mondays, June 15 to October 1; 25 cents; Dorothy Whitfield Society; Mrs. Woolsey Conover (President).

Expertly restored to its diamond-paned original appearance, the house has narrow clapboards and carved overhang, with supporting corner posts cut as corbels. Outwardly it corroborates the date given to it, but the high ceilings within have caused dispute among the experts. Its furnishing fits the early date. Very choice indeed.

DARIUS COLLINS HOUSE
(c. 1769)
56 Union Street; by written request (allow time for verification); Mr. and Mrs. Richard W. Beebe (Antiques).

A delightfully unspoiled salt box filled with many treasures collected by a connoisseur, and with a rare original Guilford cupboard built in. The woodwork and dado of the southwest parlor are painted with red buttermilk paint, much used in early days hereabouts. The entrance door is Cross-and-Bible, and other finely paneled doors open into the "borning room" and "keeping room."

HENRY WHITFIELD HOUSE *or* OLD STONE HOUSE (*1639*)
Whitfield Street; daily 10 to 5 except Mondays April to October, daily 10 to 4 except Mondays December to March; state of Connecticut, Miss Lois North (curator).

This is said to be the oldest stone house in Connecticut and is largely a reconstruction. The steep pitch of the roof reminds us that it was originally covered with thatching of rye straw. The main fireplace is immense —ten feet wide, with a lintel of oak that is monumental and a flue at either end for one or two fires, as required. The furnishing is sternly medieval. Perfectionist antiquarians may question the correctness of the 1903 interior restoration, pointing out that two rooms above and two below would have been right; however, this is a point for purists to ponder.

LYMAN BEECHER HOUSE (*1770*)
475 Whitfield Street; on written or phone request, at owners' convenience; Mr. and Mrs. Walter B. Dodge.

This house, built on the green, was moved in 1829 to its present site here near the water. The feat was accomplished by seventy yoke of oxen. The owner, himself famous, was the father of two more famous Americans: Harriet Beecher Stowe and Henry Ward Beecher, preacher and abolitionist. It is a plain white clapboard village house, typical of this section of the state, spacious and accommodating. A modern glass window at the rear of the large living room looks out on a lovely water view. Otherwise very little modernization is evident, and what there is only adds to the livability. The same may be said of the furnishings.

ISAAC STOWE HOUSE (*1743*)
77 Broad Street; on written request; Dr. and Mrs. Levin Lyttleton Waters.

An unspoiled example of the third period of Guilford architecture (1700–1750). The things to note are its massive framing, generous fireplaces, fine moldings, attic smokehouse, gun closet, and hardware made by the builder. The present owners are living in it while they restore it and taking their time so that they will make no mistakes. They already have collected some excellent pieces. (Mrs. Waters is a daughter of Mrs. Warnecke of "The Mowings," described under Moodus.)

JOSEPH CHITTENDEN HOUSE
(*1766*)
78 Petticoat Lane (Fair Street); by appointment only (phone: Glendale 3-2112); 50 cents for Dorothy Whitfield Historic Society; Mr. and Mrs. Russell M. Nichols.

This is a fine example of an integral salt-box house, in which many of the original features remain intact. These include a massive stone chimney serving three fireplaces, small panes in the windows throughout, and a "sparking bench" in the hall. It is a home which combines eighteenth-century charm and comfortable living. There are many ancestral portraits, all of descendants of Guilford settlers, as is Mrs. Nichols herself.

¶ *Madison*

NATHANIEL ALLIS HOUSE (*1739*)
Boston Post Road near library, east of town center; daily; 25 cents; Madison Historical Society.

The Allis House is one of a nice collection of seventeenth- and eighteenth-century houses in this town next door to Guilford. It has been furnished to retain the atmosphere and charm of the town from the 1740s on—which it does.

LEE ACADEMY (*1821*)
Next to town hall; Madison Historical Society.

In addition to Lee Academy take time to look from the street at the GRAVES HOUSE (1675), the MEYS HOUSE (a red salt box of 1690), and others that you can hardly miss.

¶ Clinton

STANTON HOUSE (*1789*)

*Main Street near Congregational church
green; daily 2 to 5, summer; Hartford
National Bank and Trust Company.*

The striking white clapboard house which
claims your attention in this old town,
where the brewing of witch hazel was a
major industry, is like a large-scale cottage,
extraordinarily capacious, with one of
those hinged-panel partitions that can be
swung up and hooked to the ceiling. It contains for your delectation everything from
fine old furniture, china, and early costumes to a complete post-Revolutionary
country store, attached.

¶ Old Lyme

This picturesque old parlor town, which
has for many years attracted, along with
well-to-do residents, a steady stream of
painters, photographers, and summer
visitors, was once a busy and wealthy
world port, and many of its fine early
houses were the homes of distinguished
seafarers and sea traders. There are lots
of attractive old houses to look at from
the outside, apart from the two that can
be visited.

FLORENCE GRISWOLD HOUSE
(*1817*)

*Post Road; daily 2 to 5 except Mondays,
June 15 to September 15; 25 cents;
Florence Griswold Association, Inc.*

Attribute the likeness between the chaste
Ionic portico here and that of the Congregational church nearby to the early Connecticut architect Samuel Belcher, who designed them both. The present church is a
replica of the original, which was burned
and rebuilt in 1906–1907. When, about
that time, Old Lyme became an art colony,
it was in this house that many of the
artists boarded, and their work is now
here to be seen in the charming antique
setting provided by the old house.

WILLIAM SMITH HOUSE
(*before 1778*)

*Meeting House Hill, Johnnycake Hill
Road; by appointment in advance; Mr. and
Mrs. James Madison MacDonald.*

It was from this house in 1815, when the
Third Meeting House was struck by light-

*The grand old Denison
house at Mystic grows out
of its boulder-set hillside in
typical Connecticut
fashion.*

ning, that a daughter of Mr. Smith's with the surprising name of Union Sparrow ran to rescue the hymnbooks by carrying them out in her petticoat at the risk of her life. It is a fine, large example of Connecticut Late Colonial. It is a privilege to see the owners' collections of eighteenth- and early-nineteenth-century American, English, and Oriental furnishings—the last an indication of a seafaring community.

¶ East Lyme
THOMAS LEE HOUSE (1664)
> *Boston Shore Road, Route 56; daily 12 to 5 except Mondays, May 31 to September 15; donation; East Lyme Historical Society.*

To the student of seventeenth-century American dwellings the Lee House here is of rare interest, for it shows, in unusual fashion, the full development of the salt-box type from one room to many. Much of this growth and rearrangement was due to the fact that Mr. and Mrs. Lee produced, first and last, fifteen children, proof positive of the adaptability of the salt-box type.

¶ New London
JOSHUA HEMPSTEAD HOUSE (1643)
> *11 Hempstead Street; daily 1 to 4 except Mondays, May 15 to October 15; 25 cents, no charge to members; Connecticut Antiquarian and Landmarks Society.*

This may very well be the oldest frame house in Connecticut and one of the best documented, for the builder's son Joshua entered the whole operation in his diary. The walls are shingled on vertical boarding and filled with seaweed for insulation. It shows again, in a very different way, the evolution of a salt box.

SHAW MANSION (1756–1840)
> *11 Blinman Street; daily 1 to 4 except Sundays; donation; New London County Historical Society.*

It is plain to see from the size and style of the house that Capt. Nathaniel Shaw was a wealthy shipowner, and heartening to hear that he built it partly to give employment to a band of Acadian refugees. The eaves of both the gabled main house and its big foursquare wing are elegantly balustraded. There is much to see inside, including the carefully preserved room in

which Washington once stayed. Set on fire in the Revolution, the house was saved by the bursting of barrels of vinegar stored in the attic, which came flooding down on the flames.

¶ Mystic
The waterfront village of this historic maritime community wanders off into the rocky pastureland hills; but in the village itself there is the Living Museum of the Marine Historical Association, known as "Mystic Seaport." For lovers of the sea, ships, and boating lore this is a must. For lovers of houses there are several old ones in the Seaport, of varying interest. The SAMUEL BUCKINGHAM HOUSE (1768) was brought here by barge from Saybrook to help form an attractive part of this historical establishment—a simple, clean-cut Connecticut Colonial. Then there are the houses the three shipbuilding Greenman brothers built side by side on Greenmanville Avenue—evocative of the romantically classical 1840s.

DENISON HOUSE or PEQUOTSEPOS MANOR (1717)
> *Daily 1 to 5 except Mondays May 1 to November 1, by appointment November 1 to May 1 (phone: Jefferson 6–9248); Denison Society, Inc.*

This fine old house clad in wonderfully weathered shingles has been most delightfully restored. Each of its various rooms has been made to represent, in its own period attire, one of the eleven generations of the Denison family whose home it was, producing a panorama of furnishings from early colonial times to the Gay Nineties. We consider this one of the most interesting "family" houses in the country.

CAPT. PEREZ WOODWARD HOUSE (1815)
> *Pistol Point Road; summer months, by appointment in advance; Mr. and Mrs. Paul J. Kingsley.*

When Charles Mallory, the great Mystic shipbuilder who constructed the famous clipper *Twilight*, bought this then-unadorned house from Captain Woodward in 1828, he put on the Ionic portico to be in fashion, caused the egg-and-dart motif of the columns to be repeated on the front-door panel, and placed a cupola on the roof. Thus do architectural fashions work, their wonders to perform.

PACKER HOMESTEAD (*1720*)
Irving Street; by written or phone appointment only; Mrs. Carl C. Cutler.

This pleasant colonial family home, given truly ample proportions by enlargements made before the Revolution, has been lived in ever since it was built by lineal descendants of the original Packers. It is furnished to be comfortable with many personal pieces of no particular antiquity.

OLD WOODBRIDGE TAVERN (*1745*)
On the green; daily 1 to 5, by appointment; Mr. and Mrs. E. Fletcher Ingalls II.

Dr. Dudley Woodbridge was at one time the tavernkeeper, doctor, and preacher here. There are still two tiny rooms over the taproom in which the stagecoach drivers slept. There is a most interesting gun closet on the staircase, a secret passage, and fine old paneling everywhere. The curator of the New London Museum owned this choice house until recently.

¶ *Stonington*

Here, next door to Mystic, is another seaport village—an especially trim and attractive one. It also rambles far off into the rocky hills, its houses closely related to those in and out of Mystic. These all happen to be private homes that may be seen by appointment. There are eight altogether, next in number to Litchfield, and likewise in a community very con-

The brick trimmer arch above the vast cavern of the fireplace in Stonecrop Farm is one of the structural details common almost exclusively to the Stonington area.

scious of the priceless nature of its heritage houses. Be sure to walk around the village proper—one of the loveliest in New England. Local historians from all localities will do well to acquaint themselves with the chronology of Stonington prepared by Mr. Williams Haynes of Stonecrop Farm, who has also played an important part in the restoration of the Denison Homestead in Mystic, adjoining.

HEWITT HOUSE (c. 1699)

Off Route 2 near town; by phone appointment, July to Labor Day; Mr. and Mrs. Amos G. Hewitt (phone: Jefferson 6-2154).

The owners say that the simple finish of this earliest type of salt box indicates it was built by farmers; but don't forget that farmers were the great builders of early America. The massive oak beams, girts, sills, and corner posts have improved with age. The original floors are still intact—oak downstairs, sycamore upstairs. A house of great interest to all would-be restorers.

STONECROP FARM (1750)

Taugwonk Road, off Route 84; by appointment only, 24 hours in advance; 50 cents for Stonington Tricentennial Scholarship Fund; Mr. and Mrs. Williams Haynes.

The builder, the Hon. Paul Wheeler, was chairman of the local Committee of Safety in the Revolution and a veteran of the Indian wars. One outstanding feature of this in-every-way-delightful house is the huge old kitchen fireplace, with its trimmer arch, seen only hereabouts. The rock-ledge site is superb, and inside are unique collections —old pigeon prints and unusual spoons, among the family heirlooms. In the great fireplace room, with its immense dining table, are beautiful silver and pewter pieces. Here is a chance to catch up on local history, for the owners are the experts of the neighborhood, and are deep in Stonington lore.

PELEG DENISON HOUSE (1775)

Harvey Road; upon request, when owner is there; Mrs. Helen Joy Lee.

The attic here has pegged and numbered rafters, and a door into the chimney for

smoking meat. Most of the original woodwork is still here. Across the road is the Deacon Joseph Denison Burying Ground. This, you will begin to comprehend, is Denison country.

EDWARD DENISON HOUSE
(c. 1710)

Pequot Trail, west of North Road; upon request when owner is there; Mr. and Mrs. Minot Pittman.

The wife of Edward's son John was drowned in the well. The house later became a tavern. The bar cupboard is still here, and upstairs a ballroom with a floating partition, better to accommodate an overflow of guests. The house has corner fireplaces, unusual in this section.

JOSEPH DENISON HOUSE or GREAT HEARTH (1730)

Harvey Road; by appointment, with 24 hours' notice; 50 cents for Stonington Historical Society; Mr. and Mrs. James Reid Johnson.

With some of the finest eighteenth-century interior woodwork around Stonington and furnished in English and American pieces of the same period, this house is something to see.

CAPTAIN AMOS PALMER HOUSE
(c. 1780)

24 Main Street; by written appointment at convenience of family, June through September; Mrs. Stephen Vincent Benét.

This house in the village has many distinctions, not the least of which is the fact that it is still occupied by the family of the poet, the late Stephen Vincent Benét. Earlier it was inhabited by another celebrated American, James McNeill Whistler. It is considered to be one of the best houses in this part of the state, with fine paneling, mantels, and a rather special double stairway to the front door.

PALMER MINER HOUSE (c. 1790)

Hangman's Hill Road; by appointment; Mr. and Mrs. Palmer Miner.

Owned in a straight line of descent since the 1830s, when the first Palmer Miner purchased it from Samuel Peabody, it is a Connecticut farmhouse of substance and distinction, with two upstairs rooms hung in French wallpapers brought over around 1800.

UP THE CONNECTICUT RIVER VALLEY

Essex; Moodus; Middletown; Wethersfield; Hartford;
Windsor; Suffield

¶ *Essex*

This town, on the west bank of the Connecticut River, is one of the loveliest and most colorful of the towns of this region.

LORD HOUSE (*c. 1800*)

> *28 Main Street; on request; Mr. and Mrs. Robert I. Carter.*

On a street of old captains' houses leading down to the water, this is an old captain's house itself—a charmer from the street and a beauty within.

GRISWOLD INN

> (*mid-eighteenth century*)
> *Main Street; always open; the Lovell Family (custodians).*

A grand old inn, very little changed except for the renovation of an old schoolhouse into a taproom. You can eat and sleep here.

PRATT HOUSE (*c. 1720*)

> *20 West Avenue; daily 1 to 4, Saturdays and Sundays by appointment; closed holidays June 15 to September 15; 25 cents; S.P.N.E.A.*

Among other attractions, this house contains the very fine Griswold collection of American furniture and furnishings.

¶ *Moodus*

There are many good houses to be seen from the road in this neck of the woods, even though they cannot be visited. One of the best exteriors in Connecticut is that of the GENERAL CHAMPION HOUSE in East Haddam.

THE MOWINGS (*seventeenth century*)

> *Afternoons summer months only, upon request by letter or phone (Moodus 202W2); Mr. and Mrs. Heinz Warneke.*

This mellow old farmhouse in the woods has been restored with rare feeling and

The woodwork in the dining room at The Mowings, like the woodwork all through this old house, is a glowing example of the color and finish inherent in ancient planks, paneling, and beams.

The kitchen chamber of the famous old Buttolph-Williams house in Wethersfield is furnished with great understanding in pieces that belong perfectly to its time and place.

skill by its owners, a well-known sculptor and his painter wife, who have furnished it with family heirlooms, portraits, and many unusual country pieces. Few houses anywhere have been treated with such tangible understanding, even more apparent on closer acquaintance. But get your directions straight and look out for deer.

¶ *Middletown*

ALSOP HOUSE, *now* DAVIDSON ART CENTER OF WESLEYAN UNIVERSITY (*1840*)

> *High Street; Monday to Friday 8 to 5, Saturdays 8 to 12 and 1 to 4, Sundays 2 to 4 (only when college is open, not during vacations or summer); Wesleyan University.*

In a town containing some of the most interesting Greek Revival and Gothic houses in Connecticut, this is one of the most famous examples of the former fashion, now restored and furnished to show the graceful manner of living when Middletown was a flourishing center of commerce and culture, before the Civil War. On the outside walls are lifesize paintings of mythical figures, which appear from the

street to be statues set in niches. The house is an experience not to be missed.

RUSSELL HOUSE, *now* HONORS COLLEGE OF WESLEYAN UNIVERSITY (*1828*)

> *High Street; daily, when school is in session; Wesleyan University.*

One of the country's great Greek Revival mansions, designed by Ithiel Town of nearby New Haven, with an assist from Alexander Jackson Davis. The interiors are beautifully preserved, with decorated wall painting intact. The woodwork is becomingly ornate, and the great glass gaslight chandeliers are the very essence of their period. Count it a major opus of an eminent early team of architects.

¶ *Wethersfield*

BUTTOLPH-WILLIAMS HOUSE (*1692*)

> *Broad and Marsh Streets; daily 12:30 to 4 except Mondays, May 15 to October 15; 50 cents, members free; Antiquarian and Landmarks Society.*

One of the finest examples of seventeenth-century architecture in Connecticut (which means in the country). Dark, stark, but filled with vitality, its medieval character is revealed in the narrow clapboards, overhangs, big chimney, small windows, and furnishing of period perfection. One of the most important preservations in the state.

WEBB HOUSE (*1752*)

> *211 Main Street; daily 10 to 5, Sundays 1 to 5, during winter closes at 4; 50 cents and 10 cents; Connecticut Society of Colonial Dames.*

As beautifully urbane as the nearby Buttolph-Williams House is fascinatingly primitive, this is the house that Washington headed for in the spring of 1781 to effect a meeting with the Count de Rochambeau. Its paneling is one of the prides of Connecticut, and it is furnished with all the fitness and finish for which the Colonial Dames are famous. The red flock paper Mrs. Webb put up in honor of the general's coming is still on the walls of the room wherein he slept.

¶ *Hartford*

Three houses on the corner of the block at Farmington Avenue and Forest Street are as far from Early American as the 1870s could make them. They have a romantic-period interest, but it was mostly from the people who have lived there that they derived their distinction.

HARRIET BEECHER STOWE HOUSE (*c. 1870*)

> *73 Forest Street; by appointment; 50 cents; Miss Katharine S. Day (phone: Jackson 2–8635).*

You enter this mid-Victorian gray-brick house through a gabled porch. Mrs. Stowe always referred to it as a "cottage." It is furnished pretty much as it was when the author of *Uncle Tom's Cabin* lived there.

The many-gabled and -chimneyed CHARLES DUDLEY WARNER HOUSE (1872), the home of Mark Twain's great literary friend, can be seen from the street. In the AVERY MUSEUM you will find the famous Wallace Nutting Collection of Early American furniture, many notable Early American paintings, and collections of pottery and glass.

The Webb house in Wethersfield is among the greats of Connecticut, both for its intrinsic beauty inside and out and for its distinguished historical associations.

MARK TWAIN HOUSE (1873)

351 Farmington Avenue; daily 9 to 12 and 1 to 6, except Sundays and holidays; no charge, except for one room; Mark Twain Library and Memorial Committee.

Now the Mark Twain Library downstairs and apartments upstairs, only one room at present is furnished as it was when the great writer lived here—his bedroom, with the fantastically carved Venetian bedstead he bought in Italy. But there are hopes for the future of this, the only home he ever built for himself and his wife. He had what appears to be a pilothouse fitted to the rear to remind him of his life on the Mississippi.

¶ Windsor

This inland town way up the Connecticut River, you may be surprised to hear, carried on quite an extensive seagoing trade with the West Indies during the latter part of the eighteenth century. Carpenters from around here helped build some of the best houses in New Bern, North Carolina, for a little winter work.

LOOMIS HOMESTEAD AND SCHOOL

(main house 1690, wing 1640)

By appointment (phone: 8–8191); Loomis Institute.

It is a well-preserved rural house from the latter part of the seventeenth century, but with chimneys, trim, and rooflines which have eighteenth-century characteristics. The house, furnished with family heirlooms, is in good hands, being used for faculty housing by the school.

ELLSWORTH HOMESTEAD or ELMWOOD (1740)

778 Palisade Avenue, between Windsor Locks and Windsor; daily 9 to 5 except Mondays and Wednesdays, Sunday 1 to 6, May 1 to December 1; 25 cents; Connecticut D.A.R.

This fine big central-chimney mansion in its own three-acre park was the home of Oliver Ellsworth, one of the five senators in the First Congress who made the first draft of our Constitution. He didn't even wait to sign but galloped home to see that Connecticut did its part toward ratification.

Both Washington and John Adams were visitors here when the antiques were brand-new.

HEZEKIAH CHAFFEE HOUSE or THE CHAFFEE SCHOOL (*used for faculty housing*) (*soon after 1755*)

By appointment only; The Loomis Institute.

This elegant eighteenth-century brick house, with its central chimney and its wing, where Doctor Hezekiah had his office before the Revolution, faces the old Windsor green. The little brick building in back was either a countinghouse or slave quarters; beyond were the warehouses and the landing where seagoing vessels tied up, many miles from the sea.

LIEUT. WALTER FYLER HOUSE

(one room 1640, later additions 1773)

96 Palisade Avenue; Thursdays 10 to 5, or by appointment (phone: Windsor 8–3813); Windsor Historical Society.

This began as a one-room house, but when Capt. Nathaniel Howard bought it from Lieutenant Fyler in 1772 for one hundred and seventy pounds sterling, it began to get bigger, for every time the captain returned from a voyage he added a room. From the house his wife would sell the fine silks and other foreign goods her husband brought back. Later the three Styles sisters bought it for six hundred and seventy dollars. The side walls are filled with corncobs for insulation. The interior walls are wainscoted paneling, with cupboards built in.

¶ Suffield

HASTINGS HILL (1737)

Upon request by letter or phone, if convenient to owner; Mr. and Mrs. Henry M. Clark.

On the outskirts of another lovely old town is this red salt box, furnished and finished with such fine understanding and taste that few similar houses in the state can hold a candle to it. Mrs. Clark, a restoration expert, has collected pieces that museums might envy. If it happens that the owner can let you see it, ask her about the other houses in the neighborhood, which may at least be looked at from outside; she is an authority.

WEST OF THE CONNECTICUT RIVER

Ansonia; Hamden; Northford; Wallingford; Meriden;

Farmington; Weatogue; West Simsbury

¶ Ansonia

RICHARD MANSFIELD HOUSE
(*1754*)

> *35 Jewett Street; daily 2 to 5, May 15 to October 15; 25 cents; Antiquarian and Landmarks Society.*

The builder of this fine old salt box was the first minister of the Episcopal church and made this his parsonage for seventy-two years. It has twenty-four-pane windows, a central chimney, and overhangs.

EZRA DICKERMAN HOUSE
(*early eighteenth century*)

> *3217 Whitney Avenue; upon request; Mr. and Mrs. Christopher P. Fredericks and Mr. and Mrs. Edward John Albert, Sr.*

Some of the finest paneling and woodwork hereabouts. This excellent example of an early-eighteenth-century Connecticut dwelling is being occupied and preserved with keen appreciation.

¶ Hamden

JONATHAN DICKERMAN HOUSE *or* OLD RED HOUSE (*1770*)

> *Mt. Carmel Avenue, near park headquarters; Saturday afternoons during summer; Hamden Historical Society; William A. Reynolds (President).*

This is something quite special: a one-and-a-half-story central-chimney house with a wide roof overhang which forms an effective and attractive sunshade. It has never been marred by modern improvements. Everything is original, including paint colors and wonderful woodwork.

¶ Northford

JONES HOUSE (*1700*)

> *Village Street; by appointment, May 1 to December 1; contribution for Wayside Museum, Inc., Clintonville; Mr. and Mrs. W. Spencer Smith.*

A fine salt box inside and out, with much heirloom furniture, original paneling of pine, oak, and cherry, original floors and hardware throughout, a Y stairway to the attic, and a fireplace of *black* brick.

WARHAM WILLIAMS HOUSE
(*1745–1750*)

> *Middletown Avenue; upon request, May 1 to November 1; Mrs. Victor Schaeffer.*

Two stories with a central chimney and an attic overhang, this is said to be an exact copy of Warham Williams's grandfather's house at Deerfield (listed in Massachusetts). It has a cherry-paneled buttery, one of the best entrance doorways hereabouts, and an enchanting stenciled room upstairs. Inside a closet door every painter who has worked on the house has left his

The venerable Nehemiah Royce house at Wallingford has the great stone central chimney and the gable-end overhang so characteristic of Connecticut, also its proper share of history and of interior period attractiveness.

name and date, from before 1792 up to the present.

THE RED HOUSE ON SOL'S PATH

Farm River Valley; by written appointment, July and August; Mrs. Morris E. Alling.

According to the *Connecticut Guide,* "In the early days, when this section was used as a pasture by settlers at the shore, Solomon, a colored man with an Indian wife, made a path of convenience across Totoket Mountain." A handsome old house, with a Dutch-type cantilevered hood above the entrance.

¶ Wallingford

SAMUEL PARSONS HOUSE (*1759*)

180 South Main Street; Sundays 3 to 5 July 1 to September 30, or by appointment (phone: Wallingford 9–5216); Wallingford Historical Society.

Restoration probably completed by now; if so, well worth a visit.

NEHEMIAH ROYCE HOUSE *or* WASHINGTON ELM HOUSE (*1672*)

538 North Main Street; daily 3 to 5, July 1 to September 1; donation; S.P.N.E.A., Helen E. Royce (custodian).

A fine example of a typical Connecticut Valley "leanter," with all furniture from local sources, it has a double-paneled doorway of distinction. It was under the great elm here that Washington paused to bid good-by to the people of Wallingford. He mentioned in his diary the mulberry trees, some of which are still here.

¶ Meriden

MOSES ANDREWS HOMESTEAD (*1760*)

242 West Main Street, west of center on Route 14; Sunday afternoons, 2 to 4; 25 cents; Meriden Historical Society.

Another nice central-chimney salt box, with double overhangs and good interior paneling; but still more noteworthy as a heartening example of a local restoration project, making it a house that will improve as time goes on.

¶ *Farmington*

Along with Litchfield and Old Lyme, this is one of the three principal parlor towns of Connecticut. Unfortunately only one early house is open to the public, but that is a very early one indeed. Main Street, High Street, and Farmington Avenue are by far the best for old houses.

HILL-STEAD MUSEUM (*1901*)

Farmington Avenue; Wednesday, Thursday, Saturday, and Sunday afternoons 2 to 5, or by appointment (phone: 7–9064); 50 cents; trustees of museum.

This great country mansion of twenty-nine rooms, twelve baths, two pantries, and a "Mount Vernon front," designed by the late Theodate Pope for her parents, is shown as it was when occupied by those wealthy collectors. The house is filled with fine (mostly English) furniture and furnishings—clocks, lusterware, and paintings galore by Monet, Manet, Degas, Whistler, and Cassatt. It attracts about four thousand visitors a year.

STANLEY-WHITMAN HOUSE *or* FARMINGTON MUSEUM (*c. 1660*)

37 High Street; daily 10 to 12 and 2 to 5 except Mondays April 1 to December 1, Fridays and Saturdays 10 to 12 and 2 to 5 and Sundays 2 to 5 December to April; 30 cents and 10 cents; Village Green and Library Association.

You will agree with the Landmarks Society's description of this house as "one of the best preserved 'framed overhangs with drops' in Connecticut." Its medieval character is evident even in its original corpus of hand-worked oak and hardware. The casements are authentic if not original, though the glass panes are old. The restoration was done by the famous architectural authority on old Connecticut houses, the late J. Frederick Kelly, held in high esteem by every serious antiquarian in the country.

THE ELM TREE INN

(built about 1755 around a mid-seventeenth-century house)
Open for guests.

This inn may be the oldest in the country, for it has been doing business here since 1665, when Philip Lewis was the host. The rear ell of the building encloses the ancient part of it. Today it is still a picturesque inn of brick and frame, with the west-end clapboard beaded.

¶ *Weatogue*

This is the Simsbury area, worth investigating.

JONATHAN HUMPHREY HOUSE
(*1720–1723*)
> *Route 10 (College Highway); by request at least 24 hours in advance; Mr. and Mrs. Julian I. Milliman.*

A very good salt box in fine condition and beautifully furnished with early eighteenth-century pieces. The entrance is decorated with pilasters surmounted by rosettes, and the door itself has the Cross paneling characteristic of Connecticut.

¶ *West Simsbury*

ORKIL FARMS (*c. 1781*)
> *Old Farcus Road; by appointment, May 15 to October 1; $1.00 to Antiquarian and Landmarks Society of Connecticut, Mr. Orrin P. Kilbourn.*

The basic structure of the house remains, but many characteristic features have long since been removed, its owner says. It is beautifully furnished, and the total effect is one of great charm, both inside and out. You can't entirely erase the essential personality of such a fine early house. This one is now being treated with the consideration that it deserves.

LEADING UP TO LITCHFIELD

¶ *Danbury*

ST. JOHN HOUSE *or* SCOTT FANTON MUSEUM (*pre-Revolutionary*)
> *43 Main Street; Wednesdays and Thursdays 2 to 5, or on request; Danbury Historical Society, Albert Meserve (President).*

This old village mansion is filled with many valuable American antiques of all periods and displays periodical exhibitions of contemporary painting and sculpture.

¶ *Woodbury*

Just before you get to Woodbury, there is Southbury to look at. The two villages are rare antiques in themselves, and there are a dozen early private homes of great worth in the vicinity.

GLEBE HOUSE
(*c. 1690, enlarged 1740*)
> *Hollow Road; daily 10 to 5, Sundays 1 to 5; donation; Seabury Society for Preservation of Glebe House.*

The Glebe House is known as the "birth-place of American Episcopacy" because it was the scene of the election of the first Episcopal bishop in America, Samuel Seabury. It is an engagingly simple house, with gambrel roof, center chimney, and all the original paneling. Many of the furnishings have also always been here, and there are besides many historical pictures and documents. A good place to get local old-house information.

¶ *Litchfield*

Let it be said at once that Litchfield is one of the few truly unspoiled *old* towns in America. Authorities have called it our finest example of a "live" colonial town, which simply means that people are living in and enjoying these houses as much as they did two centuries ago. Through their generosity you are now able to visit some of the finest of these houses—otherwise to be seen only once a year on the October tour sponsored by the Litchfield Junior Republic.

TAPPING REEVE HOUSE AND LAW OFFICE (*1773*)
> *South Street; daily 2 to 5 except Wednesdays June to November, by appointment in winter; 30 cents; Litchfield Historical Society.*

Of Tapping Reeve, Lyman Beecher said after his death, "Oh, Judge Reeve, what a man he was! When I go to heaven and meet him there, what a shaking of hands there will be." Reeve, the son of a Long Island minister and a graduate of Princeton (1763), founded here the first law school in America. The little building that housed the classes now adjoins the house. The beautiful old white house has been restored and furnished with taste and scholarship by the Historical Society.

OLIVER WOLCOTT, SR., HOUSE (*1753*)

South Street; by appointment, at owner's convenience; Mrs. Frederick W. Sherman.

There are many reasons why this might be called the most interesting house in Litchfield. In addition to its architectural distinction, it happens to be the earliest house in town. Its illustrious first owner was a member of the Continental Congress, a signer of the Declaration, a governor of the state, and many other things; he entertained all the notables of the day, among them Washington. His descendants are still living right here. There are so many things to observe about this house that we will note here only a few: the porch with its Ionic columns supporting a fanlighted pediment; a room in which three walls are sheathed in wide feather-edged boards, one wall horizontal, the other two vertical; and a fine bolection molding over a bedroom fireplace. Since the house has always been occupied by the family, the furniture, as you would ex-

The Tallmadge house in Litchfield, showing the wings with their two-story columns added, it is said, after its first owner's visit with Washington at Mt. Vernon.

pect, is mostly eighteenth-century, handed down. This is not a house to miss.

TALLMADGE HOUSE (*1775*)

North Street; by appointment, at owners' convenience; Mr. and Mrs. C. Van Courtland Moon.

In the early golden era of Litchfield Colonel Tallmadge, late of General Washington's staff, entertained at one time his commander in chief, thereby acquiring for the house one of its more priceless souvenirs—George Washington's signature on a windowpane of what used to be the ballroom. The central part of the gambrel-roofed mansion, with its three dormers, was built of frame in the traditional Connecticut manner by Thomas Sheldon, but Tallmadge (after a visit to Mt. Vernon, it is said) added abbreviated wings at the ends with two-story porticoes, each supported by two slender columns. The unique style has been repeated elsewhere in town, and has come to be known as distinctive of Litchfield.

SEYMOUR HOMESTEAD (*1807*)

South Street; by appointment; Mr. and Mrs. Warren P. Smith.

One of those narrow-clapboarded, simple, but spacious houses for which the town is famous, this was built by Maj. Moses Seymour for his son Ozias, and never left the possession of the family until 1950. The major, a Revolutionary War hero, held the British mayor of New York City as hostage for a time, presumably in his own family house, built in 1735. The mayor aroused a good deal of bad feeling in town, and at one time had to be spirited away to save his life. In thanks for the good treatment he gave the Seymours the first "pleasure carriage" to appear hereabouts. But having gained the family's confidence, he strolled down the street one day and neglected to return.

JULIUS DEMING HOUSE (*1790–1793*)

North Street; on request by letter or phone, May to November, at least a day's advance notice; Mrs. Ludlow Bull.

First called "The Lindens," this house was built by a wealthy merchant who helped finance the Revolution, lost money on his loans, and recouped his losses with his general store and the China Trading Company, in which he was a partner along with

Oliver Wolcott and his friend and neighbor Colonel Tallmadge, aide-de-camp to Washington. In this big white house the handiwork of William Spratt is evident. Originally the house much resembled the more elegant of the foursquare captains' houses seen in many seacoast towns in New England. Square and white, with tall chimneys, quoined corners, and a hip roof balustraded all around, it nevertheless has its unusual Spratt features, such as the pillared entrance, and the heavy eyebrows over the lower windows.

ALEXANDER CATLIN HOUSE (*1778*)

By appointment, at owner's convenience; Mr. and Mrs. Eugene H. Dooman.

The unexpected thing about this house is the widow's walk so far from the sea (though at one time there was here in town the Litchfield China Trading Company, and merchants waxed wealthy from the trade).

CHARLES G. BENNETT HOUSE (*1814*)

East Street; by written appointment, May to November; Mrs. Arthur Goodwin Camp.

This fine brick Federal house stands imposingly on East Hill as you enter town, with its gable end facing the street and an unexpected Palladian window in the gable. The plan here is still essentially Colonial, but the graceful staircase and the mantels show the attenuated detail of the new era.

What makes this house a "must" in a town of such great attractions is the remarkable collection of museum-quality furniture you will find here—most of it seventeenth- and eighteenth-century Connecticut.

CATLIN HOUSE (*c. 1770*)

3 miles east of green on East Chestnut Hill; by appointment (phone: Jordan 7–5310); Mr. William L. Warren.

The owner of this house describes it as "a good farmer's mansion unspoilt . . ." This it is, and though probably built before the Revolution, "like many Connecticut houses it was not finished at once, and the finishing of certain rooms reflects the taste of a later date." The living room and kitchen have fine pre-Revolutionary paneling. One of the rooms has molding and fireplace trim typical of William Spratt, as well as some freehand wall painting which may have been done in the 1780s by a British prisoner quartered here. Its wide doorways, paired window placements, and double overhangs on the gable ends help to make it one of the choicest places to visit in the vicinity.

DAVID WELCH HOUSE (*c. 1754*)

Milton Steading; mid-May to mid-October, by written or phone appointment; Dr. Edward Holman Raymond.

The first owner of this fine salt box was later a major in the Revolution and a close friend of Ethan Allen. They were partners in the iron-ingot business and sold the metal from this house.

You can tell from this picture of the Nathan Hale homestead in winter what a distinct advantage it was to have the whole range of sheds and barn connected to the house under a single roof.

WILLIAM HALL HOUSE
(1758–1760)
Saw Mill Road, Milton Steading; all year round, on written request; Mr. and Mrs. J. R. Busk.

The village of Milton Steading was settled by Litchfield folk about 1740, but some settlers came from towns along the shore, notably William Hall, who came here from Guilford and brought with him certain Guilford building mannerisms—thus linking the two chief architectural localities of Connecticut.

EAST OF THE CONNECTICUT RIVER

¶ *Norwich (on the Thames 15 miles above New London)*

ROCKWELL HOUSE *(1818)*
42 Rockwell Street; Wednesday afternoons July and August, or by appointment; Faith Trumbull Chapter, D.A.R.

The house, of native-stone blocks quarried on the place, was the home of Maj. Joseph Perkins, a member of the local Committee of Safety. It contains twelve rooms, a separate building for the kitchen, and a large garden. Furnished with early American and Victorian pieces, it features an outstanding collection of china.

NATHANIEL BACKUS HOUSE *(1750)*
Near Rockwell House; Wednesday afternoons July and August, or by appointment; D.A.R.

The oldest house in the city, it was moved next to the Rockwell House in 1950, with which it is shown in conjunction. It is also furnished as a home of the period.

¶ *Colchester (20 miles up from New London on 85)*

NATHANIEL FOOTE HOUSE *(1702)*
South side of Norwich Avenue opposite Hayward Street; open by request; Col. Henry Champion Chapter, D.A.R.

A historical museum and chapter house.

¶ *Marlborough (10 miles northwest of Colchester on Route 2)*

MARLBOROUGH TAVERN *(1740)*
Always open.

¶ *Lebanon*

GOV. JONATHAN TRUMBULL HOUSE
(1740)
West side of town green; Mondays and Wednesdays 10 to 5, Saturdays 2 to 5, May to November; 25 cents; Connecticut D.A.R.

Built by Joseph Trumbull, father of Jonathan and successful farmer and storekeeper, it was a pretentious mansion for those days. Jonathan Trumbull was the last Governor of the colony and the first of the new state. He was a remarkable man —so resourceful in furnishing supplies to the Revolutionary Army that Washington made him his confidential adviser. Washington's oft-repeated remark in a crisis "We must ask Brother Jonathan" gave rise to the fact that our nation was often personified in those days as "Brother Jonathan" rather than "Uncle Sam." The house in which he was born has been moved a little and, in the process, slightly remodeled. It has nine rooms and an attic. At the head of the stairs is a tiny sentry room. The furnishings, consistent with the period, include a number of Trumbull pieces.

¶ *Coventry*

NATHAN HALE HOMESTEAD *(1776)*
South Street; daily 1 to 5, except Sundays, May 15 to October 15; 50 cents; Connecticut Antiquarian and Landmarks Society.

In September of the year in which this fine old fullsized farmhouse was being built by Nathan Hale's father, the unfortunate son was caught in school-teacher's clothes behind the British lines, and suffered the fate of a patriot spy. The house that he did not live to inherit has now become his memorial. It has also been made into one of the most charming house museums in Connecticut. The paneling, the mantels, and the woodwork all through the house show the remarkable refinement and finish for which the early carpenters hereabouts were famous; and the way in which the house is furnished and fitted out by the experts of the Landmarks Society is a tribute to their skill and taste, and a joy to behold. Mary Hale heirlooms here.

One of the finest and most beautifully preserved Greek Revival interiors in America, the double parlor of the Campbell-Whittlesey house in Rochester, is shown at the top of the page; under it is the music room of Rock Hall at Lawrence and, on the opposite page, Schuyler mansion at Albany.

NEW YORK

EVEN before the Revolution, the population of New York was polyglot in character. The colony, while it was still the "New Netherlands" of the Dutch, already contained settlers of a dozen other nationalities. These included, in addition to the Dutch, their neighbors the Walloons, a French-speaking people; the French Huguenots, refugees from religious persecution, who settled on the Hudson at New Paltz as early as 1677; Germans, Swedes, Welsh, Norwegians, and Danes from Northern Europe; and English from England, as well as those from New England, coming by sea to Long Island. It is on record that in 1644 as many as eighteen languages were being spoken in the state!

All these people brought with them memories of the houses they'd come from, and all, naturally, had to adapt their building ideas to the materials and means at hand. So, while the old houses that survive have among them various national accents, the prevailing architectural language soon became as English as the common speech, and, like it, the idiom became more and more American. When finally in the nineteenth century an American Romantic Movement got under way, New York provided its two outstanding exponents, A. J. Downing and A. J. Davis, some of whose work is represented here.

It is a far cry from the surviving tall Dutch town houses with stepped gables, steep-roofed French farm dwellings, and salt boxes with mossy roofs sweeping to the ground, to the manor houses in the Hudson and Mohawk Valleys—Queen Anne, Georgian, Federal, and Regency. And even further removed in spirit from the early utilitarian dwellings are the multitudinous examples of the Greek Revival fashion, which from 1820 on put record numbers of columns not only on mansions but on farmhouses as well throughout the state. A little later, when romantic aspiration took another and even giddier flight into the Gothic, this state took the lead in the rage for the picturesque, just as it did finally in the Beaux Arts mansions for its millionaires (as will be noted).

IN & OUT OF NEW YORK CITY

Manhattan; The Bronx; Staten Island; Brooklyn; Queens; Long Island: Lawrence, Oyster Bay, Huntington, South Huntington, Mastic, St. James, The Setaukets, Cutchogue, Sag Harbor, East Hampton; Westchester County: New Rochelle, Eastview, Port Chester, North White Plains, Scarsdale

¶ *Manhattan*

FRAUNCES TAVERN (*a restaurant*)
(*1719*)
Broadway and Earl Streets; daily 10 to 4 except Sundays, Saturdays 10 to 3; Sons of the Revolution in the State of New York.

Four stories of Georgian Colonial brick nobility denoting the erstwhile nature of the neighborhood, this is the oldest house of distinction still standing on Manhattan. A Dutch note are the dormers sloping from the balustraded roof. Built as the residence of a wealthy Frenchman, Etienne de Lancey, it was purchased and turned into a tavern more than two hundred years ago by Samuel Fraunces, a French West Indian who subsequently became a steward for George Washington. Still an eating place downstairs, it serves upstairs as state headquarters for the Sons of the Revolution, with many Revolutionary exhibits to be seen. It was here that Washington said farewell to his officers in December, 1783.

OLD MERCHANTS HOUSE (*1830*)
29 East 4th Street; daily 11 to 5, Sundays and holidays 1 to 5; 50 cents; Historical Landmark Society.

The "old merchant" who built it was Seabury Tredwell, who lived here until 1865 at a time when this whole part of town was very chic, and when Colonnade Row—around the corner on Lafayette Street—was the most talked-about residential row in the city (half of it still there, at "428"). The entrance doorway of this house in the Late Federal style is something to talk about now, with a richly detailed fanlight and ornamental ironwork newels on the steps. Greek Revival indoors, with plenty of Duncan Phyfe furniture, splendid drapes and carpets, silver hardware, and all kinds of personal belongings from the past.

THEODORE ROOSEVELT HOUSE
(*before 1858*)
28 East 20th Street; daily 10 to 5 except Mondays, Sundays and holidays 1 to 5; Theodore Roosevelt Association.

This typical brownstone in which the twenty-sixth President was born represents the next architectural phase of domestic building in the city's march uptown. It is a narrow four-story house with a high stoop and "English basement," with five of its rooms fashionably furnished with Roosevelt family possessions of the Victorian era, when "Teddy" was a boy here. The room in which he was born and the

Jumel Mansion, one of the most distinguished country houses of colonial times, stands handsomely still today in the heart of upper Manhattan.

drawing rooms are much as they were when occupied; others are devoted to museum collections covering his lifelong activities.

JUMEL MANSION (*c. 1765*)

Edgecomb Avenue and West 160th Street; daily 11 to 5, except Mondays; City of New York.

This was one of the stylish Georgian country "great houses" of its day, and today it still holds its own both inside and out, standing in its small park uptown. Noteworthy features are rusticated board siding with quoins, a beautifully balustraded rooftop, and the first tall, slender classical portico on record in the Colonies. It is really the Col. Roger Morris House; Morris was a Royalist who fled the country at the outbreak of the Revolution. Washington made it his headquarters during the fall of 1776. For a while it was a fashionable hostelry, until it was bought in 1810 by the wealthy Frenchman, Stephen Jumel, whose widow lived on in it until she died in 1865. She had a brief marriage in the 1830s with Aaron Burr, whose desk is now among the many choice furnishings here.

DYCKMAN HOUSE (*1783*)

204th Street and Broadway; daily except Mondays; City of New York.

This charming old Dutch farmhouse in its present unfarmlike situation has the easy sweeping rooflines of its Flemish Colonial

Also in Manhattan, finely maintained, is the Dyckman house, a delightful Dutch Colonial farmhouse.

style, creating a long covered front porch, with posts and railings. White clapboards above, white-painted fieldstone walls below, and a little wing at a lower level add up to a pretty and picturesque effect. Filled with furnishings of the time provided by the Dyckman family, which give the house additional interest today.

METROPOLITAN MUSEUM OF ART
Fifth Avenue and 82d Street; daily 10 to 5, Sundays 1 to 5.

The American Wing here contains one of the two largest and finest collections of early American rooms in the country, reassembled here, superbly furnished and displayed.

MUSEUM OF THE CITY OF NEW YORK
Fifth Avenue and 104th Street; daily 10 to 5 except Mondays, Sundays and holidays 1 to 5.

Several rooms of various periods from the city itself.

NEW YORK HISTORICAL SOCIETY
170 Central Park W.; daily 1 to 5 except Sundays, Saturdays 10 to 5.

Three outstanding rooms and their furnishings, of seventeenth- and eighteenth-century New England origin, given by Mrs. Katharine Prentis Murphy and her brother, Edmund Astley Prentis.

¶ The Bronx

VAN CORTLANDT MANOR (*1748*)
Van Cortlandt Park at 242d Street, east of Broadway; daily 10 to 5, Sundays 2 to 5; 25 cents Thursdays, other days free; leased and maintained by National Society of Colonial Dames.

Built to be the country seat of the famous old Flemish family whose name it bears, this great early stone house has for many years now created for countless visitors a vivid impression of well-to-do home life in those distant days. This house has a rugged dignity in comparison with the graceful manners of the Morris-Jumel mansion. It is furnished with appropriate ostentation—English in the formal rooms, Dutch in certain bedrooms, and very delightful Dutch indeed in the cavernous downstairs kitchen.

POE COTTAGE (*1812*)
Grand Concourse and Kingsbridge Road; daily 10 to 5 except Mondays, 10 to 4:30 Sunday afternoons in winter; City of New York, Bronx Society of Arts and Sciences.

The poet came here to what was then the country (!) for his wife's health for a few tragic years in the 1840s; his wife died here, and he left to die in Baltimore. In this simple clapboard cottage, with its long lean-to wing, Poe wrote *The Bells, Annabel Lee,* and some of his best-remembered stories.

BARTOW MANSION (*1820*)
Pelham Bay Park, entrance at East Boulevard and Westchester Avenue; Sundays, 10 to 5; 25 cents; City of New York, headquarters of International Garden Club.

Built by descendants of lords of the Manor of Pelham, this two-story gray-stone mansion is now used as headquarters of the International Garden Club. There are excellent Greek Revival details inside and a lot of fine furniture of the 1830s.

¶ Staten Island

Richmondtown, when it was founded in 1665, was known as "Cocclestown" for the mounds of shells left by the departing Indians. Debased to "Cuckoldtown," it was obliged to change its name for the honor of its menfolk. The forthcoming Richmondtown restoration promises to be one of the outstanding evocations of our earliest history. It will show the evolution of an American village during the seventeenth, eighteenth, and nineteenth centuries—buildings, furnishings, orchards, lanes, and gardens. Most of the houses are to be existing originals, with some reconstructions. The plan includes thirty buildings in all—eight to be left standing where they are and restored, eleven to be moved in from other sections of the island, and twelve replicas. This immense project is scheduled to be completed in 1960, but already a number of houses are open to the public. The Staten Island Historical Society, ensconced in the restored COUNTY CLERK'S OFFICE (1848), at Court and Center Streets, where it is to remain, will be the information center for the restoration; the office will remain a museum for study and display.

STILLWELL-PERINE HOUSE (*1679*)

1476 Richmond Road, Dongan Hills; Sundays 2 to 5 April to November, other times by special appointment with caretaker on premises; 15 cents; Staten Island Historical Society.

This is an interesting and picturesque example of a house put together in progressive stages. The original stone section, built by Thomas Stillwell, Staten Island's first important personage, was augmented about 1710 by Stillwell's son-in-law Col. Nicholas Britton—with a still older stone house brought here from another location. Further additions in 1750, 1790, and 1830 merely add to the total picturesque effect.

VOORLEZER'S HOUSE (*1695*)

Arthur Kill Road opposite Center Street, Richmondtown, daily 10 to 5 except Mondays April through November, open by arrangement with caretaker other times; 10 cents and no charge; Staten Island Historical Society.

"Voorlezer" was the name given by the Dutch congregation to the layman chosen to teach school and conduct church services, and his house was built to be a church, school, and dwelling. This was the first building in the whole country to house an elementary school, and today three rooms are furnished as schoolrooms—one of that earliest period, one of the eighteenth century, and one of the 1840s. There are also a living room and an old Dutch kitchen with early furnishings.

BILLOP CONFERENCE HOUSE (*c. 1680*)

Foot of Hyland Boulevard, Tottenville; daily 10 to 5, except Mondays; Conference House Association.

For more than two and a half centuries the most imposing house on Staten Island, it has beautiful walls of stone masonry two feet thick and a fine rather Dutch pre-Georgian appearance. It was built by a British naval captain named Billop, and during the Revolution, when Staten Island was in the enemy's hands, Benjamin Franklin, John Adams, and Edward Rutledge came here to discuss terms with the English admiral Lord Howe. As the British terms did not include colonial independence, the conference failed; but it is memorialized in the name of the handsome and historical old house.

¶ *Brooklyn*

LEFFERTS HOMESTEAD (*1804*)

Near entrance to Prospect Park; Monday, Wednesday, and Friday afternoons; City of New York, Brooklyn Institute of Arts and Sciences.

Peter Lefferts built this ample but simple farmhouse after the British had burned him out during the Battle of Long Island. It was moved here to the entrance of Prospect Park from Flatbush when Peter's descendants gave the old house to the city in 1918. Its roof has the downswept slope of Dutch Colonial. Fittingly furnished.

THE BROOKLYN MUSEUM

Eastern Parkway; daily 10 to 5, Sundays and holidays 1 to 5.

The museum contains sixteen representative rooms, whose dates range from the 1720 paneling in a 1665 Maryland house to the smoking room of the old John D. Rockefeller House in New York City (1884). Between these extremes of taste you will soon find the Schenk-Crook House in its entirety, among the finest surviving homes of the seventeenth century in this country. All five rooms have been transported to the museum from Canarsie Park in Brooklyn, where the house had been standing since 1656.

¶ *Queens*

BOWNE HOUSE (*1661*)

Bowne Street and Fox Lane; daily, 3 to 5; Bowne House Historical Society.

Farmer John Bowne built this frame house, with its long Dutch dormers, when the settlement was under Dutch rule. He won everlasting fame by defying Governor Stuyvesant's ban against harboring Quakers, for which he was imprisoned and deported. By bringing the unfair edict to the attention of the Dutch governing body he gained religious freedom for the whole

Only a matter of minutes away from Manhattan is Long Island's finest colonial mansion, Rock Hall, at Lawrence.

colony. Quakers continue to worship in the house, and their meeting room, with its huge fireplace, may still be seen here. A couch on which George Fox, founder of the sect, rested while he was here, many of Bowne's possessions, and later acquisitions of the family furnish the house.

KING MANSION (*before 1750*)

> *King Park, Jamaica Avenue, between 150th and 153d Streets; Monday, Wednesday, and Saturday afternoons; village of Jamaica, Rufus King Chapter, D.A.R.*

This country seat of Rufus King, our first Minister to Great Britain, one of the first New York senators, and a member of the Continental Congress, was already an old place when King bought and enlarged it shortly after 1800. The white-shingled house has three stories and an attic. Its chaste portico is Georgian, while its gambrel, like those on some of the early upstate buildings, is Dutch. The house remained in the King family until 1896, when it was acquired, along with its sur-

rounding acres of park, by the village of Jamaica. The D.A.R. has supplied it with furniture, a toy collection, books, and other exhibits.

¶ Long Island

¶ Lawrence

ROCK HALL (*1767*)

> *Daily 9 to 5 except Tuesdays, May 9 to November 1; 50 cents and 25 cents, student groups free by appointment; town of Hempstead.*

This is one of the finest Georgian Colonial houses in the state. Now on the very verge of the metropolis, the imposing three-story white-shingled mansion still sits gracefully in its little park, its gambrel roof crowned by a Chinese Chippendale balustrade. The interior is truly notable, with its eight rooms paneled from floor to ceiling and most of the fireplaces faced with delft tiles. Recently and carefully restored and furnished, the rooms achieve the rare combination of museum perfection and the "lived-in" look. The color here is lovely; particularly fine, too, are the accessories, rugs, drapes, and portraits. Most of the rooms are eighteenth-century; the double drawing room, however, is as of 1810 to go with the woodwork there, whose style was brought up to date for a great wedding celebration in that early Federal year.

¶ Oyster Bay

RAYNHAM HALL (*1740s*)
West Main Street; turn north from 25A onto Route 106, to Main Street; Wednesdays, Fridays, and Sundays, 2 to 5; 25 cents; village of Oyster Bay.

Recently restored to its original colonial core, this old farmhouse is famous because of the part played by its first owner, Robert Townsend, called "Culpepper Junior," who was Washington's principal New York spy, in the capture of Major André and the exposure of Benedict Arnold's treachery.

SAGAMORE HILL (*1886*)
Cove Neck Road, off Cove Road from Route 25A; daily 10 to 5, except Tuesdays; 50 cents; Roosevelt Memorial Association.

Built by Theodore Roosevelt, this Edwardian country home, typical of the era, served as a summer White House from 1901 to 1908. It contains countless mementos of one of our most colorful Presidents. A "personality" house.

¶ Huntington

CONKLIN HOMESTEAD (*before 1760*)
New York Avenue and High Street; Wednesdays, Thursdays, and Fridays, 2 to 5, by appointment; Huntington Historical Society.

This mid-eighteenth-century house is furnished in that period and in early-nineteenth. It houses the Huntington Historical Society and its reference library on local history.

¶ South Huntington

BIRTHPLACE OF WALT WHITMAN (*1810*)
East Side of Route 110 about 1 mile north of Northern State Parkway; Saturdays and Sundays 2 to 5, May 31 to October.

Whitman's father built this two-story shingled farmhouse with his own hands. When Walt was four, the family moved to Brooklyn, where the father became a house builder. Whitman always considered himself an Islander. Eventually, after some wandering, he came back to teach school nearby and founded *The Long Islander,* a famous weekly in its day.

¶ Mastic

MANOR OF ST. GEORGE (*1700*)
In park; June 1 to November 30th; estate of Eugenie G. T. Smith.

Sitting in its own park, an original English land grant of 1693 by William and Mary, the manor was the site of Fort St. George and was occupied by the British in the Revolution. Left to the town by the last descendant of the original owners, it will remain intact, with all its heirloom furnishings of two and a half centuries.

¶ St. James

THE OLD WOODHULL HOUSE (*before 1719*)
Moriches Road near Setauket; on appointment by letter; Mr. and Mrs. Robert James Malone.

This long, low, shingled, vine-clad dwelling combines all the time-mellowed qualities of these early Island homes. Job Smith, who built it, was the son of Richard Smith (the "Bull-Rider") and patentee of nearby Smithtown.

¶ The Setaukets

Inquire about the Open House Day, usually in early September, at the Society for the Preservation of Long Island Antiquities, with headquarters at the Thompson House.

THOMPSON HOUSE (*early eighteenth century*)
In Setauket on North County Road, about 1 mile north of Stony Brook station; Saturdays 1 to 5 and Sundays 2 to 6, May 30 to October 11; 25 cents; S.P.L.I.A.

A very choice Long Island salt box which has been faithfully restored by Mr. and Mrs. Ward Melville. It is furnished with beautiful austerity, for the most part with Long Island furniture of the earliest period.

HAWKINS-MOUNT HOUSE (*c. 1750*)

Gould Road, Stony Brook; by appointment only through Suffolk Museum, Stony Brook.

This simple white frame house was the home of William Sidney Mount, one of our foremost genre artists. He and his brothers Henry and Shepherd, both also talented painters, spent their childhood here and used the familiar and charming scenes of this peaceful countryside by the Sound for their subject matter. The nearby museum contains some of William's and Henry's choice works.

JAYNE HOUSE (*1725*)

Old Post Road, which crosses Route 25A at Bailey Hollow Road, East Setauket; home of Mr. Howard G. Sherwood, not open at present; willed to S.P.L.I.A.

An early shingled house of rare quality, it was built by William Jayne, a chaplain in Cromwell's army and an Oxford graduate. Upon the accession of Charles II to the throne Jayne fled to this country and promptly acquired this property in what is now one of the most serene old sections of Long Island. Mr. Sherwood, a connoisseur, has cherished its early wall painting in two rooms, possibly the best example of unspoiled freehand wall decoration in America. The woodwork is of museum quality, and so is the furniture.

¶ *Cutchogue*

THE OLD HOUSE (*1649*)

One block west from traffic light on south side of Route 25; weekends 2 to 5 May 30 to July, daily 2 to 5 July and August; 25 cents and 10 cents; Congregational Society of Cutchogue.

As a wedding present to his daughter Anna and her husband, Benjamin Horton moved this house here in 1660 from Southold, ten miles away, where he had built it ten years before. It is one of the best of its early vintage, with four immense fireplaces, and is furnished as befits its medieval style. It should be mentioned here that the moving of early houses, which was a fairly common practice out here on Long Island, as it is in Connecticut and Massachusetts, is made relatively simple when the houses are framed, as these are for the most part, with posts and beams mortised and pegged. The houses are stiff enough to

move all in one piece, and easy to dismantle and reassemble as well.

¶ *Sag Harbor*

OLD CUSTOMS HOUSE (*1789*)

East side of Garden Street; July 4 to October 12, daily 10 to 5, Sundays and holidays 2 to 5; Old Sag Harbor Committee.

Now between the Whaling Museum and the Hannibal French House, this old post-Colonial dwelling originally stood opposite the Whaler's Church. In those days a flag flew over the lean-to, indicating that Mr. Dering's house was not only the customs house for the first port of entry in the State of New York but also the post office. The Derings, father and son, were deep in shipping enterprises, and the latter was at one time a shipping partner of James Fenimore Cooper. The gray-shingled house, weathered and solid, with its two broad chimneys, is just about typical of the way Sag Harbor homes were built in the early days of whaling. Simple and functional, the doorway shows the skill of the ship's carpenters who built it, as do the various mantels inside; for the original fireplaces are all here, and in the kitchen the old warming ovens and built-in cupboards can be seen. The early-home atmosphere has received real consideration here.

THE HANNIBAL FRENCH HOUSE (*1799 and 1825*)

Main Street; possibly shown on request; vacation home for The Servants of Relief for Incurable Cancer.

Perhaps the loveliest house in Sag Harbor, it was erected by Augustus Howell but later redesigned by Minard Lafever, who is said to have lived here himself for a period. It did not come into the French family until the 1860s. French & Hannibal was the last of the great whaling firms in the town, and its wealth brought gala days to the house. Lafever, according to Talbot Hamlin, "was perhaps the greatest designer of architectural decoration of his time in America." In the ornate exterior of this house and in its exquisite drawing room carving he left the town a legacy to be cherished. Fortunately Charles Edison, former Governor of New Jersey, pur-

In the atmospheric antique seaport of Sag Harbor, the old Customs House at the right is one of the choice early dwellings.

Opposite is the Thompson house at East Setauket, expertly restored and maintained in museum perfection.

chased the house in 1948 and undertook its restoration. His objective is to place the houses he can buy in the hands of those who will collaborate in keeping them unspoiled.

THE WHALING MUSEUM (*1846*)
Main and Garden Streets; daily, June to September.

The Whaling Museum was built as a home for the second of three Benjamin Hunttings and is said to be the work of Minard Lafever also. Lafever had the most able of collaborators in the shipwrights and master builders who executed his designs, and the beauty and elaboration of the Greek ornamentation on this building were brought to flower by skillful craftsmen here as elsewhere in the country. The house, with its great two-story Corinthian columns, was later a Masonic temple. It is fitting that the mansion should be devoted to the display of a fine whaling collection, for it was from that enterprise that the Hunttings derived their fortune.

Beside these places which are regularly open you may see four private homes—not always the same four. Mrs. Lloyd Bassett, Jr., will conduct this little tour for *Guide* readers for a fee of one dollar, provided that she is notified well in advance so that she may be able to make the arrangements with the owners. She recommends an excellent local guidebook, "A Tour of Historic Sag Harbor" (send fifty cents to the Old Sag Harbor Committee to get it), in which some eighty places of historic interest are noted and mapped.

¶ *East Hampton*

HOME, SWEET HOME (*c. 1764*)
Main Street; daily 10 to 12:30 and 1:30 to 5 and Sundays 2 to 5 June through August, daily except Tuesdays September through May; 50 cents; village of East Hampton.

This weathered old shingle salt box, under its high canopy of ancient elms, overlooks one of the prettiest village greens in the country. The chimney wall of a rather sophisticated living room is covered with ecclesiastical paneling. Moldings are emphatic in the parlor and bedrooms, and the construction of the house throughout is "for the ages." Beside the furniture, which is appropriate, the colonial kitchen and the buttery are completely equipped. A very

A portrait of John Howard Payne hangs above the mantel in the paneled parlor of his boyhood home in East Hampton— Home, Sweet Home.

fine collection of lusterware is scattered throughout the house. The old windmill behind the house also contains collections.

MULFORD HOUSE (*late 1600s*)
> *Next to "Home, Sweet Home" on green; Friday, Saturday, and Sunday afternoons in summer; East Hampton Historical Society, Edward Mulford Baker Strong (Curator).*

This remarkable old farmhouse much resembles its next-door neighbor. It was built by an ancestor of Mr. Strong, a gentleman still known hereabouts as "Old Fish Hook" Mulford in reference to his trip to England in 1704 to protest the tax on whale oil: warned to expect pickpockets in London, he providently lined his pockets with fishhooks. His eleven-room, five-fireplace house, very spacious for its time and place, was framed with the timbers of the village church when the church, which had been built in 1650, became too small for its congregation.

¶ Westchester County

The Westchester County Historical Society, with headquarters at 626 County Building, White Plains, holds a yearly Open House Day the first week in October. Eight or ten houses are displayed each year in different parts of the county.

¶ New Rochelle

PAINE COTTAGE (*c. 1800*)
> *North and Paine Avenues; daily 2 to 5, except Mondays; Huguenot and Historical Association of New Rochelle.*

Thomas Paine, the great pamphleteer of the Revolution, lived in this shingled cottage for a period of three years, off and on.

¶ Eastview (*near Scarsdale*)

HAMMOND HOUSE (*1719*)
> *Route 100C, near Grasslands Hospital; daily 1 to 5 except Mondays, April 1 to November 1; Westchester County Historical Society, White Plains.*

This very early house has the steep roof with overhang, unbroken by dormers, which characterizes the early farmhouses

The Hammond house at Eastview is one of Westchester County's most inviting colonial cottages, a pleasure to visit.

of the neighborhood. Three successive generations of Hammonds, each one a distinguished officer of the militia, were the first three owners here. The family was well known and lived with some style, for the living room is paneled from floor to ceiling on two walls and enriched by pilasters and fine cornices and moldings, probably made in New England. Three of the rooms have been furnished with early Westchester items, and the remainder contain exhibits of interesting miscellany.

¶ Port Chester

BUSH HOMESTEAD (*c. 1700*)
> *479 King Street; Tuesdays, Thursdays, and Saturdays, 1:30 to 4:30; village of Port Chester.*

Built by Abraham Bush, a sea captain, this is an interesting Georgian house which became the headquarters of Gen. Israel Putnam in 1777–1778. The bed and desk of "Old Put" are here.

¶ *North White Plains*

WASHINGTON'S HEADQUARTERS
(1738–1770)
Virginia Road; daily 10 to 4, except Mondays (closed in winter); county of Westchester, D.A.R. (custodians).

An unpretentious story-and-a-half farmhouse with a characteristic roofline, this comfortable home that Elijah Miller built was not only Washington's headquarters in the successful Battle of White Plains but subsequently, in 1778 and 1781, that of Generals Lee, Clinton, and Gates. Its secluded position—high yet out of sight of the British—made it serviceable. The floor of the room where Washington slept is now raised several inches by the roots of an ancient sycamore tree which even then gave it shade. The D.A.R. have furnished it as an eighteenth-century farmhouse with some Washington belongings of special interest.

¶ *Scarsdale*

WAYSIDE COTTAGE (1729)
1039 Post Road; being restored, open on request; Junior League of Scarsdale (custodians).

One of the eighteenth-century landmarks of Westchester County, this attractive old shingle-and-clapboard cottage, restored by the Junior League of Scarsdale and the D.A.R., was the home of the Varian family, who were driven from it, after serving in the Revolution, by the "skinners and cowboys" (equivalent of gangsters) who infested the area.

UP & DOWN THE HUDSON RIVER VALLEY

Yonkers; Tarrytown; Croton-on-Hudson; Garrison-on-Hudson; Beacon; Fishkill; Poughkeepsie; Pleasant Valley; Hyde Park; Rhinebeck; Staatsburg; Tivoli; Barrytown; Hudson; Kinderhook; Old Chatham; Rensselaer; Troy; Albany; Athens; West Coxsackie; Kingston; Old Hurley; New Paltz; Newburgh; Tappan; Monroe

¶ *Yonkers (15 miles north of Times Square)*

PHILIPSE MANOR HALL
(early and mid-eighteenth century)
Warburton Avenue and Dock Street; Monday to Saturday 9 to 5, Sundays 1 to 5; State of New York; American Scenic and Historic Preservation Society (custodians).

Frederick Philipse was lord of the Manor of Philipseborough, comprising a large part of what is now Westchester County; so, while this manor house is immense, its palatial scale was quite in keeping with the prosperity and importance of the Philipse family. The stone south wing is the earlier, though it must be somewhat later than its given date of 1682 on the evidence of its architectural details, and the brick side wing later still. There may have been an earlier manor house on this spot in which lived the first lord, who died in 1703; for the chances are that the present manor was both built and enlarged by his grandson, the second lord, also Frederick Philipse. In any event, it is one of the truly notable early American houses done in the Georgian manner (or manners). It is certainly the sight to see in Yonkers.

¶ *Tarrytown*

PHILIPSE CASTLE (*a Rockefeller restoration*) (1683–1785)
On Route 9 in North Tarrytown; daily 10 to 5, Sundays 12 to 5; $1.00 and 60 cents, combination ticket with "Sunnyside" $1.60 and $1.00.

The first lord of Philipseborough is said to have started the stone section of this "castle," in the northern part of his vast manorial grant, in the 1680s. The frame

The two main sections of Philipse Castle at Tarrytown—the stone and the frame—were built a hundred years apart.

addition was made in the 1780s, when the building was owned by the wealthy Beekmans. Now the "castle," along with its various dependencies, has been expertly restored in the Rockefeller manner— neither money nor experts spared. It is fitted with rare Dutch and English furniture appropriate to its two widely separated periods. This place and "Sunnyside" together provide a view of three contrasting periods and the ways of life of three prominent American families. Much to be learned here in an easy, entertaining way.

SUNNYSIDE *or* THE WASHINGTON IRVING HOUSE (*a Rockefeller restoration*) (*1835–1859*)

Off Route 9 between Irvington and Tarrytown; daily, 10 to 5; $1.00 and 60 cents.

Three miles from Philipse Castle a much later "castle" has been preserved—the former home of Washington Irving. The Gothic and ultraromantic residence nearly hides what remains of the original old Dutch farmhouse that Irving bought in 1835 as the nucleus for the remarkable remodeling job that he commissioned. The Victorian interior is enchantingly un-

touched and is just as Irving and his sisters occupied it during the nineteenth century, with every evidence of the taste of a cultivated family who could afford to live with a window view of the Hudson.

¶ *Croton-on-Hudson*

VAN CORTLANDT MANOR HOUSE (*a restoration*) (*1665*)
John D. Rockefeller, Jr.

This is a major restoration of one of the most important of the early Hudson River houses, built by Van Cortlandts and occupied by them until 1940—or more than two and a half centuries. Commanding a broad expanse of the lordly river, it was originally of fortress construction and was used as a refuge from the Indians. When ready, this will be one of the most important house museums on the Hudson.

¶ *Garrison-on-Hudson*

MANDEVILLE HOUSE (*1737*)
Four Corners; open on written request in late summer and fall; Miss Nancy Allan.

One of the most ingratiating houses on the Hudson, it was begun by Jacob Mandeville, grandson of a Dutch immigrant who arrived here from Holland in 1659. The original house was two rooms with an attic; next came the kitchen wing; then, still before the Revolution, a parlor was added, with a bedroom above to accommodate the family. The library was added in 1850. The ecclesiastical paneling of the chimney wall in the oldest part, now the dining room, is of a rare quality and is repeated in the doorway, reminding us that the first church services in the vicinity were held here in the fall of 1770 and were continued regularly until a church was built. Other rooms are paneled as well, and there are built-in cupboards throughout the house. Since it was on an important highway between the southern part of Connecticut and West Point, Mandeville House was an overnight stop for many of the Revolutionary generals, among them Washington himself, and it was General Putnam's headquarters from May until October (his wife died here).

¶ Beacon

Edwin R. Corwin, Beacon historian, will be glad to give assistance in the vicinity. He is familiar with all the houses and with many of the owners.

BRET-TELLER HOUSE (*1709*)

> *Van Nydeck Avenue; vacant now but restoration in progress; D.A.R.*

Dutch Colonial in feeling, with some of the walls covered with the original round-headed cedar shingles, this house is a good example of an early gambrel. Catharyne and Roger Brett built it, and their descendants lived in it until after 1940.

DE WINDT-BOGARDUS HOUSE (*c. 1790*)

> *16 Tompkins Avenue; open by request; Mr. and Mrs. Carl E. Cummings.*

This attractive early Dutch cottage was built on Peter de Windt's estate for a relative. The de Windt House itself is long since gone, destroyed by fire, as was the famous Verplanck House. This is the third oldest house in town, and has been continuously occupied. The present owner has done a faithful job of restoration even

while incorporating modern requirements and can furnish voluminous lore that does much to bring the old house back to life.

¶ Fishkill
(*just above Beacon*)

HENDRICK KIP HOUSE (*1753*)

> *On north side of road from Beacon, near Fishkill; preferably by written appointment, May 1 to November 1; Mr. Wilbur John Hammond.*

This much-written-about house is a fine example of the early Dutch stone dwellings of the Hudson Valley. Except for an extension on the rear, its one and one half stories stand much as they looked when the place was built. It is thought by some that its builder James Hussey may have erected the east section as early as 1720. Baron von Steuben made his headquarters here while he was training the raw recruits in the area for Washington's army.

COL. JOHN BRINKERHOFF HOUSE (*1738*)

> *East of Fishkill and south of road to Hopewell; by written appointment; Mrs. Eleanora M. Lagerholm.*

With one of the purest examples of a Dutch exterior of the early period in the Hudson Valley, it has only recently been restored. Its new owner assures us that it is unchanged, except for a modern kitchen. It is another of the houses that Washington slept in. The motherly colonel's lady is said to have tucked him in snugly on cold nights. Mrs. Lagerholm plans to furnish the house in period.

VERPLANCK-VAN WYCK HOUSE *or* CRYSTAL SPRING MANOR (*1768*)

> *Fishkill Plains; on request; Mrs. E. B. Stringham, Sr., R.F.D. Wappingers Falls (phone: Hopewell Junction 6–2542).*

This great brick house, high, wide, and handsome, was built by wealthy Philip Verplanck, Jr., owner of a prosperous nearby gristmill and landing on Wappingers Creek. Philip improved his fortunes further by marrying the daughter of Burgher Gerard Beekman. The gambrel roof was a not uncommon feature of the brick manors in this section, but the balustrade and circular window in the gable are decorative notes not seen as frequently.

¶ *Poughkeepsie (on Route 9, 17 miles above Beacon)*

CLINTON HOUSE (*1765, rebuilt 1783*)
549 Main Street; daily 9 to 5, Sundays 1 to 5; State of New York.

The original house, reputedly the headquarters of Gov. George Clinton during the Revolution, was burned in 1782. But the very next year Washington, out of respect for Clinton, ordered artisans from the Temple Hill camp to rebuild the house, at which time it was enlarged. A fieldstone home typical of the Hudson Valley, simple and solid, it is furnished with museum objects today as a memorial to the state's first governor.

LOCUST GROVE (*1827, augmented 1850 and again in 1901*)
370 South Road; by appointment; Miss Annette I. Young.

This is one of the countless houses designed by Alexander Jackson Davis, whose notable career in architecture occupied more than half of the nineteenth century. It is also one of his best-known works, partly because it was bought by Samuel F. B. Morse with the first money he received from his invention of the telegraph. Morse remodeled it in 1850, and Miss Young's father made the final addition in the same style. It contains many fine Early American antiques.

GLEBE HOUSE (*1767*)
635 Main Street; being restored by Dutchess County Historical Society and Junior League, open by written request and several afternoons weekly; city of Poughkeepsie.

A small brick building with one dormer whose first occupant was the Rev. John Beardsley, exiled in 1777 because of Loyalist sympathies. The house was built in three stages, and each of the rooms downstairs is being furnished as nearly as possible in the period in which it was built.

¶ *Pleasant Valley*

BRICK HOUSE FARM (*1777*)
On written request only; Mr. and Mrs. Edwin H. Keith.

As an example of how a woman can pass the time when her husband is "off to the wars," Brick House Farm was built by Sophia Newcomb while husband Zaccheus was serving in the Revolution. Sophia's slaves made the brick for her house, which she constructed handsomely with a sweeping gambrel, ample windows, and charming details of cornice and entrance. Near the house, where the slaves dug out the clay, she made a duck pond. When Zaccheus returned, it is said he was astonished to find this delightful Georgian mansion, with his initials formed in the west wall by the ends of the beam anchors. Four spacious rooms downstairs are built around a wide hallway with Dutch doors at either end. Each of the rooms has its corner fireplace, and the woodwork throughout is of the first quality.

¶ *Hyde Park (on Route 9, 4 miles above Poughkeepsie)*

ROOSEVELT HOME (*1826*)
Daily 10 to 5, except Mondays; 25 cents; National Historical Site.

This famous country seat, built in the year of Jefferson's death, has undergone many changes, adapting itself to the needs and tastes of the important family that grew up here. Basically it is a big Federal mansion, now just as it was while a Presidential home. F. D. R. was born here January 30, 1882, and buried here April 15, 1945. His parents bought it in 1867, and the house reflects their tenure—but with all the added memorabilia of a great man whose aura will always pervade it.

VANDERBILT MANSION
(*1895–1898*)
West side of Route 9; daily 9 to 5, except Mondays; small fee; National Park Service.

Not an Early American house by any means, but, like "The Breakers" at Newport and "Biltmore" at Asheville, affording not-to-be-missed opportunity to see the heights of a sumptuous magnificence which unlimited wealth can achieve. Although pleasing and enlightening, it is far from equalling McKim, Mead and White's best houses, though it may be their biggest. The Vanderbilt who built this was Frederick, brother of Cornelius, of "The Breakers," and George, of "Biltmore."

❡ Rhinebeck (on Route 9, 5 miles above Staatsburg)

GENERAL MONTGOMERY HOUSE (before 1773)

East Livingston Street; daily, courtesy of caretaker; Chancellor Livingston Chapter, D.A.R.

This is the cottage in which the general and his wife lived while they were building "Grasmere," two miles to the south, which burned before it was finished. Montgomery captured Montreal in 1777 only to lose his life in the assault on Quebec. The cottage contains some good pieces of furniture donated by chapter members through the years.

THE BEEKMAN ARMS (an inn) (1700)

Route 9.

Open all the time as a comfortable, commodious hostelry, it began as a one-story, two-room stone house. Its enlargement began in 1769. There were later additions as trade became more brisk, but the old part still preserves its original character.

❡ Staatsburg (on east bank above Hyde Park)

THE MANSION (1830 and 1895)

Ogden and Ruth Mills Memorial Park, near Staatsburg; daily, 11 to 4:30; 30 cents and 10 cents.

A sixty-five-room palace built by the late Ogden Mills in what is now a two-hundred-acre memorial park near the town. The setting is fabulous, and the mansion is completely furnished as it was during the Mills' occupancy, with antiques, paintings, sculpture, Gobelin tapestries, and many other works of art. The furniture is chiefly Louis XV and XVI. Some of the furnishings belonged to the owner of the original house and great-grandfather of Ruth L. Mills, Morgan Lewis, who served in the Revolution and was the third Governor of New York State. The first house (1795) burned in 1832. The new one built here forms the central section of the present mansion, the wings having been added and the whole remodeled for the Mills family by Stanford White in 1895.

❡ Tivoli (10 miles above Rhinebeck on the river)

CALLENDAR HOUSE (1794)

On written request; Mrs. William H. Osborn.

This impressive old country seat has one of those breath-taking views of the valley for which the Livingston houses are fam-

Montgomery Place, near Barrytown on the Hudson, set in its velvety green park, has much of the charm of a minor French chateau.

Callendar House, near Tivoli on the Hudson, like a great Regency villa, looks out across the lordly river.

ous. Choosing this choice spot for his house, Henry G. Livingston built it and sold it at once to his cousin Philip, who named it "Sunning Hill." In 1860 it was repossessed by John Livingston, who gave it the present name. When first built, it was a manor house of stately proportions, with a hipped roof crowned by a broad, flat cupola. It had one-story wings originally, but they were apparently raised about 1830, when the portico was added to the west front, to create a classical colonnade of twelve Doric columns, giving the place the look of a great Regency villa. Other features are virtually unchanged, and it is furnished with many Livingston heirlooms.

¶ *Barrytown*

MONTGOMERY PLACE

(*between 1802 and 1805*)
On written request when owner can arrange to show; Gen. and Mrs. John Ross Delafield.

In the history of the Hudson Valley the name of Livingston bulks larger than any other, and so too did their lands. Montgomery Place is one of many mansions built by this family that literally dominated the valley for a century or more,

and some of whose descendants are still living today in the homes. In this case it was Janet Livingston, the daughter of the great Chancellor and the widow of General Montgomery, the hero of Quebec, who built the house. She and her husband had begun to build their home near Rhinebeck, when the news of his death caused her to abandon the house, which burned. Later she built Montgomery Place, overlooking one of the finest views the majestic river affords. In 1844 the north pavilion, west veranda, and south wing were built; further ornamentation was added in 1860, and today it resembles nothing so much as a charming French château, set in its spacious green park. However, the interior is virtually unchanged, and the stately rooms contain nothing but the heirlooms of an illustrious family, many of the pieces purchased by the widow Janet when it was built. Not the least interesting things to see in this mellow house are the fine family portraits.

Nearby is EDGEWATER (1820), still another Livingston house, with a library by A. J. Davis, now owned by Gore Vidal, the novelist. It is one of the outstanding Federal-style houses of the valley, with a most impressive two-story Doric portico.

¶ *Hudson (on Route 9, 25 miles above Rhinebeck)*

OAK HILL
(between 1790 and 1800)
On written request at owner's convenience, summer months only; Mrs. Herman Livingston, R.D. 2.

The first manor house of the Livingstons stood scarcely more than a mile from here; built in 1699, it burned in 1800. "Oak Hill" was built by John, one of the sons of the last lord of the manor, who selected for himself one of the choicest bluffs along the length of the Hudson, with a view of the blue Catskills, rising beyond the opposite bank. The character of the Late Federal brick house has been somewhat altered by the later addition of a mansard roof and a veranda. However, within the high-ceilinged rooms all is much as it has been since John Livingston built it, for his great-grandson's wife is still residing here. The furniture which Duncan Phyfe made in his shop in New York especially for the drawing room, richly ornate in design, is placed where it has always been. Magnificent mementos of the China trade, fine carpets, family silver, and portraits of the first lord and his lady make this a Livingston house which breathes the history of the English family whose fortunes were identified with their great landholdings on the Hudson.

¶ *Kinderhook (on Route 9J, 12 miles above Hudson)*

HOUSE OF HISTORY (*1810*)
Route 9 (Main Street); daily 10 to 5 except Sundays June to November, other months by request to James E. Leath (residence across street); Columbia County Historical Society.

Built for James Vanderpoel by Barnabas Waterman, its most talented architect, this is one of the Hudson Valley's loveliest brick Federal houses. Not the least of its many charms are its livable scale and its elegance of detail. The color of the brick is a mellow russet. Marble arches frame the fanlight of the entrance door, a delicate white railing ornaments the roof, and four well-proportioned chimneys top off an exterior of real distinction. The interior is also consistently fine. The hallway is one of

the best in the state. The arch at the foot of the exceptionally graceful staircase is flanked by delicate fluted pilasters of the Corinthian order. The beauty of these flat arches, which Waterman designed so successfully, can best be appreciated here in the hall. The house is furnished as exquisitely as it is designed, fortunately having been restored by Mr. Leath, a perfectionist who understood its rare quality. The furniture, portraits, and accessories make it one of the most satisfying small house museums in the country.

¶ *Old Chatham (a few miles east of Kinderhook)*

SHAKER MUSEUM
(eighteenth century)
May to November; Shaker Museum Foundation, Mr. H. Phelps Clawson (phone: Old Chatham 5271).

Here in the eighteenth century the Shakers set up their largest and most significant colony. A carpentry shop, a forge, the medicine-making room, and the weaving room are now on view, as well as typical rooms occupied by the brothers and sisters. A very fine collection of their furniture, notable for its beauty and simplicity of design, can be admired here. Considered by connoisseurs to be American craftsmanship at its most clean-cut and functional, this furniture and the other articles of household furnishings and equipment here have a beauty all their own.

¶ *Rensselaer (across from Albany)*

FORT CRAILO (*1704*)
Riverside Avenue; daily 9 to 5, Sundays 1 to 5; State of New York.

This rare old residence of the Rensselaers was built in two sections fifty years apart, the earlier serving double duty as a fort, as shown by its gun ports. It has been carefully restored by the state, and illustrates inside and out how the great Dutch landowners lived here in the eighteenth century. The old brick walls are laid in English bond, with headers of brick laid obliquely over the narrow windows and doors. The windows have leaded diamond panes, and the roof is tile. The furniture is for the most part regional and includes

The dining room of the House of History at Kinderhook is notable for the finish and perfection of its furnishings.

One of the great early brick houses of the state, Fort Crailo was built to serve both as a home and as a place of refuge.

many fascinating Dutch pieces. The house has been popularly linked to "Yankee Doodle" by a story which has it that a British Army surgeon staying here invented the words of that immortal ditty as he watched the raw colonial recruits tramp by. It was, of course, derisive, but the "Yankee Doodles" picked it up and made it the most popular marching song of the Revolution. Ask the way here to the nearby JAN BRIES HOUSE (1723), which is not open but still of interest from the outside.

¶ Troy (on east bank 5 miles above Albany)

CLUETT HOME (1827)

59 2d Street; daily 11 to 5, probably not on Sundays; 35 cents; Rensselaer County Historical Society.

The arched doorway and lintels of this delightful brick Federal town house are trimmed with contrasting sandstone, which along with the balustrade which edges the eaves and the round-headed dormers, all adds up to a sprightly appearance. The interior is even more debonair. A stairway of remarkable grace rises from a broad hall whose scenic paper has fortunately been preserved. One of the many fanciful features of the house is the repetition of the overdoor fanlight at every possible opportunity.

¶ Albany

SCHUYLER MANSION or
THE PASTURES (1762)

Southwest corner Clinton and Schuyler Streets; daily 10 to 5, Sundays 1 to 5; State of New York, maintained by State Education Department.

This is one of the great Georgian houses of this country, with walls of beautifully patterned brick topped with a delicate balustrade of the Chinese Chippendale pattern. Built by young Philip Schuyler, later to become an outstanding Revolutionary general, a member of the Continental Congress, and an adviser and friend of Washington's, the house sits on its high knoll as handsome as ever, with its interior strikingly and elegantly restored—carved mantels, dignified paneling, and all the panoply of colonial wealth and position. In its south-

east drawing room Elizabeth Schuyler was married to Alexander Hamilton, only one of the countless colorful occasions which brought here at one time or another practically every notable of the day.

TEN BROECK MANSION (1798)

9 Ten Broeck Place; daily 3 to 4, other times by appointment; 35 cents, no charge Mondays; Albany County Historical Association.

It had to be an imposing house, for its owner, Gen. Abraham Ten Broeck, was a hero of the Battle of Saratoga and thrice Mayor of Albany. A big brick mansion with fine Georgian features, four great chimneys, and a balustraded roof, it breathes the solidity, the concern with good living that the wealthy Dutch descendants imparted to their surroundings. A certain sober splendor marked their homes, and this effect has been preserved here both without and within.

¶ Athens (just above Catskill on the Hudson)

VAN LOON HOUSE (c. 1812)

385 Franklin; on written or phone request (Hudson 8–6932); preferably warm-weather months; Mr. and Mrs. Eugene M. Van Loon.

This beautiful Federal mansion was designed by the talented Barnabas Waterman who built the House of History at Kinderhook. This one has, among other interesting features, a large oval ballroom with brick-red walls and white trim. The village was settled in 1686 by Jan Van Loon, and two other Van Loon houses still stand: a one-story house of 1724 at the north limits of the town, and a solid fieldstone house with a gabled Dutch roof (1706) at the foot of Washington Street.

¶ West Coxsackie (on Route 385, 18 miles below Albany)

PIETER BRONCK HOUSE (1663,
brick addition 1738)

On west side of Route 9W; daily 9 to 5:30, June to October 15; donation; Greene County Historical Society.

Of stone and brick, with casements and early-Dutch-style gable ends, the house was built by the only son of Jonas Bronck, who settled in Westchester County in 1639, and

*Chaste as only a fine
Federal dwelling can be,
the Van Loon house is one
of the loveliest landmarks
on the west bank of the
Hudson River.*

after whom the Bronx was named. It is actually three connecting houses, one of which was built in 1800 when a daughter refused to live under the original roof with her stepmother. In the oldest part are two large rooms with heavy-beamed ceilings, great fireplaces, and wide floorboards. The doors have all their handmade hardware, including the knockers. The fortresslike loopholes upstairs were to be used in case of Indian attack. Bronck furniture from the seventeenth down to the nineteenth century includes Revolutionary silver, fine paintings, and a rare early Bible.

¶ *Kingston (on Route 9W, 23 miles below
   Catskill)*

VAN LEUVEN MANSION (*1784,
   addition 1795*)

*Main and Wall Streets; Thursdays and
Saturdays, 10 to 5 (closed February and
March); Fred J. Johnston.*

One of the choice Federal houses of the Hudson Valley, this was built by John Suydam, an early Senator, whose portrait, by John Vanderlyn, hangs over the living-room mantel. Among the many treasures in this house, the Waterford chandelier in this room and the carpet which once graced the home of Duncan Phyfe are outstanding. The mahogany dining room is furnished in American Hepplewhite, with a sideboard that belonged to the first governor of Vermont; the library is Philadelphia Chippendale, with a serpentine

secretary made by John Goddard, of Newport, about 1760. Mr. Johnston sells antiques in his shop nearby; his knowledge of the neighborhood is extensive.

OSTERHOUDT HOUSE
(*1688 and 1740*)

*Neighborhood Road off Route 9W, 3 miles
from Kingston; by arrangement with Mrs.
Charles S. Dana (phone: Kingston
7349W); Rev. Anita Trueman Pickett
(owner).*

A long, low stone dwelling with five dormers, painted white, it was built by three successive generations of the Dutch family of this name. The beams, among the largest known to experts in these parts, measure eighteen by ten and a half inches, and are set in the stone wall. A grandson of the first builder placed a 1740 date stone in the east end. It is furnished simply, in keeping.

SENATE HOUSE (*1666 or 1676*)

*Clinton Avenue and Front Street; daily 9
to 5, Sundays 1 to 5; State of New York.*

Very snug and full of character, it had its moment of history too. In September 1777 Kingston was temporarily the state capital by the fortunes of war, and the Senate convened in this house, then owned by Abraham Van Gaasbeek. A few days later the British burned the town, but the old stone dwelling was hardly scorched.

¶ *Old Hurley*

Old Hurley is unique in its aggregation

of unspoiled old Dutch houses built of the native stone. The owners of ten of them open them yearly under the auspices of the Old Hurley Dutch Reformed Church (itself built in 1790), usually the last week in July on a Saturday, for a modest fee. The essential character of these houses has been carefully preserved by their owners, and you will find them full of unexpected treasures. Probably nowhere else will you get a better idea of what a Dutch village in America actually looked like at that time.

JAN VAN DUESEN HOUSE (*1723*)
By written request; Mrs. Ruth C. Waterbury, Hurley.

The governing body of New York State met and hid their records in a secret room here after the British burned Kingston in 1777. Built flush with the street, like so many others in the Dutch towns hereabouts, it has the usual roofline meeting the wall not far above the twenty-four-pane first-story windows. Four dormers swoop down from the peak of the gable almost to the edge of the roof. The stone is light in color and uneven in texture; it typifies the best in this sturdy style of building.

Others to note here are the OLD GUARD HOUSE (1745), where David Taylor, a British spy, was imprisoned, a tiny stone house with one dormer and a scalloped bargeboard trimming the steep gable ends of the roof; THE SOJOURNER TRUTH HOUSE (1750), with its five dormers, the birthplace of the Negro evangelist whose name the house bears and whose religious influence was so marked hereabouts; and THE PARSONAGE (1790), with its clapboarded gable over the front porch.

¶ *New Paltz (on Route 32 16 miles below Kingston)*

New Paltz, on the banks of the Wallkill River, is one of the most picturesque towns in the country. Its Huguenot Street looks almost exactly as it did in the early part of the eighteenth century, and the low fieldstone houses with their steep-pitched roofs are much like the medieval farmhouses the Walloons left behind them in Pfalz, on the banks of the Rhine. They came to escape the religious persecution of Louis XIV, some

Washington lived longer here in the Hasbrouck house at Newburgh than in any other of his many Revolutionary headquarters; a house with much architectural interest as well.

The old stone Huguenot houses of New Paltz make this one of the most enjoyable villages in the state to visit.

of them establishing themselves at Hurley and others settling here. Four of these houses stand in their original state, and there are two others of equal interest and antiquity. A tour, called "Stone House Day" and sponsored by the Dutch Reformed Church, is held from time to time, on which occasion some of the homes described below may be visited. Mr. Kenneth E. Hasbrouck, the guiding spirit here, will arrange for special visits to private homes in the vicinity if notified in advance.

JEAN HASBROUCK HOUSE, *now* MEMORIAL HOUSE (*1712*)

Daily, 9 to 12 and 1 to 4; Huguenot Patriotic Historical Society.

This is one of the bright gems of this old Huguenot settlement; of stone, of course, sharply gabled and low-eaved.

COL. JOSIAH HASBROUCK HOUSE (*1814*)

Gardiner, south of New Paltz on Route 32; Open afternoons 1 to 5, June until Labor Day; donation for Huguenot Historical Society of New Paltz; Miss Annette I. Young (owner), Mr. Kenneth E. Hasbrouck (custodian).

Formerly known as "Locust Lawn," it was built by Josiah Hasbrouck, a colonel in the Revolution who served in the House of Representatives before 1800. It is said that the reason he moved from the Jean Hasbrouck House (Memorial House) in New Paltz is because he feared the village might prove too gay for his only son Levi. His daughter, however, continued to live in that house after her marriage to Josiah Du Bois. Miss Young, the present owner, is a direct descendant of Josiah.

¶ *Newburgh* (*on Route 9W, 16 miles below New Paltz*)

HASBROUCK HOUSE *or* WASHINGTON'S HEADQUARTERS (*1750–1770*)

Liberty and Washington Streets, in a park; Monday through Saturday 9 to 5, Sundays 1 to 5; State of New York.

Famous as the headquarters in which Washington remained for sixteen months, his longest continuous residence during the war. Here he established the Order of the Purple Heart and wrote his letter of advice to the governors of the states that were forming, and from here he finally announced the end of hostilities. A steep-roofed stone house with tall chimneys, it was built in three stages, which contributes to its present attractiveness. Washington's staff was quartered on the second floor. The house was returned to the widow Hasbrouck after Washington's departure. Nearby is a museum containing many Washington items.

GENERAL KNOX HEADQUARTERS *or* JOHN ELLISON HOUSE (*1734–1754*)

4 miles south on 94; weekdays 9 to 5, Sundays 1 to 5; State of New York.

Five miles from Washington's Headquarters at Vail's Gate on a fifty-acre tract of land, is a comely colonial fieldstone house with a low wooden wing, whose rusticity is unusually pleasing. Its two small dormers, fine roofline, and twenty-four-pane windows give its plainness plenty of style. The fireplace mantels and woodwork are of unusually excellent quality, and the house is now being furnished with good period pieces. Mrs. Knox, who was noted for her hospitality, kept "open house" here for the officers encamped at Temple Hill.

¶ Tappan (on Route 303 at New Jersey line)

DE WINDT HOUSE, now GEORGE WASHINGTON MASONIC SHRINE (1700)
1 mile west of Route 9W; daily, 10 to 4; Grand Lodge, Free and Accepted Masons of New York.

This early brick and stone house was restored after many vicissitudes as nearly as possible to its original state when Washington occupied it as headquarters during the darkest days of the Revolution. Here the general signed the death warrant for Major André, who was hanged nearby.

THE 1776 HOUSE (an inn) (1776)
Tuesday through Sunday, 9 to 11; Russell and Robert Killoran.

This tailored stone house, with four chimneys, was Major André's place of confinement during his trial for treason, and from it he went to be hanged on October 2, 1780. It was an inn even then. Interesting eight-paneled shutters on the lower windows.

¶ Monroe (on Route 17, 10 miles west of Bear Mountain)

OLD MUSEUM VILLAGE OF SMITH'S CLOVE
1 mile west on Route 17; daily 10 to 5, May to November; $1.00 and 50 cents (groups less); Roscoe W. Smith.

This remarkable collection of old country buildings has been the hobby of Mr. Smith for many years. It now contains more than twenty structures, including many varieties of shops and country stores, log cabins, and farm structures, each housing collections of equipment, utensils, tools, and early machinery—a complete education in the early American rural utilities of a century or more ago.

THE MOHAWK VALLEY & VICINITY

Amsterdam; Constableville; Cooperstown; Johnstown; Little Falls

¶ Amsterdam

FORT JOHNSON (1749)
Fort Johnson Village, 3 miles west of Amsterdam on Route 5; daily 1 to 5 April to November, weekdays 10 to 5 July and August; Montgomery Historical Society.

Superintendent of Indian Affairs for the Crown Sir William Johnson lived in baronial state with his Indian wife, Molly Brant, in this great foursquare stone mansion with its tall chimney, hipped roof, and staggered dormers. Now a vine-covered house looking nothing like a fortress, it was surrounded by a high stockade during the French and Indian War. The Indians, however, trusted Sir William, and his power over them was said to be greater than that of any other white man. Here were held Mohawk and Iroquois powwows, at which the red men were liberally entertained. The paneling and all the mantels except one are the originals. An invoice shows that woodwork, as well as glass and hardware, were imported from London. The two great halls, living room, dining room, and two bedrooms are furnished; some of the pieces belonged to Sir William, and the rest are of the same early period, except for the Sheraton dining room. The third floor and four small rooms are devoted to Indian displays—a large and significant collection.

GUY PARK MANOR (1773)
336 West Main Street; daily and Sunday afternoons; Amsterdam Chapter, D.A.R.

Built by Sir William for his daughter Mary and her husband and cousin Col. Guy Johnson, who not only inherited his uncle's great fortune but also his widespread influence with Indians; he was appointed superintendent of them in Sir William's place. The house has lost much of its character, both inside and out, by the reconstruction of the roof and cornice in 1848 and of the wings in 1858. The interior trim is typical Greek Revival now.

¶ *Constableville (on Route 26, 24 miles north of Rome)*

CONSTABLE HALL (*1810–1819*)

Route 26; daily 10 to 5 except Monday, Sundays 1 to 6, June to November; 50 cents and 25 cents; Constable Hall Association.

Remote and unspoiled in its beautiful country setting, the house itself is virtually as it was when occupied by William Constable. Of gray cut stone, its two bays bracket a pedimented portico with tall columns, and a similarly generous scale and simplicity of detail mark the interior. Much of the original Constable furniture is still here. The library and family papers are of great interest, since they concern the development of a tract of four million acres purchased in part by Constable's Dublin grandfather, Dr. John, who came here in 1754—the largest land transaction ever to be made in the state.

¶ *Cooperstown (60 miles west of Albany on Otsego Lake)*

FARMER'S MUSEUM AND FENIMORE HOUSE

1 mile north of town on 80 between lake road and lake; daily 9 to 6 May through October, winter Mondays and Fridays 9 to 5; 80 cents and 12 cents; New York Historical Association.

In the words of its administrator and one of its chief architects, Louis C. Jones, "Fenimore House and the Farmer's Museum tell the story of life as it was lived by the average citizen in the years between the close of the Revolution and the Civil War." In Fenimore House, a stately replica of a Georgian mansion, the story is told by "the artists who reported the world around them," and the place also contains an outstanding collection of folk art. In the numerous buildings of the Farmer's Museum "the rural life of the earlier period is re-created in as many ways as possible." In this group stands an immense stone barn which contains a number of living exhibits; for instance, you can see the whole process of weaving, from the braking of the flax to the spinning of the cloth. The other buildings comprise a small cross-

The way the two front bays of Constable Hall advance to embrace the entrance portico recalls a similar feature of the Langdon-Cole house in Castleton, Vermont.

roads village: the country store, the doctor's office, the school, the print shop, the tavern, and the homestead. And as an indication of how credulous these folk were, there is the Giant of Cardiff, the great hoax that fooled some of the wisest minds of the 1860s. It was carved by a Chicago stonecutter, buried in the ground, and unearthed by well diggers. Some thought there had been giants in our land!

THE LIPPIT HOMESTEAD is of particular interest; for not only has painstaking research made this as nearly as possible like a comfortable upstate farmhouse of the period, but the actual uses of the household equipment are shown here. A young woman comes daily to occupy herself with a typical farm routine. She bakes bread or beans in the beehive oven in the back of the huge fireplace, in which a roast may be turning on the spit. She collects fat for burning in the Betty lamps, churns, makes cheese, or dyes yarn in the back yard. Flax, broom, and Indian corn are grown in the nearby fields, as they must have been, and you may hear the lowing of oxen or the cry of the guinea hens and peacocks nearby. All is as it was, as if time had really stood still here since 1800.

BUMP TAVERN was built at the end of the eighteenth century. In 1844 the front was remodeled, the roof raised, and the four Ionic columns added, as well as the second-story gallery with its fine railing. It was a drover's tavern originally, standing on the old Catskill Turnpike at Windham,

seventy-five miles away from its present site. It was moved here in six huge pieces.

At Fenimore House you can obtain a "talk sheet" and map which will guide you through the town itself, which is full of fascinating architecture and associations. For special houses, see Mrs. Jones.

¶ *Johnstown (on Route 67, 11 miles west of Amsterdam)*

JOHNSON HALL (*1761–1762*)
Hall Avenue; daily 9 to 5, Sundays 1 to 5; State of New York.

In 1760 Sir William built himself another mansion, leaving the fort, nine miles distant, for his son Sir John, whose lands were later confiscated because of his Tory sympathies. Johnson Hall, whose much greater pretensions better fitted Sir William's growing importance, is a large two-story white frame dwelling whose rusticated siding and heavily dentiled cornices over windows and under eaves give it the elegant severity Sir William wanted. Lemuel Baker, the housewright, was brought from Schenectady to build it, and may also have built the house at Guy Park, which Sir William gave to his daughter. There were two stone blockhouses flanking Johnson Hall (of which one is still standing), testimony to the unsettled times. On the lawn there is a lilac circle where Sir William held conferences with the chiefs of the Six Nations. Among the other outbuildings are the carpenter shop, gristmill, slave quar-

Fenimore House at Cooperstown contains a great variety of entertaining collections relating to the history of upstate New York.

ters, and houses for personal musician, surveyor, and head butler. This was indeed a feudal barony. The mahogany chair rail in the wide hall is chipped the length of the banister; the scars are supposed to have been made by the tomahawk of Joseph Brant, brother of Sir William's wife and famous Mohawk war chief. Johnson lived here a little over a decade and died after holding a council with the Iroquois under the hot July sun, in the arms of Joseph Brant, it is told. The house, restored as it was then, contains much of the original furniture and many of Johnson's personal belongings.

¶ *Little Falls (on Route 5, 22 miles east of Utica)*

HERKIMER HOME (*1764*)
> *3 miles east on south bank of Mohawk; daily 9 to 5, Sundays 1 to 5; State of New York.*

The largest home west of Sir William Johnson's mansions, it is a two-story brick house of Dutch Colonial design, built by the hero of the Oriskany battle, the son of

Offices and shops on the village street of the Farmer's Museum at Cooperstown.

Johan Joost. Gen. Nicholas Herkimer had little more than ten years to enjoy his new mansion. Ambushed with his men by Joseph Brant, the Mohawk chieftain, he died of his wounds here ten days after the battle. Some of his personal effects are still here—his chair, pistols, and bed.

WESTERN NEW YORK

Auburn; Canandaigua; Le Roy; Penn Yan; Rochester; Youngstown; Westfield

¶ *Auburn*

SEWARD HOUSE (*1816–1817, additions in 1840, 1847, and 1870*)
> *33 South Street; November 1 to April 30 Monday through Saturday 1 to 5; May 1 to September 30 Tuesday through Saturday 11 to 5 and Sundays 2 to 5; adults 25 cents, children free; The Foundation Historical Association, Inc.*

William Henry Seward was Secretary of State in Lincoln's war Cabinet and his principal adviser, founder of the Republican party, twice Governor of New York State, and Senator. The great house presents the appearance of a handsome Regency villa, while a Victorian wing and porte-cochere add to its charm. The interior is a living picture of the life of the great statesman, about whose dramatic and sometimes tragic career very little has been written. The mantel in one of the parlors was carved by

Brigham Young, the Mormon leader, who as a lad was engaged as a journeyman carpenter by Judge Miller when he built the house. The spiral staircase in the hall was a gift of the forty-niners after Seward had won the admission of California as a "free" state.

¶ *Canandaigua (23 miles southeast of Rochester)*

The town is decidedly worth a leisurely walk-around in the general neighborhood of the Granger Homestead. At least a dozen private early homes of character and charm.

GRANGER HOMESTEAD (*1814*)
> *295 North Main Street; daily, 10 to 5; Mrs. Percy Pettit (hostess).*

Built by Gideon Granger, Postmaster Gen-

The library of the Seward house in Auburn.

eral under Jefferson and Madison, this lovely Palladian country seat is one of the great beauties of this attractive old town. It has notable mantels and woodwork. The furniture has all come down from the Granger family and includes the dining-room set which Dolly Madison gave to Gideon when he was a member of her husband's Cabinet.

¶ *Le Roy*

LE ROY HOUSE *(1815)*
> *23 East Main Street; June 1 to October 1, Wednesdays, Fridays, and Sundays 2 to 5; Le Roy Historical Society.*

Built to serve both as land office and residence, this two-story house of plastered masonry played an important part in the development of western New York. Jacob Le Roy, its second owner, and owner of half of this portion of the state as well, became Daniel Webster's brother-in-law.

¶ *Penn Yan (on Keuka Lake 16 miles south of Geneva)*

POTTER HOUSE *(1790)*
> *Gorham Road, 1 mile from Keuka Lake; groups, by appointment; fee according to time consumed; Mr. and Mrs. Fenton H. Wager.*

A Georgian frame house built for Judge Arnold Potter by a Rhode Island house-wright, this was the refuge of Louis Philippe during his stay in this section.

¶ *Rochester*

By the 1830s Rochester was already being spoken of as "the young lion of the West." Mayor Jonathan Child explained its prosperity in a speech made at the city's incorporation ceremony. "It has been settled for the most part by mechanics and merchants whose capital was economy, industry and perseverance," he said. "It is their labor and skill that converted a wilderness into a City." Thus it came about that through industry the sons of mechanics and merchants were able to build themselves fine Federal mansions, romantic Gothic and Italianate villas, and impressive neo-classic temples in this bustling town, so lately wilderness. Mayor Child's own house, built in 1837 and still standing at 37 Washington Street, was not the least of these. On the monumental scale, strikingly adorned in the Corinthian order both inside and out, its gold-and-black-marble mantels and its crystal chandeliers are an indication of amazing wealth for a pioneer city. Its condition is not good at present but it is due for restoration. At the corner of Spring and Washington Streets, now used by Mechanics Institute, is the BURKE HOUSE (1840), whose portico was inspired by a sketch of the Taj Mahal from the popular book *Views of India*. On East Avenue, wide and elm-arched—whose bosomy houses, set back on deep lawns, are little enough changed to afford a complete picture of the whole gamut of taste of the latter part of the century— stand Gothic, Greek Revival, Edwardian, and rococo rubbing elbows. The HOME OF SUSAN B. ANTHONY, at 17 Madison Street, is now open for all to see how this great woman lived.

There are few cities in which the progression of styles from the 1830s on can be seen to better advantage. Nowhere were Americans more affected by the impact of the Greek Revival than in this western region of New York State, and nowhere are there more noble temple façades. The Society for the Preservation of Landmarks in Western New York, listed below, is doing a magnificent job of focusing interest on this heritage. It has recently issued a booklet and map of the houses in the city, and further plans a brochure devoted to that unique architectural expression of this area between the 1830s and 1850s, the cobblestone house, of which there are literally hundreds still being comfortably occupied. One of the most imposing of these can be seen at the intersection of Routes 20 and 5 between Canandaigua and Geneva. Built of red lake-washed cobbles carefully graded for color and size, its applied face reminds one of the jeweler's art. This particular house is in-

teresting too because of its size, its flanking wings, and the high Ionic façade that it presents to the road. It is now a tourist home.

CAMPBELL-WHITTLESEY HOUSE
(*1835*)

South Fitzhugh and Troup Streets; daily 1 to 5, except Mondays; 50 cents; Society for the Preservation of Landmarks in Western New York, Miss Elizabeth Holahan, President.

This Greek Revival mansion is a beautiful example of an imposing town house in which no expense was spared. It takes its place with the finest museum houses in the country. The ornament of the window and door frames and ceiling cornices is of unusual splendor, the lavish use of color bringing out the beauty of the decoration. The restoration has been accomplished with artistry and imagination by painstaking experts. As for the furniture, it has been assembled and arranged with the greatest skill and fidelity to the period of the place and its Empire elegance.

The dining room of the Campbell-Whittlesey house in Rochester, the double parlor of which appears on page 120.

The front parlor of the Eastman Birthplace in Rochester.

THE OLIVER CULVER HOUSE (1815)

70 East Boulevard (first house north of East Avenue); by request (phone: Browning 6675); Miss Elizabeth G. Holahan.

Oliver Culver first viewed the region when he came here in 1798. Like Washington, he was only seventeen and a surveyor of the wilderness when he came upon the land of his choice. So in 1805 he returned to it and built a story-and-a-half frame house. This in only ten years became the ell for this infinitely more impressive abode, which has been restored with great skill and elegance and furnished for the most part with early Rochester pieces. As you enter the broad hallway, the lovely stairway is seen through an elliptical arch with a remarkable sunburst boldly carved above it. Oliver Culver's portrait hangs here, returned to the house by his family, who lived here until 1945. Upstairs the great hall becomes the ballroom, with twin mantels of freestanding triple columns, a vaulted Gothic ceiling, and a "springboard" floor built especially for dancing.

WOODSIDE (1838)

485 East Avenue; weekdays, 9:30 to 5; headquarters Rochester Historical Society.

A three-story mansion of unusually fine proportions and workmanship, it was designed by Alfred Badger for Silas O. Smith, a citizen of obvious means. The Federal style combines with the Greek Revival in a most satisfactory fashion. Some of the rooms are furnished with upstate New York pieces of the period.

Nearby, at 421 East Avenue, set in spacious grounds given a mellow appearance by the great Greek Revival structure they surround, is the old ERICKSON-PERKINS HOUSE (1842), now the GENESEE VALLEY COUNTRY CLUB.

THE HERVEY ELY HOUSE (*c. 1835*)

Livingston Park; by appointment with the Society for the Preservation of Landmarks; Irondequoit Chapter, D.A.R.

Here is another beauty of the same period, designed by Hugh Hastings, with a monumental Doric portico and flanking one-story wings with railed balconies. There is beautiful plaster ceiling ornament within, and the furniture is also of the period of the early republic. The original paint colors have been recently restored.

GEORGE EASTMAN BIRTHPLACE
(*early 1830s*)

900 East Avenue; daily 10 to 5, except Mondays; 25 cents; Eastman House Museum.

A story-and-a-half Greek Revival house, small-scale and charming, it was moved from Waterville, where George Eastman, of Kodak fame, was born in 1854. Brought to Rochester in 1954 in eight separate parts, reassembled in thirty-nine days by a crew of over fifty skilled workmen, it is now furnished with the type of things that the family must have owned at the period. The original wallpapers are also being reproduced, and the parlor stoves are especially appealing.

PATRICK BARRY HOUSE (*1855*)

692 Mt. Hope Avenue; by written request through the Landmarks Society (house to qualified students only); Mr. Frederick Barry.

This engaging example of the Italianate villa, a style which was spreading rapidly westward a century ago, is built of pink brick, with stone lintels. It was designed by Gervase Wheeler, whose plans may be seen in the library. Its carriage house and stables are still standing, and so is a delightful office building of the period (of the famous firm of nurserymen, Ellwanger & Barry), designed by Davis in the Gothic style, with narrow lancet windows. Incidentally, the buildings sit in a parklike arboretum in which many of the rare plants and trees have been growing for a hundred years. The house, with its original décor and all its original furnishings, is practically pristine.

At the left, the Eastman Birthplace is seen as it appears today on the grounds of the Eastman Museum in Rochester, a real gem of the Greek Revival.

One of the more memorable of the many fine sights of Rochester's East Avenue is the mansion called Woodside, with some most impressive Greek Revival interiors.

¶ *Youngstown (on Niagara River near Lake Ontario)*

OLD FRENCH CASTLE or FORT NIAGARA (*1679*)

> *6 miles north on Route 18; open summer 9 to 9, other times 9 to 5 (guide available); 35 cents; State Conservation Commission.*

René Robert de Salle put up this extraordinary structure, with walls *four* feet thick, for use as a home, a warehouse, and a refuge. Later occupied by the French in 1725, it was rebuilt at that time to look even more formidable to the Indians. However, it fell to Sir William Johnson in 1759, and during the Revolution it was a base for British supplies. A vast and successful restoration undertaken by the state has made it one of the best preserved of all of the great historic fortifications in the United States. The "castle" is furnished with both original and period pieces, in which many patriotic societies have assisted.

¶ *Westfield (on Routes 20 and 17 near Lake Erie)*

MC CLURG HOUSE (*1818–1819*)

> *Junction Routes 20 and 17; daily 9 to 12 and 1 to 5, June to November; Chautauqua Historical Society.*

This sixteen-room brick manor, with a style faintly reminiscent of a Scottish castle, must have been cause for amazement in the countryside even while still in the log-cabin stage. At any rate, it became known as "McClurg's Folly." Fortunately little changed through the years, the plan is to furnish it in the period of the 1820s, as it was when Mr. McClurg, a wealthy merchant with grandiose ideas, made it his home.

NORTHERN NEW YORK

Brownville; Essex; Schuylerville; Ft. Edward;

Plattsburg; Oswego; Peru

¶ *Brownville (5 miles west of Watertown on Route 12E)*

BROWN MANSION (*1814–1815*)

> *Main Street; Tuesday and Friday evenings 7 to 5, Saturdays 1 to 5; Brownville Civic Association.*

An imposing two-story house with a high attic and four tall chimneys, beautifully proportioned and built of native limestone, it was Jacob Brown's stately Georgian home until he moved to Washington as Commander of the Army in 1812. About to become a museum.

¶ *Essex (on Lake Champlain 30 miles north of Ticonderoga)*

HICKORY HILL (*1820*)

> *By appointment only; $1.00; Mrs. Winfield A. Townsend.*

The builder, William Gilliland, took his own and about twenty other families to Lake Champlain in 1765 to establish a manor such as he had seen in the Hudson Valley. His grandson, the great-great-grandfather of the present owner, built this brick house with marble exterior trim. The twenty-room mansion has fine woodwork, the drawing room is Adamesque in character. The furniture was bought the year the house was built.

¶ *Schuylerville*

SCHUYLER MANOR HOUSE (*1777*)

> *Saratoga National Historical Park; Monday to Saturday, 9 to 5; 25 cents and 15 cents; National Park Service.*

The Saratoga Battleground nearby saw the defeat of General Burgoyne, in which Gen. Philip Schuyler, the builder of this manor, took a decisive part. It became his summer residence, an earlier one having been burned in the battle. The house, little changed since it was built, is a substantial but unpretentious country dwelling of frame and brick. There are seven large rooms and a kitchen on the first floor and eleven bedrooms above—ample space for the many notable visitors, among whom were Washington, Lafayette, Hamilton, Governor Clinton, and goodness knows who besides.

¶ *Ft. Edward* (*on Route 4 and the Hudson 40 miles north of Troy*)

OLD FORT HOUSE *or* PATT SMYTH HOUSE (*1772–1773*)

29 Lower Broadway; daily 1 to 5 and Sundays 1 to 8 May 30 to October 3, or on request; Fort Edward Historical Association.

Given this name because of its proximity to the fort, which was razed in 1775, the house was built of material from a hospital used in the French and Indian War. The labor of restoration was a community project, and the town is proud of it. The place contains period furniture, pictures, and other exhibits.

¶ *Plattsburg* (*on Lake Champlain*)

KENT-DE LORD HOUSE (*1797*)

17 Cumberland Avenue; daily 9 to 6, Sundays 1:30 to 6; 50 cents; Kent-De Lord Corporation, Saranac Chapter D.A.R. (custodians).

The original section of this long two-story frame house was built soon after the Revolution by James Kent, State Chancellor and Justice of the state supreme court, who was known as the "American Blackstone." Purchased by De Lord, a French refugee, in 1812, it was enlarged and inhabited by his hospitable descendants for more than a century. It was occupied by the British briefly during the Battle of Plattsburg; they left in such a hurry that they forgot a chest of table silver, which is on display here today, along with fine furniture and various family treasures, both French and American.

¶ *Oswego* (*southeast corner of Lake Ontario*)

BATES RICHARDSON HEADQUARTERS HOUSE (*1850, remodeled 1880*)

135 East 3d Street; Sunday afternoons 3 to 6 April to November, other times by appointment; Oswego County Historical Society, Charles M. Snyder (President).

Given to the Historical Society completely furnished in Victorian by the Bates heirs, this massive, ornate house is a good example of a Late Victorian mansion. The dining room is paneled in oak and the library in cherry, and the ceilings of the parlor and drawing room are molded. The society has added an "Indian Room" and an early kitchen.

¶ *Peru* (*on Route 22, 10 miles south of Plattsburg*)

KEESE HOMESTEAD (*1834*)

Rogers Old Road, 4 miles off Route 22 between Harkness and Peru; daily, 10 to 7; 25 cents; the Keese family.

Built by Pieter Keese, a Quaker, of native sandstone, this house is now occupied by the seventh generation of the family.

*Typical of South Jersey are the quite English-appearing tall brick houses
which rise from the fields that roll like the swell of the ocean. The pent roofs
that break across the fronts are part of the pattern, and the first floors are
generally well off the ground, contributing to their tallness. This is Homeland,
down near Salem, now restored with understanding and affection by its
owners. On the opposite page, and at nearly the opposite end of the state, is
the Zabriskie–von Steuben house, one of the rare remaining examples of the
Dutch Colonial houses still in practically pristine condition.*

NEW JERSEY

THE TWO most interesting architectural forms indigenous to New Jersey are exemplified, one in the upper, and one in the lower part of the state. Near the northeastern corner we have the well-known and well-loved Dutch Colonial types, an outstanding example of which is the Zabriskie-von Steuben House at North Hackensack; and down in South Jersey, around Salem, we have the distinctive tall brick houses built there by English settlers. These latter deserve to be better known than they are, just as the Dutch Colonial houses of Bergen County and vicinity deserve better fates than have befallen most of these unique dwellings. It would seem almost better to have them disappear altogether than for them to stand in a state of mutilation and disrepair, if it weren't that, while they at least exist, there is hope that some means will be found to preserve and restore them before it is too late.

The best of the big early mansions are the Trent in Trenton, the Ford in Morristown, and the Dey in Preakness Valley Park—all beauties, but comprising not too numerous a collection of well-preserved "great houses," open to the public for a state with so much historical importance.

FROM TRENTON NORTH

¶ *Trenton*

WILLIAM TRENT HOUSE (*1719*)

539 South Warren Street; daily 10 to 5 and Sundays 2 to 5 May through September, daily 10 to 4 and Sundays 2 to 4 October through April; 25 cents and 10 cents; city of Trenton.

An eighteenth-century sales bill describes this stately Queen Anne residence as "a genteel brick dwelling house, 40 x 48 feet, two stories high, four rooms on a floor, with a large handsome staircase and entry, with a cellar under the whole building, and a court yard on each front of the house, one fronting down the River Delaware to the ferry, through a large handsome avenue of English cherry trees, the other fronting up the river to Trenton." The description hardly does justice to this beautiful mansion, with its elegantly gardened grounds, much as they were two hundred years ago. In 1682 William Trent came from Scotland to Philadelphia, where he made his residence in the famous Slate Roof House, which had been William Penn's mansion—long since gone—on 2d Street. When he built his own mansion, up the Delaware on the Jersey side, he had Trent Town laid out around it. The genteel dwelling is stunningly restored, both inside and out. Most of the rooms have paneled dados and paneling over the corner fireplaces, as well as in the window reveals. Museum furniture of the early eighteenth century—William and Mary,

and Queen Anne—throughout; rugs in keeping; and distinctive curtains by the bountiful and ubiquitous Scalamandre.

OLD BARRACKS (*1758–1759*)

Willow Street opposite West Front Street; Wednesdays 10 to 5, May through August, Wednesdays 10 to 4 September through April; 25 cents and 10 cents; Old Barracks Association.

This is the only surviving one of five barracks erected during the French and Indian War to protect the colonial troops. In 1776 it quartered the Hessians. The building itself is like a long, oversize house, gaining its beauty from good construction and an aura of age. Simply furnished with antiques of the Revolutionary period, with some formal exhibits of china, silver, and costumes.

OLD MASONIC LODGE HOUSE (*1793*)

Northeast corner South Willow and Lafayette Streets; Monday to Friday, 10 to 12 and 1:30 to 4.

The first Grand Master of American Masonry was Col. Daniel Coxe, from Trenton. The lodge here was organized in 1787, and the Georgian fieldstone building with white trim is one of the oldest Masonic houses standing. The building is distinguished, and contains many relics of the day.

¶ Titusville (Washington Crossing State Park, a few miles up the Delaware from Trenton)

MC KONKEY FERRY HOUSE *or* JOHNSON HOUSE (*before 1776*)

Route 202; Tuesday to Saturday 10 to 5, Sundays 2 to 5; adults 25 cents, children 10 cents; state of New Jersey.

This is the house in which Washington and his staff spent the night before the Battle of Trenton after crossing the ice-packed Delaware. It served as a tavern then as well as a ferryhouse, and has been furnished as it was on that historic night. Across the Delaware at the other end of the bridge on the Pennsylvania side is a group of stone buildings which are a living souvenir of that historic occasion.

¶ *Princeton*

Princeton is a parlor town in the true sense of the word. Not only does it go far back into colonial times, with many landmarks and many pages of history to show for it (not quite so many lovely landmarks as in Litchfield or New Castle, say, but perhaps more pages of history), but, as with other parlor towns, it has had the good fortune of lying somewhat off the beaten path that inevitably demolishes any pristine beauty in its way.

The McKonkey Ferry House, on the left, has great appeal with its round-headed shingles.

The William Trent house in Trenton is an elegant Queen Anne mansion elegantly furnished and maintained.

Furthermore, well-directed civic pride has here, as in a few other communities, made a point of preserving as much as possible of the past and placed controls upon the worst excesses of the present. In other words, it remains a most appetizing old town and has not tried to be too pointedly picturesque. The time to see it is on the annual visiting day in spring, when many of the fine old private homes are opened. But, as dates differ from year to year, find out ahead of time from the Garden Club of Princeton or from the Princeton Book Shop.

MORVEN (1701)

Stockton Street and Library Place; will be open at specified times as Governor's Mansion (planned for 1957); state of New Jersey.

This great house of yellow-painted brick trimmed with white occupies its little park in Princeton with an air of pleasant importance. A wide porch now adds a picturesque note to the Early Georgian appearance of the fine old mansion, which has lived through a lot of history. The British ransacked and partially burned it when they retreated from Princeton in 1776. Washington and Cornwallis have both slept here (at different times) in the carved and canopied four-poster. A carved mantel in the dining room was brought to this country before 1700. Single-arm wrought-iron latches were installed before the birth of Thomas Jefferson, who visited here, along with most of the other Revolutionary notables. A colonial bath tub is still in use. Turned over to the state in 1953 by former Governor Edge for use as a permanent executive mansion, it is being restored and modern comforts added.

PROSPECT *or* THE PRESIDENT'S HOUSE (1849)

On campus; grounds during daylight hours, house on special occasions only; Princeton University.

Designed by John Notman of Philadelphia, this great brownstone mansion is romantically austere in the Florentine style that was chosen for so many of our grander Victorian homes. It has a side porch whose decorative ironwork (clusters of grapes painted blue) is in the large scale of the house. The house itself has much interest, especially as seen from the lower terraces of the extensive garden to the rear. The trees alone are worth a visit.

DEAN'S HOUSE (1756)

On campus; open only on special occasions; Princeton University.

Occupied during two centuries by ten college presidents, it was first inhabited by Aaron Burr, Sr. During the Battle of Trenton it was General Leslie's headquarters, and John Adams visited here while en route to the Continental Congress. The two giant sycamores at the gate were planted in 1765. The house was designed by Robert Smith, of the Carpenters Company of Philadelphia.

ELMWOOD (c. 1732)

Princeton Pike; on request by letter or phone (1–2879); Mr. and Mrs. William H. Jackson.

One of the loveliest early houses in the Princeton area, built of the pale ledge stone of the locality, the house has great style and has been understandingly restored. It is charmingly furnished, the owners having made it livable without changing its essential character.

YEATMAN HOUSE (1836)

72 Library Place; by advance appointment when convenient to owners; Mr. and Mrs. Phillip W. Yeatman.

Designed and built by an architect named Steadman along with four other houses in the Federal style, all of which are standing nearby. Beside being a typical urban dwelling of the period in this university town, it has other claims to distinction. Woodrow Wilson lived in it for many years while a professor at Princeton, but it came into the news in a controversial manner some time before his occupancy; for in it was installed the first indoor toilet in the vicinity, which immediately became a *cause célèbre*. The present owners have restored the house very well and have furnished it harmoniously with a number of fine late-eighteenth-century pieces.

TUSCULUM (1773)

Bayard Lane, less than a mile from town; open on written request; Mrs. Ario Pardee.

A Late Georgian house of local brownstone and singular charm, cushioned in boxwood. The great stone barn was built in 1792, and "Tusculum" has been a going farm ever since. It was the home of John Witherspoon, an outspoken patriot, a signer of the Declaration, and President of Princeton (1768–1794). Washington was a frequent visitor here.

¶ *Rocky Hill* (*5 miles north of Princeton on the Kingston road*)

BERRIEN MANSION or
ROCKINGHAM (*1730*)
Daily 10 to 5 except Monday, Sundays 2 to 5; 10 cents and 35 cents; state of New Jersey, Department of Conservation and Economic Development.

A white clapboard farmhouse which served as headquarters for Washington from August to November, 1783, while the Continental Congress was in session at Princeton. In the upstairs blue room he wrote his Farewell Address to his army, and from its balcony he later delivered it to some three hundred of his men, who sat on the lawn or leaned against the trees. Here, in the midst of these serious matters, he also had time to entertain and attend banquets in his honor, as was his wont. Furniture and other articles used by George and Martha are here.

¶*Freehold* (*23 miles east of Princeton via Hightstown*)

COVENHOVEN-HANKINSON
MANSION (*1775*)
150 West Main Street; by written or phone appointment, May 15 to October 15; Mr. and Mrs. Rhea Moreau.

The Covenhoven-Hankinson Mansion, the oldest residence in town, is a white-shingled, green-shuttered "farmstead," sitting on a broad lawn with old shade trees. It faces away from the street, run through long after the main section of the house was built by master builder John Middleton who constructed the nearby Tennant Church. The lovely proportions of the church and its many other fine details are repeated in the mansion. An unfinished overmantel painting has been attributed to the Hessians. Clinton stayed here the night before the Battle of Monmouth, forcing the widow Connover, then owner, to betake herself to the milk room with her

household to spend the night there on the brick floor. The Moreau family has occupied the house for a long time, and it is furnished with family heirlooms, many as old as the house itself.

¶ *Red Bank* (*15 miles east of Freehold*)

WHITEHALL HOUSE (*before 1776*)
Battlefield National Park near Woodbury, Route 130; daily, 10 to 12 and 2 to 4; 35 cents; National Park Service.

While the Battle of Red Bank raged around her, Mrs. Whitehall, a Quaker, kept on spinning. The famous spinning wheel is here, along with the other colonial furnishings.

¶ *Middletown* (*5 miles north of Red Bank*)

MARLPIT HALL (*1684*)
Route 35 between Keyport and Red Bank; Tuesdays, Thursdays, and Saturdays 11 to 5, Sundays 2 to 5; Monmouth County Historical Association.

In a village dating back to the seventeenth century, it is one of the rare houses of this type and age in the state, showing the strong Dutch influence. It is a long wide-shingled one-and-a-half-story house with small dormers. The interior has many interesting early features, among them a pilastered fireplace and a carved shell cupboard. Furnished with very early Jersey pieces.

¶ New Brunswick

BUCCLEUCH MANSION or
THE WHITE HOUSE (*c. 1729*)
Buccleuch Park, near intersection of College Avenue and George Street; Sundays and holidays 3 to 5 Memorial Day to Labor Day, or by appointment for fee; city of New Brunswick.

Built by Col. Anthony White of the British Army, this is a fine Early Georgian house through which have passed many important figures in the history of the state. Elizabeth Morris, daughter of the colonial governor, was its mistress. It was renamed "Buccleuch" for his royal Scotch kin by Col. Joseph W. Scott, who bought it in 1821. He was the son of Moses Scott, Surgeon General of the Revolutionary Army. There are furniture and portraits of considerable interest here, and the Dufour wallpaper of 1807 and 1815 is outstanding; on the lower-hall wall is "The Banks of the Seine"; and on the upper-hall wall "Hindustani Scenery," consisting of twenty strips. Both are the first and only paper on these walls.

WOODLAWN ALUMNAE HOUSE
(c. 1835)
Open on request to college; New Jersey College for Women.

This is a handsome building, but used as a place to entertain faculty and guests, with mostly modern equipment.

HENRY GUEST HOUSE (1760)
60 Livingston Avenue; daily, 9 to 5; apply at adjoining public library.

This house sheltered Tom Paine, who was forced to hide from the British here. It was owned by a successful tanner and whaler, Henry Guest. It is not furnished, but has an exhibit of laces and shawls.

IVY HALL or CORNELIUS LOWE HOUSE (1729–1740)
River Road; by written request well in advance; Theodore Voorhees.

Once the largest and most costly house in the busy shipping center known as "The Landing," this is one of the outstanding examples in the state of a Georgian mansion. It is fortunate that it has an owner who appreciates its rare qualities. Built of local sandstone, it has a splendid entrance, and the hall is beautifully paneled. In addition to fine paneling in many of them, each of the other rooms has a fireplace with a carved mantel, and the old tiles have been preserved in a number of them; so has much of the original hardware. Among other features are the shell cupboards. The house is furnished, says the owner, largely in period but "as a home, not a museum."

¶ *South Bound Brook (7 miles northeast of New Brunswick on Route 44)*

STAATS–VON STEUBEN HOUSE
(1690)
165 Main Street; by written request; Mr. and Mrs. Charles Gurney Hollister.

Built by a Dutch landowner as a manor house for his farmlands, it remained in his family until 1935—almost a record tenure. During the Revolution it was von Steuben's headquarters and is usually known by this name. Washington and Lafayette were frequent visitors. The house has most of its original features—the hardware, the "Holy Lord" hinges, the hand-hewn oak beams in the ceilings, the hand-carved mantels, and the bull's-eye windows. It has recently been restored and made comfortable for modern living without destroying its character.

¶ *Somerville*

WALLACE HOUSE (1778)
38 Washington Place; daily 10 to 12 and 1 to 5 except Mondays, Sundays 2 to 5; 35 cents and 10 cents; state of New Jersey, Department of Conservation and Economic Development.

Occupied by George and Martha Washington from the fall of 1778 to June, 1779, while the Army was stationed at Camp Middlebrook, now Somerville. While here, Washington planned the Indian Campaign of 1779 which broke the power of the Six Nations. It is an unpretentious white-clapboard house, the rooms not large and the woodwork simple. There is some interesting old furniture and glass. Washington's ten-foot iron army trunk, lined with oak, which stands in the hall, is memorable when you learn the reason for its dimensions: in case of Washington's death, it was designed also to serve as his coffin. The rigors of the campaigns come intensely and intimately to life when you look at its grim length. Mrs. Washington told friends later that her most vivid memories of the house were the piercingly cold nights when she huddled under the quilts while guards knelt at her windows with guns pointed out into the night, ready for the ever-present danger of attack.

OLD DUTCH PARSONAGE (1751)
65 Washington Place; daily 10 to 12 and 1 to 5 except Mondays, Sundays 2 to 5; 35 cents and 10 cents; state of New Jersey, Department of Conservation and Economic Development.

Built of brick brought from Holland, so it is said, this place stands only a short distance down the street from the Wallace House, and was frequently visited by Washington. It was built by the congregation of the Reformed Dutch Church for the Rev. John Frelinghuysen and his Dutch bride, Dinah van Bergh, who came here with him because she believed the Lord wanted her

In the Dayton Room of Boxwood Hall the portrait over the Adamesque mantel is of Jonathan Dayton, youngest signer of the Constitution, who lived here in the early 1800s.

to help in the work of the churches of New Jersey. Here young men came to study for the ministry, and the building later became the seminary that was to be the nucleus of Rutgers University.

¶ Plainfield

NATHANIEL DRAKE HOUSE (*1746*)

> *602 West Front Street facing Plainfield Avenue; Tuesdays, Thursdays, and Saturdays, 2 to 5; 35 cents and 10 cents; Plainfield and North Plainfield Historical Society.*

A Dutch Colonial white-clapboard house of two and a half stories which was a stopping place for Washington while he was reconnoitering during the spring of 1777. Exhibits only.

¶ Elizabeth

BOUDINOT MANSION *or* BOXWOOD HALL (*1750*)

> *1073 East Jersey Street; daily 10 to 12 and 1 to 5 except Mondays, Sundays 2 to 5; state of New Jersey, Department of Conservation and Economic Development.*

A well-restored shingle house with a plain exterior and twenty-four-paned windows, some of them with the original glass. This deceptive façade leaves you unprepared for the amazing interior. The entrance hall is broad enough for a ball. There are richly carved mantels, unusual cornices, blue and white delft tiles in two fireplaces, and period wallpaper copied from the original. It

was the home of the first president of the Continental Congress, the son of Elias Boudinot, a Princeton silversmith.

¶ Madison (*on the way to Morristown*)

MEAD HALL *or* THE OLD GIBBONS MANSION (*1833–1836*)

> *On campus of Drew University; open daily, including Sunday; Drew University.*

An impressive and quite beautiful brick structure, painted white, with six stately Corinthian columns thirty-six feet in height supporting a flat roof with a fine balustrade and tall chimneys. The porch, which is ninety feet long, is paved in marble and is reached by flights of stone

Mead Hall began as the monumental mansion of William Gibbons, from Savannah.

steps. The place has for the most part been made into offices, but the former ballroom and dining room serve for social purposes, and may be seen at all times. The former is the only furnished room, containing Victorian pieces. A mansion whose original builder, William Gibbons, of Savannah, Georgia, was obviously a gentleman of wealth and taste.

¶ Morristown

FORD MANSION (1774)

> 230 Morris Avenue, Morristown National Historic Park; daily 10 to 5, except Mondays; 10 cents; National Park Service.

It is one of our great white flush-boarded Georgian houses, of robust proportions and with a delightful doorway, full of sturdiness and grace. It was built by Col. Jacob Ford, Jr., with wealth acquired from the neighboring iron mines. Morristown was, in effect, the military capital during the winter of 1779–1780, and, thanks to the widow Theodosia Ford, the house was a comfortable home for the Washingtons, serving as host during those months to most of the important men of the time.

It has been beautifully restored, and its fine interior can now be seen much as it looked during the Washington occupancy. In the living room is the desk on which many of his letters were written; the looking glass, table, and Queen Anne chair were also here during his stay. The kitchen, which in very cold weather served as dining room too, has a huge and fully equipped fireplace. On January 18 Washington wrote, "Eighteen belonging to my family and all Mrs. Ford's are all crowded together in her kitchen and scarce one of them able to speak for the colds they have caught." Mrs. Ford had kept only two rooms for her own living quarters. In May, 1780, Lafayette brought the good news to the general that France was sending a second expeditionary force.

SCHUYLER-HAMILTON HOUSE (before 1765)

> 5 Olyphant Place; Tuesday and Friday 10 to 12 and 2 to 5, ring bell and ask caretaker other times; Morristown Chapter, D.A.R.

The scene of Alexander Hamilton's courtship of Elizabeth Schuyler in 1779, the building is a simple one, with flush eaves at

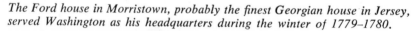

The Ford house in Morristown, probably the finest Georgian house in Jersey, served Washington as his headquarters during the winter of 1779–1780.

There aren't many of the old Dutch Colonial houses left in presentable condition, a fact which makes the little Van Horn–Branford house at Wyckoff a rare exception.

the gable ends and bracketed cornices. The porch is a later addition. Dr. Jabez Campfield, Senior Surgeon of the Continental Army and Washington's personal physician, was quartered here in 1780. Beautifully furnished as a home of the period.

WICK HOUSE (*1750*)

> *Northeast corner Mendham-New Vernon road and Jockey Hollow Road; daily 1 to 5 except Mondays, Sundays 10 to 5; National Park Service.*

An appealing old farmhouse with sweeping rooflines, low eaves, and a single chimney in which Temperance Wick, daughter of a cavalry officer, made history by hiding her horse in her bedroom to save it from the British. The house is furnished with simplicity, as it must have been.

¶ *Hanover (7 miles east of Morristown on Route 10)*

THE OLD PARSONAGE *or* ASHBEL GREEN HOMESTEAD (*1757*)

> *On left of highway; open by appointment with Mr. and Mrs. Richard P. Heppner; Stockton Green (owner).*

Built as a parsonage for Jacob Green, the great-great-great-grandfather of the present owner—a teacher, pastor, doctor, and distiller. The house is a low, rambling, shingle structure. It housed Washington's staff during the winter at Morristown. Voluminous diaries of Ashbel Green, son of Jacob, second President of Princeton, and Chaplain of the Continental Congress, may be examined here. They contain a wealth of incidents and intimate comments

on personages of the Revolutionary period never yet published.

¶ *Caldwell (around the mountain on Route 46)*

GROVER CLEVELAND BIRTHPLACE (*1832*)

> *207 Bloomfield Avenue; daily 10 to 12 and 1 to 5 except Mondays, Sundays 2 to 5; 35 cents and 10 cents; state of New Jersey.*

This was a church manse when the future President was born here in 1832. There are memorabilia of Cleveland and his period—his cradle, which was an old one given to his mother by a neighbor; a chair he used in the White House; his desk when he was the Mayor of Buffalo; and similar items.

¶ *North Hackensack*

ZABRISKIE–VON STEUBEN HOUSE (*1739–1752*)

> *New Bridge Road, ½ mile off Route 4; daily 10 to 12 and 1 to 5 except Mondays, Sundays 2 to 5; 25 cents; state of New Jersey, Department of Conservation and Economic Development, and headquarters of Bergen County Historical Society.*

One of the finest examples of an Early Dutch Colonial house to be seen anywhere. Built of tailored native stone, its rooflines, sweeping in a long, flattening curve to create the porch roofs, have an almost pagodalike effect at the gable ends. The house is of great length, with nine delicate columns supporting the roof and forming the porch. It was Washington's headquarters during the retreat from Fort Lee in

A house of unusual dignity, substance, and true architectural merit is the famous old Dey mansion in what is now Preakness Valley Park not far from Paterson.

November, 1776. Two years later it was the headquarters of General Cornwallis. And again, in September, 1780, after the war, Washington used the house on his way to Hartford, Connecticut. It gets its name from Baron von Steuben, who was given the house and surrounding land in appreciation of his services with the ragtag army into which he had drilled military precision. However, he never occupied it, and it reverted to the Zabriskie family, from whom it had been taken because of their Tory sympathies. It has Dutch and Colonial furniture, and many curios of the late eighteenth century; and the house itself remains very much as it was in 1752.

¶ *Preakness Valley Park (Wayne Township)*

DEY MANSION (*1740*)

> *Route 6, 4½ miles west of Paterson, on Totowa Road near Mountain View Avenue; Tuesdays, Wednesdays and Fridays 1 to 5, Saturdays after 1; 35 cents; Passaic County Park Commission; Mrs. R. Rauchfuss (custodian).*

Washington knew how to pick the best! This remarkable brick house, set in its small, attractive park, is another of his headquarters in New Jersey—this time during July, October, and November, 1780. A Dutchman named Dirck Dey (pronounced *Dye*), who bought 611 acres of wilderness here and who was unquestionably a man of great skills, erected this distinguished eight-room manor house with the help of his slaves

and artisans. It was inherited by his son Theunis; he brought to the place his bride Hester Schuyler, to whom were born ten children, five of whom fought in the Revolution. The beautiful exterior is unusual, with the old red brick set off by the window and door openings, framed in brownstone. Its proportions, color, and decoration are striking. The early interior has been most thoughtfully restored, with all later changes removed. The color treatment inside is excellent, and the furnishings are being carefully chosen. This is on its way to becoming one of the best house museums in the state.

¶ *Wyckoff*

VAN HORN–BRANFORD HOUSE (*1747–1760 and 1800*)

> *Lafayette and Wyckoff Avenues; by request; donation to Bergen County Historical Society; Mr. and Mrs. Ray B. Lake.*

This is a small Dutch Colonial brown-field-stone house of three parts; each part is of a different height and each built at a different period, but together they make a most harmonious and picturesque whole. The house belonged to a Loyalist, Barent van Hoorn, and was plundered in 1777 by the Whigs. It has been little altered, and its present owners, who are connoisseurs, have done much to preserve and enhance all its interesting features. As dealers in antiques (this is their home, not their shop), they have furnished it with some choice Queen Anne pieces, local slip ware, and other rare items.

¶ *Ringwood Manor Park (in Ringwood Valley, northern Passaic County)*

RINGWOOD MANOR (*c. 1780*)
> *In park; daily 10 to 4 and Saturdays, Sundays, and holidays 10 to 5, May through October; parking 50 cents summer, 25 cents winter; state of New Jersey.*

An outstanding example of how a cultivated and wealthy American family lived in the nineteenth century, the house, which has belonged to some of New Jersey's best-known families—the Erskines, Ryersons, Coopers, and Hewitts—was passed on to the state in 1936 by Erskine Hewitt, along with all of its furnishings. Of curious architecture, it seems to have been augmented and changed at will. The bays, gables, columns, and porte-cochere are all most

suggestive of its Victorian era; however, a part of it is the early house, dating back at least to 1804, when it was advertised for sale in the New York *Herald* as "an elegant mansion with a 92 foot front." Of this, two rooms and a hall remain intact. A still earlier house may have burned down during the Revolution or may have been incorporated. It too was a mansion, for Washington, who stopped there frequently on his way from Norristown to West Point (it was then the home of Robert Erskine, official cartographer of the Continental Army) notes in his Journal, "Mrs. Erskine is a sensible and accomplished woman who lives in a style of affluence and fashion; everything indicates wealth, taste and splendor. . . ." And why not? From 1740 to 1931 iron of high quality was continuously mined on this twenty-thousand-acre tract, and the owners of Ringwood Manor directed the proceedings.

FROM TRENTON SOUTH

¶ *Burlington (Route 130 at Bristol Bridge)*

Burlington was once a flourishing river-port, and the Delaware was crowded with white sails; on its green banks stood the prim brick summer dwellings of Philadelphia Quakers. Today industry and superhighways are breathing down its neck, with the Bristol-Burlington Bridge looming over the town. Yet it manages to retain a lot of its eighteenth-century character. This lingering atmosphere can best be felt under the guidance of Mrs. Hugh Pugh, who requests one week's notice in advance.

HUGH PUGH HOUSE (*1725*)
> *130 West Broad Street; any time, on tour; tour 50 cents, proceeds to Historical Society; Mrs. Hugh Pugh (phone: Burlington 1491).*

Distinctly worth a visit to acquaint you with the early brick-panel construction, typical of the small houses of the period. Unless you wish to drive your own car, Mrs. Pugh will take you on a walking tour

which will include the two houses for the Historical Society (regularly open) and the houses listed below.

F. E. BELDIN HOUSE (*1797*)
> *312 Wood Street; any time, on tour; Mrs. F. E. Beldin.*

Only the lower floor of this home may be seen.

GENERAL GRANT HOUSE (*1856*)
> *309 Wood Street; any time, on tour; Mrs. E. H. Slack.*

Occupied by General Grant for a time during the Civil War; beautifully kept up, with some handsome family furniture.

CAPT. JAMES LAWRENCE HOUSE
> *(rear c. 1767, front before 1800)*
> *459 High Street; daily 10 to 12 and 1 to 5 except Mondays, Sundays 2 to 5; state of New Jersey.*

Birthplace of the naval hero of the War of 1812, whose historic words "Don't give up the ship" were spoken when he was fatally wounded in the battle between the U.S.S. *Chesapeake* and the H.M.S. *Shannon* in Boston Harbor. The house is joined to the

Cooper House, and they are similar in style—simple, sturdy, red-brick town houses of pre-Revolutionary character, with beautiful doorways and paneled shutters. When they were built, the town consisted of perhaps two hundred houses in all, and was on the way to becoming a summer resort for Philadelphians, who came up on Delaware River steamboats and built their summer houses on the green banks of the river. The house is well restored and furnished with antiques.

JAMES FENIMORE COOPER HOUSE (*c. 1780*)

457 South High Street; Sundays 3 to 5, or by appointment; Burlington Historical Society.

This house, in which James Fenimore Cooper was born in 1789, was built by Samuel How about ten years earlier. The famous family subsequently moved to Cooperstown, New York, when the author-to-be was thirteen. The Burlington Historical Society has preserved the interior, in which old furniture, pictures, maps, and other Burlington relics make interesting exhibits.

THOMAS REVEL HOUSE (*1685*)

8 East Pearl Street; on request to C. H. McCray, 46 Riverbank Street; Colonial Burlington Society.

Often called the "Gingerbread House," this is probably the oldest in Burlington. It is a tiny red-brick structure, whose fame dates back to 1723, when a young man of seventeen by the name of Benjamin Franklin, who was walking from Boston to Philadelphia, missed his boat. The mistress of the house gave him hot gingerbread while he waited for the next one; this is the claim to immortality of both the owner and her house.

MC CRAY HOUSE (*c. 1850–1860*)

46 Riverbank Street; any time, on tour; Maj. and Mrs. Charles McCray.

A Victorian cottage with some nice paneling and some interesting French furniture.

There is still another Victorian cottage, the VAN RENSSELAER, designed by Strickland, at Talbot Street and the riverbank. It is a collector's item, though not open to visitors.

¶ *Rancocas (just west of turnpike 3 miles below Interchange 5)*

Rancocas is a charming and still unspoiled village containing an early Quaker meeting and schoolhouse. How long it can remain so in the midst of encroaching "progress" is a problem for its devoted inhabitants. Some of the owners of the old houses, other than the two listed below, will undoubtedly be glad to show them by appointment.

WILLIAM S. BAKER HOUSE (*1767, addition 1820*)

By written appointment; Mr. and Mrs. William S. Baker.

One of the five small brick Quaker-style mansions along the banks of the Rancocas, with its original interior—its paneling, mantels, cupboards, and unique staircase—intact. It is furnished appropriately, which is to say, simply.

NORMAN S. WIGGIN HOUSE (*c. 1760s*)

By written appointment; Mr. and Mrs. Norman S. Wiggin.

Also unpretentious and typical, its old woodwork and fireplaces are intact too. Mr. Wiggin may be able to help you to see some of the others.

¶ *Mt. Holly (3 miles east of Interchange 5)*

JOHN WOOLMAN MEMORIAL (*1771*)

99 Branch Street; daily 9 to 6, Sundays 1 to 6; maintained by a Friends organization.

Built on land once owned by the noted Quaker, John Woolman, one of the earliest opponents of slavery, it is a small red-brick building with adjoining gardens in which the present-day Quakers have tried to recreate the atmosphere of the place and period.

THE COURT HOUSE (1796) and the BURLINGTON COUNTY GAOL here were designed by Robert Mills; the latter was the first fireproof building in America and is not nearly so obsolete as you might think.

¶ *Bordentown*
(*10 miles below Trenton*)

An easygoing Quaker named Thomas Farnsworth established himself here on the banks of the Delaware in 1682. A little later Joseph Borden came by sailing vessel from Philadelphia and bought him out. Borden believed in progress and soon had his own stagecoach running between this place and New York, and boat service to Philadelphia as well. It was in no time a town taking his name. Even before the Revolution it was quite a famous place, with large schools whose students came from as far away as South America and the West Indies. It was also a summering place for many Revolutionary figures, among them Tom Paine and Francis Hopkinson. Such was its fame that Joseph Bonaparte, brother of Napoleon, and King of Spain and Naples, bought a large estate here in 1820, where he lived for twenty years or more. His French Colonial mansion stood in what is now Bonaparte Park; all that remains of the many buildings is the garden house.

Some of the old houses in the town are still standing. Should you want to know more about them, Mr. Orson H. Brown, 322 Prince Street, who has lived there more than 83 years, will be glad to give you directions. He must be notified in advance, and may on occasion conduct a small group personally.

The GILDER HOUSE was the home of the famous Gilder family and still breathes the atmosphere of the cultivated and remarkable people who lived here—poets, musicians, critics, explorers, and the celebrated editor, Richard Watson Gilder, of the old *Century* magazine.

The THOMAS PAINE HOUSE was used by him when he was carrying on his great work for the freedom of the Colonies.

The CLARA BARTON SCHOOLHOUSE, built in 1739, was used by Clara Barton, founder of the Red Cross, to establish the first public school in this country in 1844.

¶ *Camden*

WALT WHITMAN HOUSE (*1840*)
330 Mickle Street; daily 10 to 12 and 1 to 5 except Mondays, Sundays 2 to 5; 35 cents and 10 cents; state of New Jersey.

An unpretentious clapboard house joined to its taller brick neighbors, it sits flush with the pavement. The great poet lived in it from 1884 until his death in 1892. Many of his furnishings and mementos are here in place, as well as a valuable collection of original manuscripts.

POMONA HALL (*1726 and 1788*)
Northeast corner of Euclid Avenue and Park Boulevard; Mondays, Wednesdays, and Fridays 1:30 to 4, other days by appointment with E. H. Havens (curator); Camden County Historical Society Museum.

Built in two sections—the earlier by Joseph Cooper, Jr., and the later by his nephew Marmaduke—this impressive house of tapestry brick, with a double chimney at either end bearing the builders' initials, definitely represents one of the noteworthy pieces of New Jersey Colonial. Fortunately the staircase, fireplaces, partitions, and Colonial fittings are intact. The newer section (1788) typifies the post-Revolutionary changes in style. Its main function now is as a museum for the Camden County Historical Society, and it has on display exhibits of maps, Indian relics, and files of old newspapers, with only one room furnished in facsimile as this is written.

¶ *Haddon Heights*

GLOVER MANSION (*c. 1705*)
In park; Camden County Park Commission.

Much of its appearance was lost in remodeling. It was built by John Glover, who arrived in 1703 after being discharged from the British Navy. He sought and found his sweetheart Hannah Thorne, who had come to America earlier with her father, and brought her here as his bride. It is now an office of the Camden County Park Commission.

¶ *Haddonfield*

HADDONFIELD HISTORICAL SOCIETY (*1836*)

231 Kings Highway E.; daily Monday to Friday, 2 to 5; Haddonfield Historical Society.

This is a tall, narrow town dwelling much like those in Burlington and typical of the Jersey and Pennsylvania town houses of the well-to-do burghers of the period— plain and substantial as the Quakers who lived in them. It is well stocked with items of local interest, which include furniture, household decorations, and some of the belongings of Elizabeth Haddon, the town's first settler, sent here alone from England by her father when she was only twenty to look after a large property he had purchased in this area.

Old Indian King Tavern near Haddonfield.

INDIAN KING TAVERN (*1750*)

232 Kings Highway E.; daily 10 to 12 and 1 to 5 except Mondays, Sundays 2 to 5; 35 cents and 10 cents; state of New Jersey, Department of Conservation and Economic Development.

A landmark when Haddonfield was just another Jersey crossroads village during the Revolution. Among the distinguished figures who stopped over here were Gen-

eral Greene, Lord Cornwallis, Lafayette, "Mad Anthony" Wayne, Count Pulaski, etc. Innkeeper Creighton's niece, Dolly Payne, became President Madison's wife. Rescued and restored in 1903 by the state, the tavern is now maintained as an inn of its period. It houses a library of six thousand volumes, some Washington manuscripts, and earlier memorabilia.

¶ *Woodbury*

JUDGE JESSUP HOUSE *or* GLOUCESTER COUNTY HISTORICAL SOCIETY (*1750 or 1765*)

58 North Broad Street; Mondays 11 to 3, Wednesdays and Fridays 2 to 4, or by appointment with L. L. Lammert (phone: Woodbury 2–02111); Gloucester County Historical Society.

Built by either John Tatem or Judge John Sparks, this is a typical early South Jersey house with Dutch Colonial features and Tudor touches. It has in all eighteen rooms, eleven of which are furnished, none in any one period, but with many interesting antiques. Records show that it was the boyhood home of the young naval hero, Captain Lawrence, born in Burlington. A mansard roof has been added to the house as well as a portico, though the building was better off without them.

¶ *Salem*

HOMELAND (*1729, wing 1784*)

By appointment; $1.50 to Salem County Historical Society; Dr. and Mrs. A. Ralston Green.

Built by a Whig colonel, Benjamin Holme. this is a perfect example of the red-brick manor house found only in this part of Jersey and in Delaware, usually with descending wings. They have fine style and proportions, and their personality is prim and English. Colonel Holme owned sixteen hundred acres and the ferry nearby, which was the terminus of the old King's Highway. Both the house and ferry were set afire by the British in March, 1778; fortunately the exterior of the house remained intact. It was the custom to carry the furniture to the waiting British ships before the houses were burned. A clock from this house, made by Wagstaff of London, was later recovered from British headquarters in New York. The house and

The dining room of Homeland is large enough to include a coffee-table grouping before the fireplace. The kitchen lies beyond.

grounds have been beautifully restored, and the charming interior has been treated with taste and skill. The kitchen and dining room are of particular interest, the kitchen containing modern equipment so artfully placed as to be practically invisible. The rare collection of molds here on the mantel shelf centers the attention on the vast hearth.

ALEXANDER GRANT HOUSE (*1721*)
81 and 83 Market Street; by appointment with Harry A. Crispin; Salem County Historical Society.

This is a typical South Jersey brick town house with a wing. It is not furnished as a home at the present time, but has large collections of furniture, glass, china, and apparel.

The kitchen at Homeland has become an extremely pleasant all-purpose room for dining, sitting, but primarily for cooking, filled with fascinating antiques.

The brickwork is a remarkable feature of the fine old Hancock house.

¶ *Hancocks Bridge* (*south of Salem*)

HANCOCK HOUSE (*1734*)

> *Daily 10 to 12 and 1 to 5 except Mondays, Sundays 2 to 5; 35 cents and 10 cents; state of New Jersey, Department of Conservation and Economic Development.*

This Quaker house was the scene of a ferocious massacre of American patriots on March 21, 1778. A band of thirty men sleeping here was trapped by three hundred of the enemy and bayoneted. Still visible on the floor are the bloodstains. This was in reprisal for the food that was being sent to Washington's army at Valley Forge from this area, which is said to have prevented their starvation. As in a number of the houses in this area, the initials of the owner William and his wife Sara and the date are laid in the masonry which on one wall of this house forms a unique zigzag pattern with the use of only blue glazed bricks, while the front alternates red and blue. This use of bricks, an early brickmasons' fancy, can be seen as far west as the William Whitely House in Kentucky. The interior, furnished in antiques, has carved panels, moldings, and mantels, elaborate grillwork on a closet, and early Venetian blinds. In addition, there are such commonplaces of the day as bedbug traps, hoopskirt chairs, and tailors' gooses.

CEDAR PLANK HOUSE (*c. 1700*)

> *Behind Hancock House; daily.*

This tiny one-story structure stands behind the Hancock House. It was built of cedar from the nearby swamps by the Swedes who settled here in 1643. The hand-hewn planks are dovetailed in Swedish fashion at the corners.

¶ *Greenwich*

RICHARD WOOD MANSION (*1797*)

> *Wednesdays and Sundays 2 to 5 April through December, other times by appointment; contribution; Mr. Theodore Wood.*

This fine old house stands unchanged on a street laid out in 1684, and while it is not furnished as a house, it contains exhibits of local items and various private collections, changed from time to time. Mrs. Sara Sheppard Hancock, president of the Salem County Historical Society, lives a few miles distant in Bacon's Neck upon the land her ancestor Samuel Bacon bought from the Indians in 1682. Her own home is of interest, having been in her family since it was built.

THE ANCHORAGE *or* WHEATON HOMESTEAD (*1848*)

> *By request; Maj. Frank Ankenbrand.*

Built by Providence and Ruth Foster Wheaton on the site of a library which stood here 1821–1838, it is a large frame house with a widow's walk and iron balustrades made by a local smith. The house has twenty-three rooms, twelve furnished with a variety of antiques and an unusual collection of paintings and prints, which include Morlands, Rowlandsons, and Knellers. One room contains a bedroom set identical to the one in the Lincoln Room in the White House. It was once the property of Charles Willson Peale's son, and the present owner purchased it from Peale's granddaughter. There are also some Lincoln and Peale items.

¶ *Somers Point*

SOMERS MANSION (*1720–1730*)

> *Shore Road and traffic circle at Somers Point; daily 10 to 12 and 1 to 5 except Mondays, Sundays 2 to 5; 25 cents; state of New Jersey, Department of Conservation and Economic Development.*

John Somers, a Quaker born in England, purchased a three-thousand-acre tract from Thomas Budd in 1695; when he died in 1723, he left his "home lands" to his fourth child, Richard. He had been an important figure, operating a ferry from Great Egg Harbor to Cape May, and thence to East Jersey. Richard built the mansion of hand-made brick between 1720 and 1730. There are records of Quaker meetings held here in those days. The mansion remained in the family until 1937, when the heirs deeded it to the county historical society. It was renovated by WPA workmen, who removed the stucco and exposed the Flemish-bond brickwork; an original eight-foot fireplace in the great room was restored, disclosing a herringbone pattern in the back. The deck roof is particularly interesting, supported by hewn timbers which taper from a width of seven inches at the ridge to one or three at the heels, where they are pinned to the timbers supporting the steeper slope—undoubtedly an example of a shipwright's work. The mansion has been restored with great care to reveal as many as possible of its original features, including the paint.

Nothing could be more typical of the country furnishings and appearance of southeastern Pennsylvania than this children's dining room in Pottsgrove Manor, with one of the stone dwellings of the Furnace beyond. On the opposite page is Mt. Pleasant in Fairmount Park, considered by all and sundry to be one of the four or five greatest Georgian houses in the country.

PENNSYLVANIA

THE MANOR houses, such as ING-HAM MANOR near Lahaska and POTTSGROVE at Pottstown, are pure, unadulterated Pennsylvania, not to be found anywhere else. And it is unmistakably the same with the farmhouses that are so closely related to the manors. Then there are the celebrated country seats like MOUNT PLEASANT in Fairmount Park and CLIVEDEN in Germantown, which for all their striking individuality also have a common character. All of these—the manor houses, the farmhouses, and the country seats—are boldly built and detailed, most of masonry. But there is more to it than

173

that; each one of them also has a quality of firmness and a generous scale, which helps to endow them with their robust regional character.

It is only when you come to the early town houses of downtown Philadelphia, such as the POWEL, SHIPPEN-WISTER, and MORRIS HOUSES, which are direct descendants of eighteenth-century London town houses and of the later, more delicate Georgian, that you feel these more sophisticated homes could have been built as easily almost anywhere else in the Colonies.

It goes without saying that the richest region for fine early houses is the old southeastern section, fanning out from Philadelphia across the adjacent counties and into the farmlands that sweep in a wide arc from the Delaware, through the Pennsylvania Dutch country, past York and Gettysburg to the Maryland border. The barns and houses are colorful to look upon, and the countryside is bountiful.

The best way to see some of the interiors is to attend the tours, which are numerous. Spring and fall are the best times of the year as far as visibility, brightness, color, and comfort are concerned, and it is during these two seasons that most of the visiting days in the various localities occur, all noted below in their proper places. The biggest is the Pennsylvania House and Garden Tour, taking place at the end of April and the first week in May and lasting three days; write for full information to the Penn-Sheraton Hotel, 39th and Chestnut Streets, Philadelphia. Also the guidance you get on these occasions is something to be grateful for, especially in the environs of Philadelphia, if you happen to be a stranger there.

IN & OUT OF PHILADELPHIA

While walking through the streets of present-day downtown Philadelphia, especially east and south of Independence Square, bear in mind that this was by far the largest of all our colonial cities. In 1775 its population was forty thousand, as compared with New York's twenty-five thousand and Boston's sixteen thousand. In fact, according to Carl Bridenbaugh in *Cities in Revolt,* "it was larger than any city in England except London itself and had taken its place not only with the largest provincial cities of the British Empire but with those of western Europe." The narrow lots in which the crowded city was laid out resulted early in a close-order formation of houses standing right up from the sidewalks, a characteristic that is not only historical but still current today on Philadelphia streets miles distant from downtown. It is a characteristic that gives great charm to Elfreth's Alley down below Independence Hall, where a Visiting Day is held in the spring by the Junior League of Philadelphia, 1715 Rittenhouse Street, to which you should write for dates; their tour also takes in other historic houses. It is a characteristic that gives both elegance and charm to several fine blocks on Clinton and Delancey Streets, which you will find by following Spruce Street a short way west after you have seen the POWEL, WHARTON, WISTER, and MORRIS HOUSES, in that order. With due respect to the houses, the noblest display of early American architecture downtown here (or anywhere in the country) is of course INDEPENDENCE HALL (1738–1741), a building which, with its entourage, contains many delightful details that are truly domestic in quality.

¶ The downtown houses

POWEL HOUSE (1765)

> *244 South 3d Street; daily 10 to 5; 25 cents; Philadelphia Society for the Preservation of Landmarks.*

This is the only early house of high distinction in downtown Old Philadelphia which is regularly open to the public. Samuel Powel, who bought it shortly after it was built, was a cultivated gentleman, *bon vivant*, entertainer of celebrities, world traveler, and mayor of colonial Philadelphia. The house was beautifully suited to the social brilliance brought to it by the Powels and their friends, but for many years in its later life its handsomeness fell into such low esteem that it was on the point of disintegration. Its restoration came just in the nick of time, for dismantling had begun. Fortunately its marvelous drawing room got no farther away than the Philadelphia Museum of Art, where it can now be compared with the stunning re-creation of the room in the house itself done by the late H. L. Duhring, Jr., architect of the restoration.

WHARTON HOUSE (c. 1795)

> *336 Spruce Street; open on written request to The Mutual Assurance Company, 240 South 4th Street.*

Somewhat similar to but not quite in a class with the Powel House, this building with its beautiful brickwork is being used for business purposes, but with a keen appreciation of its interior beauty. Well worth seeing.

SHIPPEN-WISTER HOUSE (c. 1750)

> *4th and Locust Streets; open on written request to The Mutual Assurance Company, 240 South 4th Street.*

A charming Georgian town house, larger and earlier than the Powel House, though again not quite its equal, it is, as is the Wharton House, owned and occupied for business purposes by the same appreciative and thoroughly "Old Philadelphia" firm.

ROBERT MORRIS HOUSE (1786)

> *225 South 8th Street; by appointment with N. W. Ayer & Son, Inc.*

Perhaps the most impressive of these four fine Georgian houses is being used to good effect by the old Philadelphia advertising firm of N. W. Ayer as a house in which to

Downtown Philadelphia is given distinction by its notable early town houses, of which the Powel is a superb example.

entertain out-of-town guests. Throughout, the house is nicely maintained.

BETSY ROSS HOUSE (1700)

> *239 Arch Street; daily, 10 to 4:30; American Flag House and Betsy Ross Memorial Association.*

The story goes that George Washington, Robert Morris (of the house above), and George Ross called at this very early unpretentious little town house to discuss the making of the first American flag with the seamstress who lived there. Both Betsy and her home have been famous forever since. The finely molded substantial cornices at roof eave and pent eave give the small-scale façade real Pennsylvania character. The rooms are all furnished for simple Philadelphia eighteenth-century living.

Nothing quite as remarkable in terms of the early German dwellings remains still standing in the Pennsylvania countryside as the house from which these rooms, now at the Philadelphia Museum of Art, were taken.

This house was at Millbach in Lebanon County, and the kitchen opposite, with its walk-in fireplace, and the stair hall, left, indicate the medieval quality of the first Pennsylvania "Dutch" homes.

EDGAR ALLAN POE HOUSE (*1800*)

530 North 7th Street; daily, 10 to 5; 50 cents; Richard Gimbel Foundation for Literary Research.

The poet lived for two years during the 1840s in this city dwelling typical of its date, meaning that, although plain, it has some personality. There are many possessions of Poe's here, and there is a fine research library for Poe students.

BARTRAM HOUSE (*1731*)

In Bartram Gardens, 54th Street and Eastwick Avenue, below Elmwood Avenue; daily, 8 to 4:30; no charge weekdays, Sundays and holidays 10 cents; city of Philadelphia.

Speaking of personality, this house is bursting with it, and most of it is John Bartram's, who built the place with his own hands of beautiful local stone laid up in ashlar courses. The tall Ionic columns were added, no doubt, when he remodeled it later in its century. One of the greatest of the early botanists, self-taught, his original touches—a recessed porch and carved-stone window casings—give the house its personality. The gardens are famous, of course, with rare and exotic plants, which his son-in-law continued to collect after

his death. This is in many ways one of the most rewarding old places to visit in the whole Philadelphia area.

WOODLANDS (*cemetery office*) (*c. 1770*)

Woodland Avenue and 39th Street; not open; Philadelphia Society for the Preservation of Landmarks.

This extraordinary "great house," of stone, was the community seat of the distinguished old Philadelphia family of Hamilton when the banks of the Schuylkill here were a lovely landscape of gardens and lawns. It is now surrounded by a vast city cemetery and occupied by the cemetery offices. There are immense porticoes front and back. Still quite a sight.

PHILADELPHIA MUSEUM OF ART

On hill overlooking river at entrance to Fairmount Park; daily 10:30 to 5.

1. Hall from the House of the Miller, Millbach, Pennsylvania.
2. Bedroom from the House of the Miller, Millbach, Pennsylvania.
3. Drawing room from the Powel House, Philadelphia, Pennsylvania.
4. Room from the Ezekiel Hersey Derby House, Salem, Massachusetts.

The rooms from the Millbach house are heavy, dark, and dour, with much medieval beauty and dignity. You won't see anything more pure in the whole Pennsylvania Dutch region, but there will be a lot out there which is more colorful and kindly. Here too is the original drawing room from the Powel House. And of extraordinary interest is the room from the great Ezekiel Derby House, in Salem, the one on which McIntire and Bulfinch collaborated, and which was torn down fifteen years after it was built. The room is mostly McIntire, furniture and all.

¶ The Fairmount Park houses

LETITIA STREET HOUSE
(1703–1715)

Daily 10 to 5 (closed holidays); admission by written (address bursar) or phone (Poplar 5-0500) request to Philadelphia Museum of Art; 25 cents and 10 cents; Fairmount Park Commission (custodians).

Not a country seat, obviously, but a little beauty of a brick town house brought out here in the 1880s from Letitia Street, in deep-downtown Old Philadelphia near Elfreth's Alley (noted above). Furnished in Queen Anne in accordance with its early date. The house is often called "Penn's Cottage," but it was never owned or occupied by William Penn.

SWEETBRIER MANSION *(1797)*

On right of park 300 yards along Landsdowne Drive; daily 10 to 5, except Sundays; 25 cents; Fairmount Park Commission (custodians).

A foursquare white-painted stone house with a lot of style, built by a man from Boston named Samuel Breck and now most handsomely maintained and furnished. Breck was a man with great social inclinations, and at Sweetbrier Mansion he lavishly entertained the *haut monde* of his day—royalty, nobility, and even Presidents. A perfect house for the purpose.

CEDAR GROVE MANSION
(1721 and later)

Beyond Sweetbrier Mansion on right fork; daily, 1 to 5 (closed holidays); 25 cents and 10 cents; Fairmount Park Commission (custodians).

As the date indicates, this fine sandstone house has developed in various stages; the end result is a sense of rambling informality. An unusually deep ground-level porch, brick-paved and roofed over, was an 1830 idea, and very becoming too. The house was moved here in 1927 from what is now the industrial section of Frankford, over by the Delaware. It contains the family furniture, and the old colonial kitchen is a favorite feature.

BELMONT MANSION (*a restaurant*)
(*before 1742, 1745, 1755, and 1760*)
Daily 5 to 8 except Mondays September through May, daily 5 to 9 June, July, and August, Sundays 1 to 8 year round; Fairmount Park Commission (custodians).

This distinguished old country mansion, built of stone, with early brick additions, has an interior that furnishes much pleasure along with the food. Outside the effect of the house suffers somewhat from an upper story added in the nineteenth century.

STRAWBERRY (*1798–1830*)
Near 33d and Dauphin Streets; daily, 11 to 5 (closed August); 25 cents and 10 cents; Fairmount Park Commission (custodians).

The older central section is oddly flanked by the two high later wings, one of them added, they say, to "entertain the City Troop." The ballroom, or music room, is a period chef-d'oeuvre done in richly colorful French Empire. The interior offers a complete change of pace from the other Fairmount Park houses. The original 1750 house here was called "Somerton" and was burnt by the British during the Revolution. The present central section is the second "Somerton," built in 1798 by William Lewis, a famous Philadelphia judge.

Joseph Hemphill was later responsible for the neoclassical wings and for quite a few other extravagant features, which contributed after his death to a foreclosure on the mortgage. It was the next owner, an energetic country woman, who made "Somerton" a going enterprise, with great fruit gardens and a dairy herd; she served refreshments on the side to the carriage trade from town, making a name for herself with her strawberries and cream. The house soon became known as "Strawberry Mansion," and "Strawberry" it still is, now delightfully restored.

WOODFORD (*1742–1756*)
Daily 1 to 5, except Mondays; Fairmount Park Commission (custodians).

This formal Georgian mansion, of tawny brick trimmed with white, is the personification of cultured elegance, true to type for early Philadelphia. It is one of the finest colonial houses in the country, and furnished to absolute perfection. "Woodford" had become a park guardhouse when it was restored under the direction of the Pennsylvania Museum and entrusted with the Naomi Wood Collection that helps to give the interior its present-day distinction.

MOUNT PLEASANT (*1762*)
Daily 1 to 5 (closed holidays); 25 cents and 10 cents; Fairmount Park Commission.

Another great magnificent Georgian mansion, richly done in stone, brick, and stucco, and complete with flanking dependencies, it is far and away the most

The music room of Strawberry in Fairmount Park is brilliant with the bright satins of its Empire furnishings.

"important" house in the park. As "Woodford" comes closest to perfection, "Mount Pleasant" comes closest to grandeur. And it is just as imposing inside as out. The John Macpherson who built it in 1762 was lavish with the money he made from privateering, and expense was no object. Seventeen years later it passed from Macpherson to Maj. Gen. Benedict Arnold, the American commander at Philadelphia, who bought it for his bride, the famous Philadelphia beauty Peggy Shippen. But before the couple had a chance to occupy it, the general was exposed as a traitor and fled over to the British Army.

HATFIELD HOUSE (*c. 1760–c. 1835*)
Daily except Thursdays, 10:30 to 5; Fairmount Park Commission (custodians).

This stalwart old country house of 1760, which gained its impressively formal Greek Revival portico in 1835, was brought here in 1930 from what is now an industrial section of the city, originally named "Nicetown." A decidedly attractive addition to the fine assembly of Fairmount Park houses.

¶ The Germantown houses

STENTON (*1728*)
In the small park at 18th and Cortland Streets; city of Philadelphia, Society of Colonial Dames (custodians).

This was one of the first great houses you would have come to approaching Germantown in colonial days, and one of the finest. Standing now in its little six-acre park surrounded by city, this noble old mansion, of brick laid in Flemish bond, once lorded it over a grand country estate. The wide brick-paved entrance hall, like a loggia, is a notable feature. James Logan, who built it, accompanied William Penn to America in 1699. Penn left him in charge of the Province of Pennsylvania during his long absence in England. He was one of the greatest Philadelphians of them all, and his house has the same stature. Washington stopped here during the Brandywine and Germantown battles. The Colonial Dames maintain it, and a recent job of restoring original wall colors and furnishings does them credit.

Woodford is another of the great coterie of Fairmount Park mansions.

WAKEFIELD (*1798*)
16th Street and Lindley Avenue; may be seen by special arrangement; city of Philadelphia, Fairmount Park and Colonial Dames, Chapter VI (custodians).

This large, attractive stone house, with a lovely railed porch below the pediment, looks down on a small public park, almost as it must have appeared in its distant past. It is used largely for meetings, and not all of it is furnished.

HACKER HOUSE (*1772*)
5214 Germantown Avenue; Tuesdays, Thursdays, and Saturdays 1 to 5, except Saturdays in August; Germantown Historical Society.

Typical of Germantown—meaning warm-tinted, wide-jointed stonework, handsome woodwork within, and reeking with history. It houses the library and museum of the Historical Society.

GRUMBLETHORP (*1744–1808*)
5267 Germantown Avenue; daily, 1 to 5; Philadelphia Society for the Preservation of Landmarks.

Somewhat more manorial, this is the house John Wister built. Wisters occupied it until 1940, during which period it was called the "Big House"; then they gave it to the Landmark Society. It is the house in which British General Agnew died of his wounds

The parlor of the Morris house, where the Washingtons lived when this was the Presidential residence.

The Morris house faces the site of the old market square in Germantown where Martha Washington did her marketing.

after the Battle of Germantown. The fine old house is now in gradual process of restoration and refurnishing.

MORRIS HOUSE (*1772*)

5442 Germantown Avenue; daily 9 to 5 except holidays; National Park Service.

This brownstone house on the square is famous as the place that Washington made his Presidential residence at the time when Philadelphia was the capital. In 1793 he

Upsala, another of the fine stone mansions that lined the old "Great Road."

brought his family here because of the yellow-fever epidemic in Philadelphia and the next summer rented it. His Cabinet met here often. A smallish house, it must have been bursting at the seams with guests, aides, etc. Washington comments on the fact that the cook might be seen from the dining room, where he was wont to receive. The house was well built but without any ostentation.

UPSALA (*1798*)

6430 Germantown Avenue, between Johnson and Cliveden Streets; Tuesday and Friday afternoons; 10 cents; Upsala Foundation, Frances A. Wister (President).

This beautiful house of ashlar-cut masonry is a lot simpler and less manorial than "Cliveden" across the street, but it stands as "Clivenden's" rival at this end of the "Great Road," for it has a graciousness and livability that the other lacks. When fully restored and furnished (a slow process for lack of funds), this is bound to be one of the Philadelphia "musts."

WYCK (before 1760), at 6206 Germantown Avenue, stands at right angles to the street behind its wall. It is one of the oldest and grandest but not open now. And farther out, opposite UPSALA, stands CLIVEDEN (1760), the most famous of them all in this area. Still belonging to a member of the Chew family, it is not open now, but at least you can get a good look at it from the street.

THE ADJACENT SUBURBAN COUNTIES

¶ *Delaware County: Upland; Essington; Chadd's Ford;*
Dilworthtown ¶ *Chester County: West Chester; Wayne;*
Bryn Mawr; Valley Forge; Pottstown ¶ *Montgomery County:*
Audubon; Whitemarsh; Hatboro

The number of houses listed for these three "Philadelphia counties" is no indication of how numerous the fine old houses are in this whole region. There are myriads of them, with a warm stone beauty all their own, making any rambling back-road drive rewarding. There are hardly any that are better than the houses listed here, but if you would like to see more, and particularly more private homes, you should send for the program of the annual house and garden tours managed by the Pennsylvania House and Garden Tour, Penn-Sheraton Hotel, 39th and Chestnut Streets, Philadelphia, which includes "Down the Brandywine." There are also local visiting days, which are mentioned below.

¶ Delaware County

Delaware County Day, usually in late May, shows as many as fifty historic buildings; the tickets are about two dollars and fifty cents, or four dollars including transportation. For dates, etc., write to Delaware County Day, 47 Long Lane, Upper Darby, Pennsylvania.

¶ *Upland (just out of Chester)*

CALEB PUSEY HOUSE (*1683*)
> *Race Street; private.*

This is not open ordinarily, but it does happen to be the oldest English-built house in Pennsylvania. Of brick-and-stone construction and of more than mere archeological interest.

¶ *Essington (down Broad Street, Philadelphia, onto 291)*

JOHN MORTON HOMESTEAD
> (*1654, 1698, and 1806*)
> *Prospect Park; daily, 9 to 5; state of Pennsylvania.*

If you have a taste for the truly primitive, these two log houses, with a later stone section in between, will be interesting. John Morton, a signer of the Declaration, was born here in 1724. The house is furnished in an appropriately primitive Dutch fashion and well cared for.

¶ *Chadd's Ford (322 over to Route 1)*

WASHINGTON'S HEADQUARTERS
> (*as of 1777*)
> *Battlefield Park, on Brandywine River 15 miles from Wilmington on 202, 1½ miles south of intersection; weekdays 11 to 5 except Mondays, April through September, Fridays, Saturdays, Sundays, and holidays 11 to 5 October through March; state of Pennsylvania.*

LAFAYETTE'S HEADQUARTERS GROUP (*as of 1777 with later additions*)
> *Same.*

HOWE'S HEADQUARTERS GROUP (*1754*)
> *Same.*

On the Brandywine Battlefield, where Howe's and Washington's armies met on September 11, 1777, these constitute three historically interesting and increasingly attractive groups of houses and outbuildings. They are being furnished as of the Revolutionary period under the direction of Henry F. du Pont, of Winterthur, Delaware, one of the country's outstanding collectors of Americana.

¶ *Dilworthtown (on 202, 4 miles south of West Chester and about 1 mile from the Brandywine Battlefield)*

THE 1704 HOUSE (*1704*)
Old Westchester-Wilmington Pike ¼ mile from Dilworthtown; Tuesdays, Thursdays, and Saturdays 2 to 5 except holidays, also by appointment; 50 cents; Chester County Historical Society.

In the spring of 1648 Quaker William Brinton embarked with his wife and son William for Penn's colony, refugees of the religious struggle in England. Brinton in time prospered, acquiring more than a thousand acres of land. His son William married Jane Thatcher at the Birmingham Meeting, then held in the Brinton cabin. His father deeded the farm to him in 1697, and here he built a stone house for his wife and six children; the stone was taken from a nearby quarry. The walls were twenty-two inches thick, and the steep roof was pierced by dormers and pent eaves over the first-floor windows on the north and south sides of the house. In all there were

A recent remarkable restoration is the 1704 House near West Chester.

twenty-seven windows (an unusual number for the times) with leaded sash. Little of this early house remained when the society received it in 1947 from descendants of the builder, who had purchased it for preservation. The many descendants of the family have formed an association which has helped the Historical Society to finance the restoration. The restoration architect, Mr. Edwin G. Brumbaugh, made a careful study of the old house that existed under the modern wood and plaster after the removal of a large serpentine wing. It now stands much as it was originally—a medieval dwelling. The selection of furnishings is based on actual inventories taken after the death of the builder; only a very few of the original items have been located so far.

¶ *Chester County*

Chester County Day, the first Saturday in October every year, is the time to see the Chester County houses. Send for the illustrated program of nearly forty houses so that you can pick out the maximum of twelve houses which they advise you to attempt to see. This is truly a house-tour treat, beautifully organized. Address Chester County Day, Box 1, West Chester, Pennsylvania.

¶ *West Chester*

DAVID TOWNSEND HOUSE
(*c. 1790–1830*)
225 North Matlack Street; Tuesdays, Thursdays, and Saturdays 2 to 5 (closed holidays), or by appointment (phone: 4755); 25 cents; Chester County Historical Society.

This tall town house was a small farmhouse in 1785; it had a three-story-front face lifting in 1830. It is well furnished with Hepplewhite and Sheraton pieces.

¶ *Wayne*

THE HOMESTEAD (*1789*)
Beech Tree Lane and Bellevue Avenue; open on request; Mrs. E. Dorothy Finley, Radnor Historical Society.

A tenant house put up on his Revolutionary farm by Squire John Pugh, this interesting

The best known and one of the most endearing of all of Washington's Revolutionary headquarters is this erstwhile ironmaster's residence at Valley Forge.

house has been for many years the home of the present owner's family.

¶ *Bryn Mawr*

IDLEWILD FARM (*1717*)

Follow Morris Avenue to Williamson Avenue; by appointment (phone: Lawrence 5–1234); Mr. and Mrs. Lawrence Saunders.

One of the very early Welsh stone farmhouses, beautifully kept and furnished. It is on a farm that has been in continuous operation since 1717, when the Welsh were beginning to filter into this part of Pennsylvania. There is a fascinatingly equipped early kitchen.

¶ *Valley Forge*

WASHINGTON'S HEADQUARTERS BUILDING (*1758*)

Daily; Valley Forge Park Commission.

This was built to be the ironmaster's residence for what was then the "Mount Joy Forge," but by the time John Potts bought it a few years later, the name had changed to "Valley Forge," which is the name that

has become immortalized by the man who occupied the house during the winter of 1777–1778 and the men who were encamped around it in the cold. It is a house so familiar in appearance that, paradoxically, few people really have a clear picture of it in their minds. To see it with your own eyes is to draw closer to that fateful winter. It is furnished mostly as it was at the time; much of the furniture belonged to the Potts family. Colonel Dewees' house and General Varnum's quarters are in the Park.

¶ *Pottstown*

POTTSGROVE (*1752*)

Route 422; daily 10 to 4, Sundays 1 to 4; state of Pennsylvania (owner), administered by State Historical and Museum Commission.

This, in a way, is "Valley Forge" five times as large—one of the great remaining manor houses of Pennsylvania. Built by the wealthy father of the John Potts who owned the Valley Forge house, it also served as Washington's headquarters—for

Pottsgrove is the embodiment of all that is most appealing among the stone country mansions of the state.

five days in September, 1777. This immense, handsome dwelling of mellow masonry is a thrilling house to visit; the colors inside and the furnishings couldn't be finer. It combines the best qualities of the early Pennsylvania manor and farmhouses.

¶ Montgomery County

¶ Audubon (from Jeffersonville, on 422, take Egypt Road)

MILL GROVE FARM (1762)
Pawling Road; daily, 10 to 5; Montgomery County Park Board.

This big stone house, with characteristically pented gables, was built by James Morgan, an iron man, who allowed the north wing to stand becomingly on a lower level. In the 1790s it was owned by Jean Audubon, the French father of the naturalist, and in 1804 it was occupied by the naturalist himself. It was at the Bakewell country place nearby, called "Fatland," that under tender circumstances John James met his future wife, Lucy.

FATLAND (1845)
Adjoining Mill Grove Farm; private (see above).

The house in which the Bakewells lived when Audubon was at Mill Grove Farm, of which no picture exists, was torn down

in 1845, and on the same foundations was erected the remarkable Greek Revival mansion which today somehow manages to survive—an immense, bleak romantic edifice, with Ionic porticoes front and back, and one wing to match. It may or may not be preserved.

¶ Whitemarsh

HOPE LODGE (1721)
Route 309 on outskirts of town (house well marked); June 1 to November 1, Wednesday through Sunday, 12 to 5; no charge; Hope Lodge Foundation.

This is by all odds one of the finest Early Georgian houses in the country. Its fine five-bay brick façade bears some resemblance to "Wilton" in Richmond. A slightly recessed brick arch above the doorway is notable, and its interior woodwork is deeply molded, bold, and vigorous. The scale is lofty throughout. It was built by a wealthy, prominent Quaker named Morris for his English bride-to-be; but somehow the marriage never took place, and Morris lived and died here at Hope Lodge, a bachelor. An interesting house to see at any time, and when it is fully restored, it will be one of the prizes of Pennsylvania.

¶ Hatboro

KEITH HOUSE (1722)
Graeme Park, Keith Valley Road; by appointment; Mr. and Mrs. Welsh Strawbridge.

Built by Sir William Keith, this long, narrow, high stone house has a tall gambrel roof and two tall brick architectural chimneys rising from the central section of the roof. We agree with Wayne Andrews that "Keith's country home was an inspired creation of carpenters and masons (presumably Swedish) . . . an occasion when artisans were as eager as artists to stress the beauty of the materials with which they worked." While the exterior is unadorned, though with fine pattern and color in the wide white-jointed stonework, the interior is rich with paneling—in many rooms from floor to ceiling. The house is not at present maintained as a lived-in dwelling, but the passage of time has done wonders to the woodwork color.

Keith house is an edifice for connoisseurs. It is the work of Swedish artisans building proudly with the beautiful Pennsylvania fieldstone.

LANCASTER COUNTY

You are now in the country of the "plain people"; the villages, the countryside, and the people hereabouts are as picturesque as any in America. On market days in Lancaster the country people flock in, and it is something not to miss; they are Tuesdays, Fridays, and Saturdays (the five markets being open on different days). Out of town, try to get off the main roads once in a while. Lancaster farms are famous for their painted decorations as well as for their productivity.

You can get the current date (generally in mid-October) for Lancaster County Day by addressing the Lancaster County Art Association, Box 967, Lancaster, or else the Stevens House, Lancaster—a fine, old-fashioned hotel with a lot of style. Then, by writing the Women's Club of Ephrata, you can find out just when in May they'll be holding their Hospitality Day for Ephrata and northern Lancaster County. Not all the houses will be old, but don't let that stop you!

¶ *Lancaster*

WHEATLAND (*1828*)
> *Marietta Avenue; daily 9 to 5 April through October, weekdays 9 to 5 rest of year; The Buchanan Foundation.*

This handsome brick Federal mansion was purchased in 1848 for $6,750 by James Buchanan when he was Secretary of State in the Polk Cabinet—a bargain even then.

Wheatland, home of President Buchanan, in Lancaster, is now handsomely restored.

He lived here with a niece, who acted as hostess while he conducted the first "front-porch" campaign in our political history, becoming our first and only bachelor President. The house is furnished throughout in a style appropriate to its period, and contains many Buchanan-family pieces. The grounds, like the house, have been beautifully restored.

¶ *Ephrata (13 miles northeast of Lancaster on 222)*

EPHRATA CLOISTER (*1733–1749*)
> *Daily, sunrise to sunset; 50 cents; guides; state of Pennsylvania.*

The cloisters comprise a set of buildings put up by the Seventh Day Baptists, a communal society founded by Conrad Beissel in 1732: the SAAL, the SISTERS' HOUSE, the CONRAD BEISSEL HOUSE, and others. A re-

markably preserved, picturesque group of buildings, with a rich flavor of the Rhineland; not to be missed.

¶ *Reinholds (10 miles beyond Ephrata on 222; turn left on 897)*

MRS. HATTIE BRUNNER'S HOME AND ANTIQUE SHOP
> *On request to owner.*

Mrs. Brunner's old Dutch house is a museum of wonderful Pennsylvania antiques. She has been a collector, connoisseur, and dealer for more than fifty years, and has made notable contributions to the Metropolitan Museum and others.

¶ *Manheim (10 miles northwest of Lancaster on 72)*

BARON STIEGEL MANSION (*c. 1762*)
> *Town square; by appointment (address: M. Luther Heisey, 237 North Lime Street, Lancaster); Lancaster County Historical Society.*

Stiegel was no baron, but a glassmaker and iron founder of great fame who came here from Germany in 1750, laid out the town of Manheim, and built this remarkable house with a band platform on the roof. He owned the entire glassmaking town by 1770 but died penniless four years later. When, during the Revolution, Congress met at York, forty miles west, Robert Morris made this his residence; and Washington stayed here overnight on occasion.

BERKS COUNTY

The barns or the houses! Which are better here you will have to decide for yourself.

¶ *Baumstown (6 miles southeast of Reading on 422)*

DANIEL BOONE BIRTHPLACE
(*c. 1735–1779*)
> *Birdsboro, R.D. 2; daily; 25 cents; state of Pennsylvania.*

The wilderness scout of renown spent his youth in this beautiful example of an early Pennsylvania stone farmhouse. Small windows—for lack of glass and for protection—give it an ancient look. Now faithfully

restored (by architect Brumbaugh), it contains early benches, tables, and other primitive furnishings. West of town is the house built by Lincoln's great-grandfather Mordecai, marked but private.

¶ *Birdsboro (a few miles beyond Baumstown)*

HOPEWELL VILLAGE (*c. 1740–1750*)
> *6 miles southeast of town in hills back on Schuylkill River; daily 8 to 4:45, Saturdays, Sundays, and holidays 9 to 6, May through October; National Park Service (superintendent in charge).*

This represents one of the early manorial

ironmaking communities, built around a cold-blast charcoal-burning furnace. The community was medieval and self-sustaining, and stayed pretty much that way until the furnace was closed in 1883 after one hundred and thirteen years of activity. A fascinating, out-of-the-ordinary restoration, well worth seeing. (See Saugus, Massachusetts, for the ironworks restoration there.)

¶ *Douglassville (just beyond Birdsboro)*

MOUNS-JONES HOUSE *or*
OLD SWEDE'S HOUSE (*1716*)
> *Will be open when restored; R. H. Schurr.*

This fine stone house is the oldest in the region. It is being, or has just been, restored with the help of the Berks County Historical Society. The plan is to have it furnished with eighteenth-century pieces. It would be well worth finding out if it is ready.

¶ *Oley (5 miles northeast of Reading on 73)*

HENRY FISHER MANSION (*1801*)
> *By written or phone request (Yellow House 9–3276), preferably Saturday; Mr. and Mrs. Frank S. Fisher.*

Probably the finest example of a Georgian manor house in this section, it was three years a-building. A few family pieces are left. Each mantel is differently carved by master craftsman Gottlieb Drexel.

¶ *Womelsdorf (12 miles northwest of Reading on 422)*

CONRAD WEISER HOUSE (*1751*)
> *East of town in Conrad Weiser Memorial Park; Historical Society of Berks County, administered by Pennsylvania Historical and Museum Commission.*

This early stone house, typical of the region, was the home of the famous pioneer treatymaker and Indian interpreter.

BUCKS COUNTY

Bucks County is not only one of the biggest counties in Pennsylvania but in its venerable way one of the most beautiful. In covering the houses listed below you will pass through its finest towns and countrysides and see its early stone houses and barns at their best.

¶ *Tullytown (a few miles up from the Bristol bridge off Route 13 on the Delaware and near the Levittown development)*

PENNSBURY MANOR (*1683–1938*)
> *Well marked; daily, 10 to 4:30; state of Pennsylvania.*

When William Penn returned from England in 1736, he found his great country establishment "very near falling, the roof open as well as the windows, and the woodwork almost rotten." For two centuries after that it was left untouched; so the restoration which began in 1936, by the late R. Brognard Okie, had to be undertaken nearly from scratch. The manor is in fact a re-creation by this well-known architect, who was an authority on early Pennsylvania domestic architecture. The result is a grand success, comprising not only the manor house itself but many dependencies on the parklike estate by the bank of the wide Delaware. It is furnished appropriately.

¶ *Fallsington (near Washington Crossing)*

At this historic point ten miles up the Delaware from Trenton there are state parks on both sides of the river (see Washington Crossing, New Jersey) marking one of the more famous episodes of the Revolutionary War.

THOMPSON-NEELY HOUSE (*1701*)
> *East of Bowman's Hill section of Washington Crossing Park, at Clarksburg.*

The central part of this typical early brownstone house was built by John Pidcock, the first white settler in these parts. Here Washington had a meeting just before crossing the Delaware on Christmas night with his generals. The original part of this engaging house is furnished with pre-Revolutionary pieces, and more is being done.

The Thompson-Neely house in Washington Crossing Park is one of the handsome landmarks of this historic locality.

OLD FERRY INN (*1812*)

At the Crossing; daily April 15 to November 1, or upon special request during park hours; Washington Crossing Park Commission.

At the Pennsylvania terminus of McKonkey's Ferry, which played a vital part in the crossing, is an impressive brownstone of the period which was superimposed on the original ferryhouse by Mahlon Taylor. It was, of course, the scene of great activity that Christmas night when the Americans launched their desperate "Victory or Death" attempt, and also the scene of their triumph—the Hessian officers spending their first night of captivity here. The commission plans to make the Ferry Inn into a museum too.

TAYLOR MANSION

Across from the Old Ferry Inn.

This old stone beauty is now the Washington Crossing Park Administration Building.

¶ Newtown

One of the truly choice old towns of Pennsylvania, it is neither perfect nor spectacular but has plenty of mellow warmth and atmosphere. Charming old stone house rows and individual houses and inns line the main street. There is an Open House Day, generally in mid-May (address Open House Day Committee, Newtown). And let us suggest the drive from Newtown to Buckingham on 413 as one on which you will see any number of distinguished old stone country homes, delightful to look at as you pass. The town was Washington's headquarters before and after the Battle of Trenton.

LAVENDER HALL (*1742,*
older part prior to 1709)

Left on 532 just out of town; open as an eating place.

BIRD IN HAND (*1690*)

Near the Temperance House; Edward R. Barnsley.

Formerly a tavern, it is one of the oldest frame houses in the state.

FRIENDS' MEETINGHOUSE (*1817*)

The meeting held here was organized by Edward Hicks, the famous primitive painter.

¶ Solebury

A charming crossroads village with a fine Friends' meetinghouse, east of Buckingham via 202 and 263.

INGHAM MANOR (*an antique shop*)
(*pre-Revolutionary*)

Back on 202 between Aquetong and New Hope about 1 mile from New Hope.

One of the most likable and unspoiled tailored stone houses in the county, the massive exterior walls, the paneled living room, and the huge fireplaces reflecting the finest features of the local architecture.

LEHIGH & NORTHAMPTON COUNTIES

¶ Allentown

TROUT HALL (*museum and library*) (*1770*)

Allen Park, 414 Walnut Street; Wednesday and Saturday afternoons; city of Allentown, headquarters of Lehigh County Historical Society.

The impressive stone exterior of this two-and-a-half-story country place shows how well the early settlers here managed to set themselves up. This was the house of the son of the William Allen who laid out the town, and was named from a nearby stream in which trout abounded. Allen ignored the "Dutch" architecture of the neighborhood and built a Georgian Colonial mansion. It once housed Muhlenburg College.

¶ Egypt

TROXELL-STECKEL HOUSE (*1756*)

Daily (caretakers' house nearby); Lehigh County Historical Society.

This is the real thing, a big early fieldstone farmhouse, with pent eaves, a heavy-beamed kitchen with an enormous walk-in fireplace, and fine early-farmhouse furniture. There is a wonderful cast-iron German stove of 1758 inscribed "Verachte das Alter ni" ("Never despise old age"), an appropriate motto for most of the entries in this book.

¶ Catasauqua

GEORGE TAYLOR HOUSE (*1757*)

Lehigh County Historical Society.

This fine old stone house, now in process of restoration, was the home of the signer

of the Declaration of Independence after whom it is named.

¶ Bethlehem

There is a group of old stone buildings in the vicinity of the Moravian church which housed one of the many early communal religious sects. While all are being used, it is possible that some of them may be seen on request. They are well worth seeing from the street at any rate, and be sure to pay a visit to the Moravian burying ground above the church, where the famous Easter Dawn Service is held each year.

¶ Easton

MIXSELL HOUSE (*1833*)

Southwest corner 4th and Ferry Streets; Saturdays 2 to 5, or by appointment; Northampton County Historical and Genealogical Society.

The Mixsell House was occupied by the family until 1928, when it was willed to the Historical Society, which exhibits here county historical items, Indian artifacts, pottery, books, old deeds, and furniture.

GEORGE TAYLOR HOUSE (*1757*)

4th and Ferry Streets; national holidays, or by appointment; D.A.R.

The George Taylor House was built by William Parsons, founder of Easton, and then became the town house of the signer of the Declaration after whom it is named. Some of the original furniture is here, along with other pieces of the period.

CENTRAL & NORTHERN PENNSYLVANIA

¶ Harrisburg

JOHN HARRIS MANSION (*1766*)

219 South Front Street; daily 2 to 5, except Sundays; headquarters of Historical Society of Dauphin County.

This fine stone mansion was built here on the banks of the Susquehanna by the

founder of Harrisburg, and is the oldest building in the city. Now a most rewarding historical museum, it was from its front porch that John Harris in 1775 watched the final review of the Harris Ferry company of Thompson's Rifle Battalion when this body of Pennsylvanians marched off to join Washington at Cambridge, among them Harris's namesake son, who was later killed at Quebec. From the same spot a year later Harris called the people of Harris Ferry together and read to them the Declaration of Independence, two days after it was signed in Philadelphia.

¶ *Sunbury*

HUNTER MANSION (1852) and FORT AUGUSTA (scale model)

Open daily; Pennsylvania Historical and Museum Commission.

Fort Augusta was Pennsylvania's stronghold in the Upper Susquehanna Valley from the days of the French and Indian War to the close of the Revolution. It was an extraordinary wilderness construction, containing considerable living accommodations within the fortifications. Residing in the fort during the Revolution was Col. Samuel Hunter, County Lieutenant of Northumberland, who occupied the commander's quarters while the fort disintegrated. Finally this last log building burned, and Capt. Samuel Hunter, the colonel's grandson, built the present Hunter Mansion, now a museum containing many fascinating relics of Fort Augusta and early Sunbury. Not the least interesting feature is the large-scale model of the fort which has been built on the lawn in front of the mansion.

¶ *Boalsburg*

BOAL MANSION (1789–1798)

Estate near Route 322; being restored, partially open daily May to November; 60 cents and 25 cents; Pierre L. Boals.

It is probably best to begin by quoting a historical note furnished by Mr. Boals.

"The first of the Boals family came to this country before the Revolutionary War. Its ancestors had lived in Ireland after one of the captains of the Spanish Armada was shipwrecked on the coast of that country and married and settled there. Always an adventurous family the Boals served in nearly every war and became allied in a later generation with a French family of equally romantic history. Through the present owner's mother, Mathilde de Lagarde Boal, the family has inherited the

family chapel, complete with all its antique furnishings, works of art and religious accessories, of Christopher Columbus's descendants in Spain. . . . The house, the chapel, and the museum contain many heirlooms which are rich in historical association, from chain mail of Crusading days to Simon Bolivar's pistol. . . . The house is especially rich in fine china and crystal and objets d'art. The museum at present contains examples of both early Pennsylvania furniture and elegant European pieces."

Not only does the estate here, now on display, live up to the promise implicit in this description, but there is a further inducement to visit the vicinity if you can arrange to be on hand for the annual Old Boalsburg Day, generally held in May or June and sponsored by the community's P.T.A. In addition to ten or more old houses, taverns, and schools in Boalsburg itself, the tour takes in old buildings of interest in the nearby villages of Oak Hall, Linden Hall, and Shingletown. Here is an opportunity to get a rounded picture of the past and present of one of the most appealing countrysides in Pennsylvania. (Observe the enthusiasm taken here in the local history.) Write to Dr. D. W. Russell, Boalsburg, for dates and further information.

¶ *Altoona*

ELIAS BAKER MANSION (1844)

Baker Boulevard, near 36th Street; Saturdays and Sundays, 1:30 to 4:30, June to October; Museum of Blair County Historical Society.

Baker was an ironmaster, and he built a house in keeping with the importance of his status—limestone walls, all interior trim of black walnut, Italian-marble columns in the drawing room, carved furniture, inlaid piano, and so on. Renovated in 1951, and a good job.

¶ *Northumberland*

DR. JOSEPH PRIESTLEY HOUSE AND MUSEUM (1797)

Open by arrangement with Pennsylvania State University.

On a dramatic eminence where the Susquehanna divides into its east and west branches, there is a house of considerable size, built in 1797 by Dr. Joseph Priestley, the celebrated English chemist who discovered oxygen and other gases. The house is of clapboard, with many interesting details and some of the doctor's furniture. It is preserved as a memorial, and the small adjacent brick laboratory is a museum. The view is magnificent.

WESTERN PENNSYLVANIA

¶ *Farmington (near the southern border of western Pennsylvania 15 miles southeast of Uniontown on Route 40)*

MOUNT WASHINGTON TAVERN (*1816*)
On site of Fort Necessity; daily, 8:30 to 5; National Park Service.

The tavern is a big beautiful brick house with great double-chimney gable ends, one of the more impressive of the early-nineteenth-century stagecoach inns that lined the famous old National Road leading from the Atlantic to the West. And don't miss the old tollgate house a few miles farther east with its cut-stone octagonal tower. The tavern, of course, contains many relics of the battle as well as the furniture of its early inn days.

¶ *Ambridge (about 15 miles northwest of Pittsburgh on Route 88)*

OLD ECONOMY (*1824–1826*)
In the town; daily; 50 cents; state of Pennsylvania.

Here is not only the relic of an interesting experiment in communal living and industry but a fascinating museum of the domestic manufactures of the early nineteenth century. The Harmonist Movement began in Wurttemberg, then a kingdom in southern Germany, whence the adherents of lay preacher George Rapp followed their leader to this country in 1803. They made their first settlement at what is now Harmony, twenty miles north of Ambridge, where there are some interesting remains. Ten years later they sold their Harmony holdings most advantageously and moved to the banks of the Wabash in Indiana, where they founded New Harmony (see Indiana). This successful settlement they also sold again ten years later, and again to good advantage, this time to the English social theorist Robert Owen, and moved

back to Ambridge here. The thirty-five-room "great house," built by the Harmonists with their own handmade brick, was originally two separate homes for Father Rapp and his chief lieutenant, Frederick Reichert Rapp; it was made one house in 1832 by a connecting wing. Decline followed the adoption of celibacy in the colony and the death of Father Rapp. The society was finally dissolved in 1905. But in its halcyon days everything the Harmonists did, from weaving to wagon-making, could hardly have been done with more skill and enterprise. This is evident here at Ambridge.

¶ *New Geneva (a few miles north of Point Marion, on the West Virginia border, on Route 166)*

FRIENDSHIP HILL (*1789–1823*)
Daily, May to November; 75 cents and 50 cents; Mr. and Mrs. Sherwood C. Martin.

Albert Gallatin, who came as a young man to this country from Geneva, Switzerland, and later became Jefferson's Secretary of the Treasury, built the brick first section of "Friendship Hill" just before his marriage. Then, thirty-four years later he added the stone mansion to the earlier house, making of it today, in its ivy-covered beauty, a pleasant memento of this colorful and famous figure of our republic's early years.

¶ *Scenery Hill (on Route 40 between Brownsville and Washington near both "Friendship Hill" and Fort Necessity)*

CENTURY INN (*1794*)
Daily; Dr. G. F. Harrington.

This is said to be the oldest tavern on the entire length of the National Pike. Built as an inn by Stephen Hill, founder of the village, it has been operated continuously as a tavern ever since. It is a cut-stone structure, typical of the region, and if it has not been preserved exactly as it was originally, we must bear in mind that concessions have to be made now and then to the changing necessities and tastes of the patrons.

¶ *Pittsburgh*

CROGHAN HOUSE, *now* PICNIC HOUSE (*1830s*)
Daily; state of Pennsylvania.

The main feature of this great Classical Revival mansion is the remarkable quality of its interiors, ornamented with Corinthian details of a very high order, if a little heavy in places. But it was meant to be a house in which to entertain, and the name it now enjoys fits it to perfection.

¶ *Russell (8 miles north of Warren on Route 62 near New York State)*

THE LOCUSTS (*1835*)
Just out of town; by appointment, June 1 to October 30; Mrs. W. A. Walker.

This historic old Warren County house was built in 1835 by Guy Irvin, who was one of the largest lumber operators in western Pennsylvania at the time. On his many raft trips down the Allegheny, Ohio, and Mississippi Rivers, which carried him into the Deep South, he found the houses he passed to his liking and decided to make his own home a composite of those which he liked the best. And though he made a

Unfortunately not many of the fine western Pennsylvania early houses can be opened on occasion to the public. The Locusts, near Warren, is luckily an exception.

remarkably good job of the house, to tell the truth it turned out to be more than anything else a rather choice example of western Pennsylvania Georgian. The brick was made on the place, the lumber came from Mr. Irvin's own forests, and the stone from nearby quarries. The restoration and furnishings are well done.

¶ *Washington (at junction of Routes 19 and 40, southwest of Pittsburgh)*

LE MOYNE HOUSE (*1812*)
49 East Maiden Street; daily, 1 to 5; Washington County Historical Society.

This cut-stone domicile, with its rather severely classical details, stands flush to the sidewalk and has a dignified if slightly dour appearance from the street. A smaller door to the left of the somewhat monumental entrance led at one time into what was the office and pharmacy of Dr. Francis J. Le Moyne, who built the house and later made of it a station of the Underground Railway. He was a leading abolitionist and at one time an unsuccessful candidate for the Vice-presidency.

¶ *West Overton (near Scottdale on Route 119 about 30 miles southeast of Pittsburgh)*

OVERHOLT HOUSE (*1838*)
Just out of village; Saturdays and Sundays 2 to 5, other times by appointment; Westmoreland-Fayette County branch of Western Pennsylvania Historical Society, Richard T. Darsie (Secretary).

This charming old brick hillside house, with its high white porch, was built by Abram Overholt, maternal grandfather of Henry Clay Frick, who was born in a cottage on the place and became one of the greatest steel magnates and art collectors of his day. The rooms are furnished with more than usual interest, and a Federal room, a Mennonite room, and a historical room with wallsize murals of the French and Indian War are especially notable.

Ohio is famous for its broad, flat-arched, fanlighted doorways, many of them much more ornamented than this one that belongs to the Mower house in the very good town of Granville. And within the tall, two-story portico of the President's house at Marietta, on the opposite page, is another doorway of similar form and proportions.

OHIO

*I*F YOU had been planning to try your fortunes in the wilderness that was then Ohio in the late eighteenth century, and had been making your way from Tidewater Virginia, Maryland, or the Carolinas, you would have struck for the Ohio River; there at some point you would most likely have loaded your worldly goods on a barge or flatboat and floated down the river toward your destination. But if you had been coming from the New England states, you would in all probability have trekked along the southern shore of Lake Erie on horseback, if you were lucky enough to own a horse, your family jolting along behind in a Conestoga wagon. After

1798 there was yet another route—Zane's Trace, which connected Wheeling, West Virginia, with Maysville (then Limestone), Kentucky—a vital road for those determined to settle in the central portion of the state. In fact, later it was to be known as the "National Road," and today it stretches across the continent from Atlantic City to San Francisco under the designation "Route 40."

Naturally the influence of the New Englanders is plain to be seen in the early building in the northern part of the state, still known as the "Western Reserve," and many of the place names too are of Yankee origin. In the southern part occasional stately Georgian houses

195

and even a few columned mansions of the plantation type have survived. But it was to accommodate the great influx that came surging over Zane's Trace, swelling to still greater proportions after it became a highway, that the characteristic Ohio building—the inn—sprang up; in fact, it seems that almost every house in the state today has been an inn at some time during its career. Of the old houses that have survived the blights of commerce and fire, there are actually more inns than private dwellings. But the inns were, after all, built exactly like any large-family house of the period; and thus, even when there are few other old places in a neighborhood, the inn tells us quite as much about domestic building as would a private dwelling.

In recent years, Ohioans, increasingly conscious of their architectural heritage, have been restoring not only the early homes but many of the inns as well. Together they are a reminder of one of the most fascinating episodes in America's development.

¶ Northeastern Ohio

¶ Kinsman

ALLEN HOUSE (1820–1830)
Open as a tearoom; Miss Alice Logan.

Built by Dr. Peter Allen and inherited by his grandson Dr. Peter Dudley Allen, this can be truthfully described as one of the most delightfully unusual exteriors in Ohio. Richly but lightly ornamented, the exquisite carvings on window frames, doorway, and entablature are something to behold. The four full-height fluted pilasters with Ionic capitals are echoed by the short pilasters which stand on either side of the door, whose entablature is a little master-

Another familiar feature so typical of early Ohio houses is the pilastered front. The Matthews house at Painesville is a particularly fine example, with good Greek Revival details.

piece of sunbursts and delicately carved moldings. It is a mansion in miniature, and its interior detail is equally fine in quality.

¶ *Unionville* (*between Painesville and Ashtabula*)

SHANDY HALL (*1815, enlarged 1825*)
   Near Cleveland on Route 84, 1 mile east of Unionville Tavern; daily 10 to 5 except Mondays, May 1 to November 1; 50 cents and 15 cents; Western Reserve Historical Society.

A pioneer homestead of weather-beaten clapboard, of whose rambling seventeen rooms the banquet hall is the chef-d'oeuvre. It has a flat, barrel-vaulted ceiling, and between it and the low dado is a magnificent French wallpaper that made this room the wonder of the frontier countryside.

¶ *Painesville*

MATTHEWS HOUSE (*1829*)
   497 Mentor Avenue; campus of Lake Erie College; by appointment to limited groups; Mrs. Dean C. Matthews.

This house is one of a small group in the town built by the Western Reserve's architect-builder Jonathan Goldsmith, who came here from Connecticut in 1811 and died here thirty-seven years later. His work also survives in Mentor, Willoughby, and Cleveland. The Matthews House was moved to the campus of Lake Erie College and restored. It is a choice Greek Revival house whose owner has furnished it appropriately with antiques, some of them here originally. The stairway with its carving and delicate spindles is a good example of Goldsmith's fine detailing, as is the ornate exterior of the doorway with its drape carvings.

LUTZ'S TAVERN (*1822*)
   792 Mentor Avenue (Route 20); open all the time; Park and Gerald A. Lutz (proprietors).

Originally Rider's and Randall's Tavern, it was first a stopping place on the Indian trail between Buffalo and Cleveland. Its "Mt. Vernon" front was added shortly after the inn was first built. Its six square piers are built around rough-hewn posts; a small door has been cut in one of them so that the guest may examine the construc-

tion. The inn has been well restored fairly recently and is furnished with antiques.

¶ *Cleveland*

DUNHAM TAVERN MUSEUM (*1842*)
   6709 Euclid Avenue; daily 12:30 to 4:30 except Mondays; contribution; Society of Collectors.

An important stopping place on what was the old Buffalo-Cleveland-Detroit stage road, it was built by Rufus and Jane Pratt Dunham, immigrants from Massachusetts. A tavern until 1857, it was a country home from then until 1930. Meanwhile, Cleveland had swallowed up almost everything of this nature, and the Society of Collectors there did a great service to the community in preserving this fascinating old landmark. There are appropriate period furnishings as well as special exhibits.

¶ *Hudson*

SEYMOUR HOUSE (*1841*)
   15 Prospect Street; by written or phone request; Mr. and Mrs. C. K. Reynolds, Jr.

Nathan Perkins Seymour came to Western Reserve Academy in 1834 from Yale, of which his grandson was later President. Nathan brought his bride, joined the faculty here, and built this finely proportioned brick house. Its construction was in the competent hands of the Connecticut carpenters, the Porters, who had come here to build the college buildings. It is said that, in spite of their excellent reputation, young Dr. Seymour watched every brick being laid; since he was a classical perfectionist, he wanted his home to be perfect. The present owners mean to keep it that way too and have left some of the rooms completely unchanged. The furniture is antique, with occasional contemporary pieces.

The PRESIDENT'S HOUSE and the BLISS or SLAUGHTER HOUSE on the campus of Western Reserve Academy are occupied by members of the faculty, and while no particular attempt has been made to furnish them in keeping, they are houses with much period charm whose interior woodwork has been left intact. Requests may be made to the residents, Mr. and Mrs. E. Mark Worthen, and Mr. and Mrs. Richard MacFarlane, respectively.

OLD STAGE COACH INN or
SINGLETARY HOUSE (*an antique shop*)
(*1828*)
> *Near Hudson at Streetsboro; Mr. and Mrs. Carlton Close.*

Considered a showplace throughout the area, like so many others of an early vintage in this state, it was built as an inn. It is a handsome white clapboard dwelling with possibly one of the most interesting doorways in Ohio.

¶ *Zoar* (*near New Philadelphia*)

This historical village was established in 1817 by a group of three hundred Separatists from Wurttemberg, led by Joseph Baumeler. Although the Zoarites came for religious freedom, they were not a severe sect, and their houses reflected German comfort and color. They were roofed with red tile, and both interior and exterior were brightly painted, several colors sometimes being used in one room. Painted decorations may be seen on the furniture, much after the manner of the Pennsylvania Dutch. The town was surrounded by apple orchards and a magnificent community garden, much of which is still maintained. Love of flowers and music seems to have predominated in this industrious community, which soon became self-sustaining. Its beer has become legendary.

WILLIAM AND LILLIAN BIMELER HOUSE, NUMBER ONE HOUSE, JOSEPH BAUMELER'S HOUSE
(*all prior to Civil War*)
> *Daily 9 to 5 except Mondays, April 1 to October 30; state of Ohio.*

These homes were built simply, with the exception of Baumeler's house, which was originally intended as a home for the aged and certainly reflects the success of the colony. Of red brick, and two and a half stories high, it is an ornate mansion in the Late Georgian Colonial style, pillared, porticoed, and iron-railed. The Bimeler House, a plain two-story brick, is more typical. Both houses have indigenous collections of Zoar products of all kinds, including interesting pottery, weaving, and musical instruments. A few rooms are furnished.

¶ *New Philadelphia*

SCHOENBRUNN MEMORIAL STATE PARK
> (*Thirteen log cabins, church, and school*) *daily; state of Ohio.*

Three Moravian missionaries from Pennsylvania led a band of Christian Indians to the banks of the Tuscarawus River, where they founded the first village in what is now Ohio. Here all the Christian Indians were killed and scalped by whites—one of the uglier episodes in our frontier history. The village is an expert and edifying reconstruction.

¶ *Central Ohio*

¶ *Mt. Vernon*

CURTIS-DEVIN HOUSE (*1834*)
> *208 North Main Street; by written request; Fletcher M. Devin, 208 North Main Street.*

This house was altered in 1850 according to the prevalent Greek Revival fashion, at which time the balconies to the front, the huge scrolled acroteria surmounting the gable, and the balustrade at the eaves were doubtless added. The marble mantels were probably done by two English stonecutters in Gambier who came here to work on Kenyon College. The staircase is particularly noteworthy, with its simple, delicate spindles and its finely carved stringers. The narrow paneling which forms the wall beneath is repeated in the deep dado broken by a niche midway up the stairs. The whole thing is executed with real taste and skill.

¶ *Granville*

AVERY-DOWNER HOUSE (*1842*)
> *221 East Broadway; on request; Denison University.*

Now a sorority house, this is a remarkably

pure example of Greek Revival, built by Benjamin Morgan for Alfred Avery. The central two-story portion has four fluted Ionic columns supporting a deep unornamented pediment. The one-story wings repeat the central design. The effect of the place is chaste and charming.

MOWER HOUSE (*1824*)

> *233 East Broadway; open with advance notice; Mr. and Mrs. A. H. Heisey.*

This was the residence of Granville's leading citizen back in the second quarter of the nineteenth century. Later it was used for many years as a local bank, but it is now again a very gracious and attractive home, beautifully furnished in periods preceding the date of the house itself.

¶ Newark

DAVIDSON HOUSE (*c. 1815*)

> *In Moundbuilders Park; Wednesday and Sunday afternoons; Licking County Historical Society.*

A white clapboard house moved here from downtown Newark in 1948 and now set in a green park with its own walks and brick-walled gardens, this is a delightful and unusual piece of architecture with strong Federal feeling. The delicacy of the detailing on the doorway is extraordinary, and the recessed bay under the side gable, with its flat-arch form and its gallery, is a striking feature. In fact, it is considered one

of the finest doorways in the Middle West. It is furnished in period, many of the articles having been made in Newark or nearby, and there is an interesting collection of Ohio primitive painting.

¶ Zanesville

HEADLEY INN (*now a restaurant*) (*1802–1865*)

> *Between Zanesville and Springfield on Route 40; daily 9 to 5 except Mondays, June 1 to October 1; Mrs. Harry Ackerman and Mrs. E. B. Howard.*

One of the most famous of all the famous early inns of Ohio, it was originally a drover tavern. Mrs. Uzdal Headley was known the whole length of the old National Road for her cooking. Built of huge blocks of dressed sandstone two to three feet long, a foot high, and eighteen inches wide, it is a kind of Ohio landmark, whose owners have preserved much of the early atmosphere. Big open fireplaces in the dining rooms still glow cheerfully in cold weather. In one of the beamed rooms the old sassafras tables and benches are still in use. See the upstairs rooms and the narrow, enclosed stairway that leads to them, with its rare grapevine pattern painted in polychrome on the riser baseboards—the work of Amos Edgerley, who married Uzdal's sister. A fascinating old inn, and the fare deserves its fame.

This early example of split-level planning is the Headley Inn outside Zanesville on Route 40— one of the most popular stopping places along the old National Road to the West from pioneer days to the present.

HILLSIDE (*1834*)

> *461 Luck Avenue; May 15 through July, by appointment only; Mr. and Mrs. Clarence Graham.*

This impressive house with its classical portico crowns a hilly section of the city which was nicknamed "Natchez" by the river boatmen because it reminded them of the famous Mississippi town on its hill. There is a notable pair of mantels in the immense living room.

ROBBINS HOUSE

> *115 Jefferson Street; by written request; Mrs. R. M. Taylor.*

Occupied for sixty years by the owner's parents but not lived in now. The unusual cornerstones and quoins draw the attention of many passers-by. Other houses to note are the GUTHRIE HOUSE (1842), a stunning brick house with a classical portico supported by four fluted columns; the BUCKINGHAM HOUSE and the MATTHEWS HOUSE, with their very good Ohio doorways.

UNITY FARM (*1834*)

> *McConnelsville, 15 miles south of Zanesville; April and May, by appointment; Mr. and Mrs. E. C. Jones.*

Unity Farm was built as a stagecoach inn on the banks of the Muskingum when the mail route ran between Zanesville and Marietta. It is a long white building of simple distinction which has been thoughtfully restored by its owners. It has some of the original stenciled walls, as well as firebacks of museum quality.

¶ *Chillicothe*

ADENA (*1806–1807*)

> *April 1 to October 30, Daily 9 to 5 except Mondays, balance of year, daily 1 to 5; state of Ohio.*

"Adena" was known first as Mt. Prospect. Thomas Worthington, one of the first two United States senators from Ohio, made the acquaintance of Benjamin Latrobe in 1805, when the famous Baltimore architect was at work on the south wing of the Capitol. He commissioned Latrobe to design this twenty-room mansion for his fifteen-thousand-acre estate. It remained in the family until 1903. Worthington, who came from Virginia, was Governor of Ohio from 1814 to 1818. He was buried in a Duncan Phyfe casket; the governor desired good cabinetry at all times. "Adena" has been beautifully restored. The chastity of the interior is enlivened by the wonderful color treatment of walls and ceilings. Six of the rooms have handmade wallpapers and authentic draperies in which the materials are at least a hundred and fifty years old. The family has returned many of the original pieces of furniture, and the collection now includes an outstanding set of Duncan Phyfe and other pieces of Sheraton and Hepplewhite used

The hand of a truly talented architect is apparent in the north front of Adena near Chillicothe—one of the best country houses Benjamin Latrobe ever designed.

Adena is now strikingly furnished with heirloom pieces that have been returned to the house; one of the handsomest early houses in Ohio.

by the governor. The masons were the two Morris brothers from Virginia; the iron, carpets, and brasswork came from Philadelphia; the window glass from Albert Gallatin in Gallatin, Pennsylvania; and the wallpapers from Baltimore. Local carpenters made many of the chairs, bedsteads, bureaus, wardrobes, tables, sofas, and clockcases, using mahogany and local cherry. This is a house that illustrates its own story to perfection.

¶ *London*

RED BRICK TAVERN (*1837*)

> *Halfway between Columbus and Springfield on Route 40; open March to January; Mrs. Nell Brasket (phone: London 401).*

A handsome red-brick tavern with double end chimneys and spanking white trim, this old inn is one of the best-looking in the state. It can boast of having served six Presidents, beginning with John Quincy Adams and ending with Warren Gamaliel Harding. Harrison and Van Buren met here in a "smoke-filled room," and the famous slogan "Tippecanoe and Tyler too" is said to have been hatched here.

¶ *Lakeview*

MANARY BLOCKHOUSE MUSEUM (*1812*)

> *On Route 69, at northern end of town; May to September; 25 cents.*

A log house built by Captain James Manary during the War of 1812, it served as a refuge for pioneers following the Hull Trail. In 1823 James McPherson bought it, plugged its rifle ports, and made it into his home. It now contains more than 1,000 relics of the period 1800–1825, rare cotton prints of the 1770s, and willow and hickory chairs.

¶ Northwestern Ohio

¶ *Norwalk*

STURGIS-KENNAN-FULSTOW HOUSE (*1834*)

> *99 West Main Street; by written appointment during summer months; Col. and Mrs. Philip H. Fulstow.*

One of the finest homes here, and Greek Revival, of course. The pediment, supported by four octagonal columns, is decorated with an oval sunburst. Said to have been designed by William Gale Meade, who also built the Vredenburgh House that is owned by Mrs. Fulstow's brother. Contemporary furnishings.

Other good examples are the VREDENBURGH-GARDINER HOUSE (1832), 133 West Main Street; the WOOSTER-BOALT HOUSE (c. 1830s), 114 West Main Street; the KIMBALL-WOOSTER-MARTIN HOUSE (c. 1830s), 54 Main Street, a real Greek Revival beauty; and the OLD BAKER HOUSE (1830), 207 East Main Street.

¶ *Waterville* (*southeast of Toledo on 24*)

THE COLUMBIAN HOUSE (*1837, wing 1828*)

Ethel N. Arnold, 405 West Sandusky Street, Finley, Ohio.

Built as an inn by John Pray, one of the earliest settlers in the Maumee Valley, it was a stagecoach stop between Detroit and Dayton, and the social center of the community. An old lady told the owner that she could remember riding horseback over forty miles as a girl, her party gown in the saddle bag, to attend the balls given here. It is a fine-looking three-story building, well proportioned, with three doorways flush with the pavement. It has all its original woodwork: six-panel black walnut doors, dados in almost every room, and carved moldings in the ballroom on the third floor. Reopened as an inn some years ago, its owner hopes to open again soon.

¶ *Milan* (*a few miles north of Norwalk*)

In the 1840s, thanks to the canal that linked it with the Great Lakes, Milan was one of the leading grain ports of the world—for ten prosperous years. Then came the railroads!

MITCHELL-TURNER HOUSE (*1828*)

128 Center Street; not open now; Mr. Jay Fenn.

This is a charming Greek Revival house with a most handsomely wrought Ionic portico, as ornamental and appealing as an old-fashioned valentine. A lovely sight from the sidewalk. May be seen at some later time.

GALPIN HOUSE, MILAN HISTORICAL SOCIETY (*1840s*)

10 Edison Drive; May 1 to October 1, daily 1 to 5 except Mondays; Milan Public Library and Milan Historical Society.

A three-story red-brick house of substance and distinction, with the white trim and white shutters typical of the better Ohio town houses of the period, it was owned by Dr. Loman Galpin, who delivered a neighbor's baby christened Thomas Alva Edison. The parlor and kitchen are furnished in the period, and there is an In-

dian room. The remaining rooms are used for collections and exhibits but are due to be furnished.

EDISON BIRTHPLACE (*1841*)

11 Edison Drive; April 1 to December 1 Tuesday through Saturday 9 to 5, Sundays 1 to 5, January 1 to April 1 Thursday through Saturday 9 to 5 and by appointment (closed December); 50 cents and 25 cents; Mrs. Madeleine Edison Sloane.

This charmingly simple little brick house was designed and built by Samuel Edison, father of Thomas, when the town was a flourishing grain port. The family lived here until 1853, when they moved to Port Huron, Michigan. The house is appropriately and very pleasantly furnished, and contains many of the great inventor's personal possessions. Very engaging.

¶ *In & out of Lebanon*

GLENDOWER (*1836*)

Route 42; daily 9 to 5 except Mondays; 25 cents and 10 cents; state of Ohio, Ohio State Architectural and Historical Society, Mrs. William Mason Phillips (curator).

This is the chef-d'oeuvre of the Lebanon area. Greek Revival was going great guns when Amos Bennett, carpenter and joiner, built "Glendower" for J. Milton Williams, an outstanding lawyer and public figure of his day. Its recessed panels and entrance columns, its window grille in the attic, and the frieze on its low flanking wings are typical manifestations of the fashion which produced this truly distinguished brick mansion. It has been beautifully restored and furnished with original pieces from Warren County homes.

THE GOLDEN LAMB (*an inn*) (*1815*)

Mr. and Mrs. Robert H. Jones (proprietors).

This is a landmark—the oldest hostelry in the state, licensed December 23, 1803. It is known that in 1807 a two-story log inn existed on the spot, for, when the first copy of *The Western Star* came out in that year, advertisers located their shops in relation to Mr. Seamon's tavern. Ichabod Corwin built the present commodious brick building. "Charles Dickens, Esq. and Lady" registered here in 1842. Ten Presidents and many other celebrities have also been guests; some have had rooms named for them.

LEWIS HOUSE (*1846*)

144 East Mulberry Street; by written or phone request (Lebanon 3–2306); Mrs. Hazel Brookes, Lebanon.

The house has been occupied by the present owner's family since it was built, and, except for the 1900 porch, nothing has been added. The present owner's thrice-married mother was her thrice-married father's last wife; she was alive until 1945. Thus the house was occupied continuously by one husband and his wives for ninety-nine years—probably a record. Aunts and uncles moved in from time to time and in passing left their things in the house. "Therefore," says Mrs. Brookes, "it is a conglomeration and we are sentimental about some of the most insignificant items." The double parlors are impressive, and the walnut railing of the three-story open-well staircase has an unusually free form and newel post, spokes, and rail of rare finesse. There are fireplaces in almost every room; in the parlors the mantels have rare tile facings. Twin Venetian-glass chandeliers are reflected in pier glasses reaching to the ceiling. The original cornices and draperies, the excellent furniture and old family portraits all create in this fine period piece an atmosphere of well-to-do Midwestern family life in the mid-nineteenth century.

BRYNFRYD (*1840s*)

Cincinnati Avenue; by written or phone request; Mr. and Mrs. Wallace S. Howell.

A most impressive foursquare Greek Revival mansion in its own little park. With two-story columns across the front and a balustraded deck on the flat hip roof, it is engagingly romantic, yet eminently livable. A nostalgic touch is the old coach house on the grounds with its iron window grilles.

THE GOTHIC (*1840s*)

Cincinnati Avenue; by written or phone request; Mr. and Mrs. J. Alfred Jackson.

The ornamental bargeboards, sharp rooflines, balconies, and narrow Gothic windows provide the romantic flavor that gave this house its name. Victorian can be winning when it wants to be. The detail is equally attractive inside, with finely designed Gothic arches in the halls, spacious rooms, and antique furniture, some of it much earlier than the house.

BRANSBY FARM (*1855*)

Route 48, 5 miles north of Lebanon; on written request; Mrs. William Mason Phillips.

This well-proportioned white frame colonial is as sound today as when it was built a hundred years ago by John Plunkett, a native of Virginia. Among the rare items here is a pressed-glass punch bowl, one of a pair that belonged to Henry Clay; the other is in his home "Ashland" in Kentucky.

Stately and stylish, Glendower is one of the outstanding country mansions in the neighborhood of Lebanon.

ASHLEY (*1850*)

> *Maple Street, Harveysburg, northeast of Lebanon; on request; Mr. and Mrs. J. E. Welsh, Box 81.*

Colloquial Greek Revival, with a tall central section with foursquare columns and pediment, and low flanking wings, this was an active station on the Underground Railway. Furnished entirely with fine antiques.

OAK HILL (*1838*)

> *9 miles south on 48 at Morrow; open on request; 50 cents toward public library and upkeep of extensive grounds; Mr. and Mrs. Richard S. Whitacre.*

The house might be called "Ohio antebellum," exemplifying as it does the days of the 1840s and 1850s. The present owners' great-grandfather, who built it, was General Superintendent of the Little Miami Railroad (now the Pennsylvania), which ran nearby, and was the son-in-law of Cincinnati's pioneer cabinetmaker and clockmaker, accounting for much of the furnishings. The original draperies in the drawing room are of East Indian sailcloth, more than a century old, and painted in exquisitely faded colors. The crystal chandeliers are still lit with candles. Servants' quarters and carriage houses are also on the lovely grounds.

FERNEYCROFT (*1842*)

> *Lebanon; by written request, 1 to 5; voluntary donation accepted; Mrs. Georgette Glosser Stubbs, R.F.D. 3.*

As Mrs. Stubbs remarks, "The outstanding fact is that 'Ferneycroft' has been owned and occupied by the family for five generations. Visitors enjoy the evidence of how 'living the hard way' was accomplished a century ago."

¶ Up the Ohio from Cincinnati

¶ Cincinnati

SINTON-TAFT HOUSE (*a museum*) (*1820*)

> *4th and Pike Streets, near center of town; weekdays 1 to 5, Sundays and holidays 2 to 5; Cincinnati Institute of Fine Arts.*

This is in many ways the most unusual Classical Revival house west of the Eastern seaboard states. Said to have been designed by Benjamin Latrobe, it is quite Adamesque in its delicacy and adornments. Full of Federal-period style and dazzling white, its impressive entrance portico is approached by a graceful flight of steps. Steps and porch are guarded by ornamental iron railings. It contains much excellent furniture, creating a homelike but palatial setting for its fine collections, including Rembrandts, Turners, Goyas, and Corots.

KEMPER LOG CABIN (*1804*)

> *Zoological Garden, 3400 Vine Street; daily 10 to 5 May to October, rest of year Sundays, weather permitting; 10 cents and 5 cents; Colonial Dames.*

Really a two-story log dwelling, reputed the oldest within the Miami Purchase, it is furnished with primitive pieces of the pioneer variety.

¶ Pt. Pleasant (*on the Ohio southeast of Cincinnati*)

GRANT HOUSE MUSEUM (*before 1822*)

> *Grant Memorial State Park, junction of Routes 52 and 232; daily 9 to 5 April 1 to October 30, rest of year 1 to 5; state of Ohio.*

The house in which the President was born is tiny and unpretentious. It contains many personal belongings, including his cradle, his Bible, the trunk he took to West Point, and his favorite cigar case.

¶ Ripley (*on the Ohio northeast of Cincinnati*)

JOHN RANKIN HOUSE (*date unknown*)

> *Daily 9 to 5 except Mondays, April 1 to October 30, rest of year 1 to 5; state of Ohio.*

The state honors the Reverend John Rankin, a great abolitionist, by making his small brick house into a memorial for him. It was a station on the Underground Railway and because of its high location could cast a light which might be seen for miles across the Ohio River. Local legend claims that Eliza of *Uncle Tom's Cabin* crossed on the floating ice near here and was one of the many slaves to be succored at this house. After the war Ripley became a haven for freed Negroes, who also made, across the river, settlements named "Pomposity" and "Africa."

The Sinton-Taft house in Cincinnati, the home of two distinguished Ohio families, and now the home of a distinguished art collection.

¶ *Marietta*

Named in gratitude for Marie Antoinette, the Queen of our Revolutionary allies, this town at the junction of the Ohio and the Muskingum is the site of Marietta College and was one of the most important pioneer outposts during the western migrations after the Revolution. It is the oldest surviving Ohio settlement.

RUFUS PUTNAM HOUSE
(before 1788)
In the Campus Martius State Memorial Museum; daily, 9 to 5; state of Ohio.

Putnam is the man who led an important early group of settlers to this section where an elaborate scheme of dwellings in the form of a hollow square, which they called the "Campus Martius," served as a fortification. His house was one of the four substantial corner houses and is the only structure of the development still standing. It is now in the Campus Martius Museum. The framework is mortised and braced at the corners with dovetailed diagonal pieces held in place by wooden pins. The house is furnished in keeping with the style of its period. In it are some of Putnam's possessions, many others being in the museum itself, along with a host of relics from this extraordinary pioneer project. In the rear of the museum is the little 1788 land office of the Ohio Company, a fascinating restoration by the Colonial Dames.

THE PRESIDENT'S HOME *(1818)*
301 5th Street; on request to President's office; Marietta College, W. Bay Irvine (President).

Built by Henry P. Wilcox, who came here from Alabama in the early part of the century, this house is a small Southern Colonial mansion, even to the high-terraced approach with its double flight of steps, whose wrought-iron railings are supposed to be the midcentury work of a professor at the college here. The inside stairway, which terminates in a dome, or shell, is sculptured of wood. In 1825, a year after the house was finished, the builder departed, leaving a few debts to be settled. The property went to the Mills family, in which it remained for more than a hundred years, after which the college acquired it.

¶ *Gallipolis (junction of 7 and 23, on Ohio River)*

OUR HOUSE *(1819)*
434 First Avenue; daily except Monday 9 to 5, rest of year 1 to 5; state of Ohio.

Of Late Georgian colonial design, this two-story brick house with its end chimneys and two arched and paneled doorways was built as a hostelry by Henry Cushing, whose hospitable "Come up to our house" created the name. Much of the interior is original; the carving on the mantels is unusually refined for a tavern in the wilderness, as are the arched doors with their graceful fanlights. Beautifully made also is the circular stairway of walnut and cherry. The original lighting fixtures are in place, as well as the taproom chairs, tables, and settees, and the bed in which slept Louis Philippe, later to become King of France. Lafayette stopped here in 1825, and Jenny Lind in 1851. The third floor has possessions of the ill-fated early French refugees, who arrived in these parts in 1790, five hundred strong. Mostly small tradesmen from cities, they were unable to cope with the wilderness and were practically wiped out by disease, starvation, and Indians.

One of the best hunting grounds for good early houses in Indiana is down along the Ohio River, and one of the best towns along the river is Madison, where stand both Shrewsbury House and the Lanier home, two of Indiana's best, both the work of the remarkable early carpenter architect, Francis Costigan. The staircase in Shrewsbury House, above, is one of his tours de force; the Lanier home opposite one of his most monumental mansions.

INDIANA

HOOSIER is the name given to a state which has its own strong individuality, yet seems more typically American than almost any other. Pioneer traffic east and west flowed unceasingly through it, and earlier still it flowed north and south as well, for the French fur trappers and traders who first settled around Vincennes came north from New Orleans and south from Quebec. At that time they did not go farther west because the prairie lay beyond. Thus it was here that the English, German, and Scotch-Irish pioneers met up with the French; consequently a melting pot for our dominant ancestral strains came into being. Yankee shrewdness and toughness of fiber were to combine with the politesse of gentlemen adventurers from Virginia and the Carolinas to produce a kind of special type: a sturdy and substantial individual who was knowing rather than shrewd, and friendly rather than polite— a man in essence democratic. All this does not explain how he came by the name Hoosier but it does throw some light on the particular meaning the name has taken on—a name which next to Yankee seems to be a kind of joking symbol for "real American."

From this confluence of different peoples you might expect to find several styles of home building, and indeed you will. For once the necessary log-cabin stage was in the past; the early houses and buildings that are found in the state represent a wide range of influences. On the whole, Hoosiers do not seem to have amassed the great fortunes encountered in many other sections of the country during the days of cheap land and cheaper labor. Nor, for the most part, were they a folk given to ostentation. Mansions of the Lanier variety in Madison occurred infrequently. But of comfortable town houses on the modest scale there were numbers, and we can see some of them today in the Ohio River towns such as Madison and Vevay, neat, stylish, well-built, denoting a pleasant way of life.

¶ Bruceville

BRUCE HOUSE (1811)
Open any time; Mrs. Ruth McClure Ashby.

This is the house in which Lincoln slept one night when he came here to address a political meeting for Henry Clay. Lincoln's host had twenty-five children, who bedded down on the unfinished second floor, since then removed. The famous guest's bedroom on the first floor is still intact with the bed he slept in; so are the wide plank floors, deep window sills, heavy hinges on the doors—everything as it was, very simple and utilitarian.

¶ Corydon (25 miles west of Louisville on Route 62)

The site of Corydon, on a steep hillside, was originally owned by Gen. William Henry Harrison. After the Northwest Territory had been divided, the seat of the government was moved here from Vincennes and in 1816 it became, for a time, the state capital, which accounts for some of its fine little buildings.

STATE TREASURY (1817)
Mulberry Street; by phone appointment; Mr. and Mrs. William B. Doolittle.

Occupied until recently by the Doolittles, descendants of Amzi Brewster, the original householder. The Doolittles are glad to show this most interesting early example even though the interior is not presently in exhibition form.

See also the old STATE CAPITOL between Beaver and Walnut.

HENDRICKS-PORTER-GRIFFIN HOUSE (1817)
Walnut Street; upon written request; Miss Olive Griffin.

William Hendricks, third Governor of the state (1822–1825), lived here. In 1841 Judge William A. Porter purchased it, and his granddaughter now occupies it. A small brick house with a two-room wing of limestone two feet thick, the house has its original woodwork, and has been little changed since the days when it was the governor's residence.

MANSION OF COL. THOMAS LLOYD POSEY (1818)
Oak Street at west end of Cherry; weekdays, 9 to 4; Hoosier Elm Chapter of D.A.R.

The Colonel Posey in question was the son of the famous territorial governor Thomas Posey, and was known as a great church worker. He never married, but as part of his good works he reared fourteen orphan children. He was the state Adjutant General. The brick house is furnished with local material dating from the early part of the century—pioneer relics for the most part.

¶ Crawfordsville (Home of Wabash College, 45 miles northwest of Indianapolis on Route 34)

HENRY S. LANE PLACE (1836, remodeled in 1845)
212 South Water Street; weekdays, except Mondays; 10 cents; city of Crawfordsville (headquarters of Montgomery County Historical Society).

The builder was the first chairman of the Republican Party, a Governor of the state, and a United States Senator; he was a potent factor in the nomination of Lincoln as well. The house, a handsome fourteen-room brick mansion, sits in a little park which is beautifully landscaped. The detail of the interior has considerable style. There is a large and interesting collection of furniture of the 1845-to-1865 vintage, a doll room, and a pioneer room, among others. The rooms are well arranged and the whole place well kept up.

¶ Greenfield (20 miles east of Indianapolis on Route 40)

RILEY HOMESTEAD (1849)
304 West Main Street (Route 40); April 15 to November 1, daily; 25 cents and 10 cents; city of Greenfield.

Birthplace of the poet, this is a simple but

The unpretentious Posey house is one of the many attractions of the old river town of Corydon.

spacious and comfortable ten-room frame house situated in the heart of the farm land. With large fireplaces and walnut woodwork, it is furnished as it was when Riley was a boy. It contains his pictures, letters, and manuscripts.

¶ *Hanover (5 miles west of Madison near the Ohio River)*

BIRD HAVEN (*1858*)
> *In summer and early fall; to visitors not staying here, 25 cents; Miss Jane Rogers, Box 153.*

Now a guest house, this is Victorian Gothic at its most charming, with steep roof, gables, and lacy scroll trimming. Its furniture is heirloom, some much earlier than the house.

¶ *Indianapolis*

BENJAMIN HARRISON HOME (*1874*)
> *1230 North Delaware Street; daily 10 to 4 May 15 to October 15, daily 1 to 4 October to May (closed two weeks in March and during Christmas holidays); 30 cents and 10 cents; Arthur Jordan Foundation.*

Built by the most illustrious son of Indiana, the twenty-third President of the United States, descended from the long line of Harrisons who have served the country with such distinction, this house offers a beautiful demonstration of the differences in architecture and decoration between the pioneer days when William Henry Harrison built his home near Vincennes (see "Grouseland") and the plush period of Benjamin Harrison, when Indians and buffaloes were a thing of the legendary past and life in these parts was established and prosperous. Here you have the fashionable house of its period—a two-story brick Regency with bay windows and ornate stone trim; its draperies, mirrors, carpets, and ornaments, stiff gilt and carved furniture evoke the gaslight era.

JAMES WHITCOMB RILEY HOME (*1872*)
> *528 Lockerbie Street; 10 to 4 daily except Mondays, open Sundays; 25 cents; James Whitcomb Riley Association.*

Riley, the pride of Indiana, whose poetry is now part of our cherished regional literature, lived in later life in this tall, stately Victorian house with its high-arched, stone-trimmed windows and doors. Definitely the dwelling of a successful man, it is furnished exactly as it was when the poet lived here, the atmosphere unique and personal.

The Riley home in Indianapolis has much to offer admirers of the Hoosier poet as well as the nostalgic eccentricities of Victorian.

¶ *Madison*

(on Ohio River halfway between Cincinnati and Louisville)

When the Ohio River was a main artery of commerce, Madison, located almost midway between Cincinnati and Louisville, was the most prosperous town in the state. Two remarkable houses survive this era, and a number of others of considerable interest line the streets near the river. Francis Costigan, who learned his trade as a carpenter's apprentice in Baltimore, is responsible for the two mentioned. Much of the elaborate carving in the Costigan houses was his own handiwork. Both are distinguished not only for their opulence but for the bold skill and ingenuity of their execution. They were built only thirty years after Madison was hacked out of the wilderness.

JAMES F. D. LANIER HOME (*1844*)

1st Street between Elm and Vine Streets; daily; 25 cents and 10 cents; Indiana Department of Conservation.

Sitting on its eminence facing the broad, brown Ohio, the south portico is impressive in every way. Richly carved are the capitals of the four great columns, which support a deep two-story portico whose ceiling is stunningly ornamented with three enormous squares centered in medallions. Engaged columns of the Tuscan order flank the ends of the front entrance and

The famous Lanier home is furnished completely in character.

the windows. The noble scale of this façade is further accented by the graceful iron grille, which repeats the octagonal pattern used in the windows of the frieze and used again in the glass cupola to which the spiral staircase in the hall ascends. Lanier, a North Carolinian by birth, and a financier and patriot who is said to have financed Indiana's part in the Civil War, built the place, and it remained in his family until it was given to the state by his granddaughter in 1925. She was then over eighty. She helped to furnish it as it had looked when her family lived there. The substantial carved furniture of the period of her childhood suits the massive scale of the house. It was a completely successful re-creation, for, in spite of its great size, this house has a wonderfully homelike quality. The emphasis is on the solid, comfortable impression of good living.

SHREWSBURY HOUSE (*1849*)

Southwest corner 1st and Poplar Streets; during January and February advisable to make appointment; 25 cents for house only; Mr. and Mrs. John T. Windle (antique dealers).

In many ways just as much a masterpiece as the Lanier Home and actually built before it, the two-story brick mansion cost about fifty thousand dollars (a tidy sum in those days), which indicates that the Shrewsburys were, to say the least, prosperous. Shrewsbury, as a member of the state supreme court, was one of Madison's outstanding citizens then. Set close to other houses, it has large side galleries and a very fine Regency doorway framing a twelve-foot door; this sets the scale for what follows. As you enter the hall, therefore, the grace and lightness of the staircase is astonishing. Freestanding, it spirals upward like a climbing vine, and is considered something of a structural marvel. There are twelve large rooms in the house and thirteen fireplaces. The ceiling height is impressive. The division between the twin drawing rooms, with their black-marble mantels, is made by double pairs of Corinthian columns, and the heavy framing of the windows reflects the Empire forms and figurations which were a result of Napoleon's Egyptian Campaign. All the woodwork is of temple proportions, yet it is paradoxically domestic in feeling. The first coats of white paint on these walls have never been covered and still look perfectly fresh. Here too are the original Louis Philippe crystal chandeliers. Architecturally the house is unaltered; indeed, this would be a job terrible to contemplate in these times. It is still in excellent condition. The Windles, who house their antique collections here, have been fortunate in acquiring the four Shrewsbury portraits, which hang in the drawing room.

OLD SULLIVAN HOME (*1816*)

> *1st and Poplar Streets; open by request; Mrs. Louise K. Gibb.*

The first two-story brick house in Madison, this neat Federal-style home was built by Judge Jeremiah Sullivan, who named Indianapolis. Floors, woodwork, and carved mantels are all original. Care has been given to conforming to the period in the furnishing.

¶ *Mitchell (between Bedford and French Lick on Route 37)*

SPRING MILL VILLAGE

> (*restored houses of early-nineteenth-century Indiana*)
>
> *Route 60, Spring Mill State Park; state of Indiana.*

The following buildings were moved here from various places and restored in order to give an authentic picture of a typical village as it might have developed between 1815 and 1830: the APOTHECARY SHOP (c. 1830), the DISTILLERY (1825), the GRANNY WHITE HOUSE (1824), the GRISTMILL (1814), the HAT FACTORY (1816), the MILL OFFICE (1818), the MONTGOMERY TAVERN (1816), the MUNSON RESIDENCE (c. 1830), the POST OFFICE AND GENERAL STORE (c. 1830), the SAWMILL (1825), and the SPRINGHOUSE (1840).

¶ *New Albany (across Ohio River from Louisville, Kentucky)*

SCRIBNER HOUSE (*1814*)

> *East Main Street; open on application to caretaker, daily 9 to 5; Piankeshaw Chapter, D.A.R.*

This is a simple frame house, restored and furnished with pieces of the pioneer period

The great double parlors of Shrewsbury House are big-scale Greek Revival.

given by friends, and with a few Scribner family pieces brought from New York (probably by covered wagon). A typical pioneer home of the time.

¶ *New Harmony (in southwest corner of state on Illinois line, on Route 460)*

OLD FAUNTLEROY HOUSE (*1816*)

> *West Street, on Route 460; weekdays 1 to 5, Sundays 2 to 5, summer 9 to 12; 35 cents; New Harmony Memorial Commission.*

This is an historic community and the birthplace of two of the most widely known utopian experiments ever tried in this country. The first was under the leadership of George Rapp (see Ambridge, Pennsylvania) from Germany, and the second under Robert Owen, a Scotch reformer, who, in association with William McClure and other early scientists, helped to bring their idealistic brand of culture and education to the Middle West. There are a number of houses here built by the Rappites, of which one of the first is the Fauntleroy House, a spacious dwelling later the home of Owen's sons David Dale and Robert Dale, which derived its name from Robert Fauntleroy. Incidentally, it housed the first women's club in this country, the Minerva, founded by a granddaughter of Robert Owen.

The RAPP-MC CLURE HOUSE, the OWEN HOUSE, and the SCHNEE HOUSE, all built around this time or a little later, are all of interest, but privately owned at present. However, the New Harmony Community is a big restoration project of the Indiana Department of Conservation, and eventually there will be much to visit here.

¶ *Rockport (32 miles east of Evansville on Ohio River)*

THE LINCOLN PIONEER VILLAGE
(*a replica*) (*1816–1830*)
> *7 to 5 daily; 50 cents and 25 cents; city of Rockport, Park Department.*

This is a memorial to Lincoln and to his fourteen boyhood years spent in this neighborhood. The Lincoln home was seventeen miles north of Rockport, and he often walked from it to John Pitcher's law office here to borrow or return books. The Village, a replica of the way the village looked at that time, was originally built as a WPA project under the direction of the sculptor, George Honig. Gentryville, a mile and a half from the Lincoln cabin, was where Lincoln spent much of his time. The well-to-do Gentry family were his great friends, and among the jobs that he was hired by James Gentry to do was taking a flatboat with cargo down the Mississippi to New Orleans—at a salary of eight dollars a month.

Of particular interest are JOHN PITCHER'S LAW OFFICE, where Lincoln spent his spare time reading, and the JONES STORE, where Lincoln clerked. Note the courting tube lovers used in the crowded one-room

log cabins; with the family all sitting around they could whisper into it. The AARON AND SARAH GRIGSBY HOME, where Abe's sister Sarah came as a bride, contains a bridal bed made of boughs. The GENTRY MANSION has been furnished by the Gentry family with pioneer pieces. The LINCOLN HOMESTEAD and a dozen other replicas complete this evocative museum of Lincolniana.

¶ *Terre Haute*

PRESTON HOUSE (*1820–1823*)
> *1339 Poplar Street; by appointment, between May and September; Miss Natalie Preston Smith.*

Built of stone in the Georgian Colonial style, the mansion's furnishings were brought from Baltimore in 1835. The house, on its shaded grounds which were once the very edge of the prairie, is now a landmark in the city.

¶ *Vevay (20 miles above Madison on the Ohio River)*

Vevay, settled by a group of Swiss in 1801 and upriver about fifteen miles from Madison, has somehow managed to escape the "blight of progress" and remains a town of many charming old houses. It was early known for the wine produced in its vineyards. Edward Eggleston, a native son whose novel *The Hoosier Schoolmaster* is a classic of early days in Indiana, lived here. Vevay had its architect too—a builder-carpenter named George A. Kyle, who inserted silver plates with his name inscribed thereon in the newel posts of several of the houses he built—a very handy device for remembering himself to posterity. The houses are for the most part rural brick, versions of Georgian, neat and serviceable. The MOREROD HOUSES, the DUMONT HOUSE, the HENRY HOUSE, the FERRY HOUSE, as well as a number of others, form an interesting group with a certain homogeneity, thanks to Mr.

Kyle. They were built between 1810 and 1820, or thereabouts. The SWISS INN has been open for business since 1823. The homeowners are hospitable to interested visitors.

¶ *Vincennes (on the Wabash halfway between Terre Haute and Evansville on Route 41)*

This town, the oldest in Indiana, was the capital of the Old Northwest. It was first a thriving French trading post on the Wabash where hunters and trappers, arriving with their "bag" after days or weeks spent in the green depths of the forests, were blinded by the sunlight and overcome with the joy of seeing sparkling white houses and other men. Then it became the seat of the government for an area greater than the original thirteen states—so great, indeed, that no one quite knew its boundaries at that time.

WILLIAM HENRY HARRISON MANSION *or* GROUSELAND
(1803–1804)
3 West Scott Street; 9:30 to 5 weekdays, 1 to 5 Sundays; 30 cents and 15 cents; Francis Vigo Chapter, D.A.R.

Called "Grouseland" by its master and known also as "The White House of the West," it was the home of the dramatic and adventurous son of the illustrious Harrison family of Virginia, whose seat was "Berkeley," on the James. Chosen to govern the vast territories, he held a kind of dictatorial sway over lands which at one time included the whole Louisiana Purchase, west of the Mississippi to Wyoming and Oklahoma, so distant from the center of government that his power was virtually autonomous. The house, with twenty-six rooms and thirteen fireplaces, is built largely of black walnut and tulipwood. To the left of the hallway as you enter is what was formerly the council chamber, a bow-ended room in which many treaties were

The William Henry Harrison mansion in Vincennes is one of the most impressive presidential homes west of the Alleghenies.

concluded with the Indians, and which the great Indian Chief Tecumseh refused at one time to enter. An unsolved mystery are the two false windows in the front.

At 505 Main Street is the BONNER-ALLEN MANSION (1824). Like a large number of impressive early homes throughout the country, this excellent brick colonial house has become a funeral home. On the whole, it is perhaps a happier fate for a fine old house to be, so to speak, "embalmed" in this fashion, with its outward aspect preserved, than to be hopelessly disfigured or destroyed. This one has been called one of the most perfect examples of Colonial architecture west of the Alleghenies. A friend of Lincoln's, Cyrus A. Allen, purchased it from David Bonner, the Virginian who built it. Lincoln once passed the night in it. He was also often entertained at the old JUDGE ELLIS MANSION (1830), at 11 North 2d Street.

The Greek Revival fashion in the thirties and forties wended its way with Eastern pioneers as far west as Wisconsin, leaving its mark in the so-called Southern Peninsula of Michigan with classical gems of charm and naïveté, of which the Wilson-Wahr house in Ann Arbor is one of the excellent few that remain in anything approaching mint condition. On the opposite page, a relic of the rich early fur-trading days in a picturesque part of the Northern Peninsula is the beguiling old Beaumont house on Mackinac Island.

MICHIGAN

*A*S INDICATED by the headings above, the houses now to be found in the Northern Peninsula either represent military installations, both British and American, or are relics of the fur trade and trapping which flourished there. Those in the Southern Peninsula towns designated above represent the influx of settlers from the Eastern states, and the fervor with which Eastern fashions in home building were utilized. It is unfortunate that so few examples of residential Greek Revival architecture have been preserved here in their original quality and condition, for few states have dealt with this thoroughly American style in such a charming way

and with the naïveté that is so essential to it.

What happened architecturally in the settlement made by Antoine de la Mothe Cadillac at the *place du détroit* ("place of the strait") between its founding in 1701 and 1760, when the British took over from the French, or even what happened up to 1796, when the United States took over, is anybody's guess. But we do know that, during the nineteenth century, easy going and well-to-do Detroit was famous for its comfortably housed, home-owning population. Someone who has carefully examined old photographs made in the neighborhood of the original 1850 NEWBERRY HOUSE long before its

1876 transformation has described the pictures for us.

"They show a peaceful, tree-lined Jefferson Avenue with large homes, well-kept lawns, a dirt road and what seems to be a board sidewalk. At its edge, in regular rhythm, ran horse-blocks, hitching posts, and, at the top of their poles— gas street lamps. Among the trees down toward the river, could be seen pleasant streets and comfortable frame houses."

And then [as historians are fond of repeating] came Ford!

The automobile industry transformed Detroit as few cities other than Pompeii have ever been transformed in so short a time. The transformation left us with but one "early" house to list for the city: the Newberry House, as remodeled in 1876. But it must be said that in return for what the industry took away, Ford gave us GREENFIELD VILLAGE. The Village is Henry Ford's own very personal statement of American homes, schools, factories, and products. But his remarkable conception has done one thing: it has given to Michigan a collection of Americana that is scarcely equaled in scope and variety anywhere else.

¶ In & out of Detroit

¶ Detroit

NEWBERRY HOUSE (1860–1876)
1363 East Jefferson Avenue; open by request; Louisa St. Clair Chapter D.A.R.

The 1850 mansion that was handed down to John S. Newberry and his bride can now be examined in the wonderfully flamboyant form it took on in 1876. In that year Newberry, a man of wealth who had made railway cars for the Union Army in the Civil War, engaged a Detroit architect, Gordon W. Lloyd, to enlarge the original house. Lloyd was an Englishman, and was said "to favor, in design, the French influence." He faced the house with two sets of bay windows rising from the sidewalk to

the roof, which he crowned with a cupola from which an excellent view could be had of pleasure boats and barges going by under sail on the river. He ended up with thirty rooms, "not counting closets, storerooms, lavatories, and toilets." A Louis XV flavor dominated the drawing room. Birch, maple, rosewood, and mahogany were effectively employed in the mantels and cabinetry of the reception room and in the dining salon, where the walls and ceiling were entirely paneled in birch. Now the house is rapidly being restored to its former exuberant appearance, with furnishings being returned and restorations made where required, and it will soon take its rightful place as an exemplar of the period somewhere between the Campbell House in St. Louis and the Victoria Mansion in Portland, Maine.

DETROIT INSTITUTE OF ARTS
Tuesday through Friday 1 to 10, Saturdays and Sundays 9 to 6, in summer 9 to 6 except Mondays (closed holidays).

Incorporated in this interesting four-room exhibit are some of the amazing rooms from Whitby Hall moved here from Philadelphia, where Col. James Coultas built his home at what is now 58th Street and Florence Avenue. He named it "Whitby Hall" after his ancestral home in Yorkshire, England. In addition there is a bedroom from "Vauxhall Gardens," a seventeenth-century stone house which stood in Salem, New Jersey, and another bedroom from Spring Garden Mansion, built in 1760, in New Castle, Delaware.

¶ Dearborn

GREENFIELD VILLAGE
9 to 4 weekdays, 9 to 4:30 weekends and holidays; nominal fee. (It is suggested that you ask for the guidebook Greenfield Village, which describes the whole area and the buildings, and offers a good map with the buildings located.)

Greenfield Village is unique in America. It covers over two hundred acres and takes in over ninety buildings. Many old buildings of Michigan and the country at large have been bodily transported to it. The Village was planned by Ford to show the development of American customs, institutions, and early industry. He said of it that "by looking at things people used and that show the way they lived, a better and truer impression can be gained than could be had in a month of reading . . ." Maybe so; at any rate, it is an easy and entertaining way to learn. The streets of the Village are lined with mills, shops, schools, stores, and homes; some of the shops are "in business." There are planing mills, sawmills, cider mills, carding mills, silk mills—just about every kind of mill that existed in the old days (some of them running too). There is a weaving shed, a blacksmith's shop, a tintype studio, a toll house, a post office, a Sandwich glass plant, a pottery, a boiler shop, a carriage shop, and a brickworks, and there are other buildings too numerous to mention. In addition there are the actual (not facsimile) homes of Ford's heroes and friends: Luther Burbank's (homeplace), Stephen Foster's, George Matthew Adams's, McGuffey's (of primer fame), Noah Webster's, and, most important in this group, Edison's. The Edison complex includes his Menlo Park laboratory, office, and library, as well as several other buildings in which he made his experiments and discoveries—and even the boardinghouse where some of his workmen stayed; all these are structures of the '70s and '80s. The Edison Illuminating Company plant where Ford himself worked in the '90s, a very sizable factory, is part of this group. Nor has Ford forgotten to commemorate his friend George Washington Carver in a log cabin such as the great Negro agronomist was born in. An attempt has also been made to trace the development of domestic architecture in America as well as to preserve the homes of those whom Ford thought worthy of such notice. The development starts with a group from the Cotswolds in England—cottage, barn, forge, and dovecote—and is followed by the PLYMPTON HOUSE from Massachusetts, one of the oldest in America. Next comes the SUSQUEHANNA HOUSE (1652) from southern Maryland, with its wide veranda and dormers, and then the SECRETARY HOUSE from Exeter, New Hampshire, typical of early-eighteenth-century New England. Another group is all Michigan architecture and shows the development there from the log house to the fine Greek Revival mansion lifted bodily from Ann Arbor. Ford's own birthplace (1863)

stands where it did originally near 58 Bagley Street, with barns, sheds, and picket fences arranged as they were in his boyhood, as are the pictures and furniture inside. The emphasis, it is evident, is on historical and social interest, but there is also an architectural and esthetic appeal. A number of the Michigan buildings are used in the public-school system of Dearborn now and may not be visited inside for that reason. However, there are plenty of houses which are furnished in their period, just as the shops and barns are; for Ford was as tireless a collector of Americana as he was a creator of it—in his own fabulous way.

¶ *Toward Farmington*

BOTSFORD INN (*1836*)
> *Route 16, 16 miles from Detroit; open all year, lunch and dinner; same management as Dearborn Inn.*

One of the oldest landmarks in the state, this inn was serving the public when Detroit was a dusty village. It was built as a home for Orrin Weston before Michigan became a state, and stood on the Grand River Road, soon to become a much-traveled highway for stagecoaches and covered wagons. With the advance of the motor age the inn fell into disuse, but Henry Ford—whose nostalgic pleasure it was to preserve the evidences of the horse-and-buggy age in which he grew up—acquired it in 1924 and had it completely rehabilitated. Today a spacious, old-fashioned place with double porches, sitting well back from the humming highway, it maintains its tradition of hospitality and good cooking. The taproom and the huge old cooking hearth are much as they were when the inn was frequented by trappers and traders.

¶ The Greek & Gothic Revival houses of the Southern Peninsula

¶ *Ypsilanti*

BALLARD HOUSE (*1830–1842*)
> *218 North Washington Street; by appointment; The Ladies Literary Club.*

Built by Arden Ballard at the height of the Classical Revival, this house is fronted by four great Roman Doric columns, an order that is repeated in smaller scale at the doorway. The house is an entertaining example of the fashion that made its mark on this part of Michigan and one of the rare examples that have remained relatively unscathed. It is furnished with a feeling for its place in the past.

¶ Ann Arbor

WILSON-WAHR HOUSE (c. 1840)
126 North Division Street; by written request; Mrs. James A. Sallade.

Considered the finest example of Greek Revival in the state by many authorities, this house has chaste and classical details and elegant proportions, and is furnished with the taste it deserves.

There are other good houses of the period to be seen here, where once the Greek Revival flourished; and at Dexter, nearby, there is one that was the finest of all—the JUDGE DEXTER MANSION—though now there is only just enough left of its former glory to stir the pulse.

¶ Adrian

GOVERNOR CROSWELL HOUSE (c. 1840)
228 North Broad Street; upon request; Lucy Walcott Barnum Chapter, D.A.R.

Home of an early Michigan governor who served two terms from 1876 to 1880, this is an attractive, smallish red-brick house, Greek Revival in character, with an odd and interesting set-back one-story wing ex-

actly duplicating the main portion. The furnishings are early-nineteenth-century.

¶ Marshall

Marshall is a town where the Greek Revival flourished early. Of its several fine examples of the style, there are two adjoining houses which are outstanding: STONE HALL (1837), the home of Mr. Louis E. Brooks; and the JABEZ FITCH HOUSE (1839), owned by Mr. Harold C. Brooks. At this point we can only call attention to the houses. Both have impressive Ionic porticoes with magnificent columns two stories in height; both have their entrances on the side, through a small one-story portico; and each sits in its own little park. They have been preserved by connoisseurs well known for their fine collections.

¶ Grand Rapids

GRAND RAPIDS ART GALLERY (1840)
230 Fulton Street E.; daily 10 to 5, Sundays 2 to 5 (closed Mondays and holidays); Grand Rapids Art Association.

This is one of the outstanding Greek Revival houses in Michigan, built by Abram Pike and occupied as a family residence until 1922. The fine fluted columns, repeated in miniature in the one-story match-

The fine Greek Revival house built by Abram Pike in 1840 now houses the Grand Rapids Art Gallery.

Remarkable for the fact that it is not only still standing but well cared for, the Sanford house in Grand Rapids exemplifies a style of architecture that was once to be found in great abundance all through the Southern Peninsula of Michigan; now a rarity.

ing wings, were brought from the abandoned Ottawa House at Port Sheldon. The interior has been completely changed, and is used for exhibits of painting and sculpture.

SANFORD HOUSE (*1847*)
540 Cherry Street S.E.; open by written request; Mr. H. P. Dix.

This very good example of the Greek Revival indicates the fervor with which this fashion was applied in what were then such out-of-the-way places. The scale of the Doric portico is almost monumental.

¶ Niles

In Niles the Greek Revival jostles the Gothic Revival, and for picturesque interest the latter wins out. When that romantic style comes into its own, as it is bound to with the passage of time, some of the best examples of it will be discovered in the Middle West. Many of us remember them or their like in the towns where we were born. They symbolized a type of comfortable family life that just managed to straddle the gap between the age of the ice pond and that of the Frigidaire.

While the owners of a number of Gothic houses have offered to allow visits by advance appointment, a stroll along Grant Street might be pleasure enough. Look at the CASPER GROTHWOHL HOUSE (c. 1850), at "552," a brick house, crisp with white trim. The porch, with its daintily railed second-story gallery, un-

If present plans materialize, the old fort and the buildings of the early fur-trading post on Mackinac Island will soon combine to form a vivid reminder of an era that was filled with many colorful characters and occasions.

covered, is like a starched lace petticoat standing out around this solid mansion; the brackets of the wide roof overhang, make a kind of ruching. Then there is the COTTAGE OF DR. JOHN W. STRAYER, at "553," a small gem of board-and-batten construction, steeply gabled; and the RALPH KING HOME, at "1218," a stately dark-brick mansion in a parklike setting, which presents a façade that is almost ecclesiastical. At 519 BOND STREET, shorn now of some of its Victorian lacework, is a house to include in this collection of Gothic heirlooms if only because it was the birthplace of Ring Lardner.

For further local information here, inquire of Mrs. Gertrude MacAhan, curator of the Fort St. Joseph Museum. An authority on the Niles homes, she

lives at 991 South 3d Street in a tiny well-preserved log cabin of the 1830s.

¶ The outpost houses of the Northern Peninsula

¶ Mackinac Island

Proposals were made by the state historian in 1956 for developing the historical features of this fascinating old resort island (pronounced *Mackinaw*). Already certain restorations have been started, as will be noted.

THE STUART HOUSE *or* **AGENT'S HOUSE** *or* **JOHN JACOB ASTOR HOUSE** (*1822*)

June 1 to September 15; 25 cents; city of Mackinac Island.

This long, large Colonial building, with its double-stairway approach, served, like most agents' houses in fur-trading days, as both office and home. It is now furnished and fitted out as nearly as possible the way it was when Robert Stuart and the great Henry R. Schoolcraft were the factors here, and the American Fur Company an Astor monopoly. The warehouse buildings of the company, restored also, serve now as a community house, while the log Biddle House, oldest on the island, is in process of restoration. The home that belonged to William Backhouse Astor (1817) is now used to accommodate employees of the hotel.

THE BEAUMONT HOUSE (*1820*)

Daily 10 to 4, during summer; city of Mackinac Island.

This attractive old-stone-house restoration was the retail store of the American Fur Company and the house in which Dr. William Beaumont first treated the gunshot case that enabled him, because the wound refused to heal, to do historic research on the activities of the stomach.

¶ Sault Ste. Marie

THE JOHN JOHNSTON HOUSE (*1815–1827*)

Daily, 10 to 4; city of Sault Ste. Marie.

The builder of this recently restored house of the trading-post period was an Irish aristocrat who married an Indian princess. The legends she passed on via her son-in-law, Henry Rowe Schoolcraft, found their way to Longfellow, a cousin of Schoolcraft's, who wove them into *Hiawatha.*

ELMWOOD *or* THE INDIAN AGENCY HOUSE (*1827*)

Daily, 10 to 4; headquarters of Chippewa County Historical Society.

Considerably changed since it was built as a large agency house, it is interesting for having been the home into which Henry Schoolcraft moved with his bride, the daughter of John Johnston and the Indian princess. The skillful restoration has made the house interesting also as a piece of true pioneer Colonial.

This is the front parlor of the house in which the Abraham Lincolns lived for seventeen years just before the momentous move to Washington from Springfield. Many of the furnishings belonged to the family; the rest are from friends and neighbors of the President. The Gothic stove is a piece to cherish. On the opposite page is the Gen. John E. Smith house in Galena.

ILLINOIS

*A*CCUSTOMED as we are to thinking of Illinois as having been settled mainly by pioneers of the early 1800s, it is easy to forget that the French were masters here more than a hundred years before, and that the oldest permanent settlement the whole length of the Mississippi Valley is Cahokia, which was established by the French in 1698 and was soon to become a great trading center and the most populous place on the river. The long French occupation accounts for the fact that the few buildings left from the early 1700s might easily have been built in Louisiana.

The next period of settlement, when young America began to stream across the continent, was a long barren time as far as building was concerned, for pioneers had to think in terms of shelter, pure and simple, and conditions were not conducive to furbelows. Few of the early crude structures have stood the test of time, but you will see that in New Salem a careful re-creation has been made of the log-cabin village where Lincoln lived as a young man.

At about the time Lincoln moved from a log cabin into a frame house, the Greek Revival was beginning to sweep the country in epidemic proportions. As a fashion, it constitutes the flower of what remains of Illinois architecture of the pre-Civil War period, and while only a few examples of these homes are presently in a state of preservation to be listed in this book, more are bound to be restored. The State Historical Society has plans of large scope and can be expected to add houses to the following list from time to time. Since this movement is rapidly gaining headway in Illinois, it is suggested that you write to Illinois State Historical Library, Springfield, Illinois, for current information in addition to that concerning the houses listed here.

¶ *Bement*

BRYANT COTTAGE (*1856*)
9 to 5 daily, except Thanksgiving, Christmas and New Year's; state of Illinois.

A small house of historical interest, for it was here that Lincoln and Douglas, friends of the owner, hatched the great debates and decided when and where they should be held. The owner was Francis E. Bryant, a cousin of William Cullen Bryant.

¶ *Bishop Hill*

BISHOP HILL (*1848–1860*)
On Route 82, 18 miles from Kewanee

Near Bishop Hill at an intersection with Route 34 the state has placed a marker which reads, "At Bishop Hill two miles north of here, Eric Jansen and Jonas Olson founded a colony of religious dissenters in 1846. Organized on communistic lines the colony at one time had 1,100 members and property worth a million dollars." The venture ended with internal dissension and the murder of Jansen. In spite of this, thirteen of the sturdy buildings erected by these pioneers are still standing. The largest one was a four-story structure which had ninety-six rooms, but this burned down in the 1920s. South of the four-acre government-owned park, which makes this such a pretty spot today, stand three large brick houses, neatly faced with cement trim, with a style all their own. One was a hotel and the other two were communal apartment houses, which is pretty much what they all remain today. Many of their occupants are descendants of the settlers who, since the break-up of the colony in 1862, have owned their apartments cooperatively. This may be the earliest example of cooperative apartment dwellings in the country. In town there are the old bakery, the brewery, the cheese factory, and the Steeple Building, which, to give you an idea of its size, houses several stores, a garage, the phone exchange, and the post office. The Old Colony Church (1848), owned by the state, is a frame structure, one of the few, for most of the first buildings were made of a soft adobe brick until a local clay was found suitable for firing. These were industrious people, for their record shows that once they had got under way with their brick making, they were turning out five million a month. No wonder the colonists sometimes worked eighteen hours a day, women included; and no wonder the colony broke up in dissension. To get a brilliant picture of how these people lived and worked, look at the exceptional collection in the church of primitive paintings, by Olaf Kraus, which depict the life in homely detail. Talbot Hamlin was greatly impressed by these buildings. He speaks of their excellent proportions in spite of crude detailing and says that "Their efforts have that true impressiveness which good proportions and adequate size always produce . . . they show the architectural amenity and formal grandeur for which the colony was striving." If this may somewhat exaggerate their qualities, it is none the less true that they constitute an unusual group of buildings, perhaps unique in this section of the country.

¶ *Cahokia* (*on Route 3, 4 miles south of East St. Louis*)

JEAN BAPTISTE SAUCIER HOUSE (*1737*)
Daily, 9 to 5, except Mondays; state of Illinois.

Since this is the oldest private dwelling in the Middle West, it has great interest for those who are concerned with antiquity as such. With the distinctively French stamp that the early fur traders and *coureurs de bois* left on this section of the Mississippi, it is built like some of the houses in Ste. Genevieve and certain other early ones in lower Louisiana. The walls are vertical logs, plaster-filled. Its bonnet roof projects out on all four sides, making a wide covered terrace surrounded by supporting posts. This seemingly primitive structure, built by the French military engineer, who built Fort de Chartres, has unexpected niceties inside, for the walls were plaster on split lath, and the windows had glass

Note the vertical log construction—à la française—*of the Jean Baptiste Saucier house in Cahokia.*

panes when oiled paper was customary out here. The floors are of sassafras puncheons on walnut beams. The house went to the St. Louis World Fair in 1904, then stood until 1939 in Jackson Park, Chicago. It is now back home to stay.

¶ Cairo

If the houses of the 1860s and the 1870s in Cairo continue to be occupied—and there is no reason why they should not, for they were built to last—Cairo will some day be a museum town, exhibiting that flavorsome period to perfection. Cairo was "a steamboat metropolis," situated where the Ohio and Mississippi meet; as such it was wealthy, and its surviving homes of the era tell the story well.

MAGNOLIA MANOR (*1869–1872*)
2900 Washington Avenue; daily 9 to 5, Sundays 2 to 4; 50 cents; Cairo Historical Society.

The Charles A. Galigher House is a perfect example of this ornate style as well as the solidity of building, for the walls are of double brick with a ten-inch air space between. The exterior with its heavy eaves, heavy cupola, double arched lintels, and New Orleans ironwork railings on porch and upper balcony, is also decorated in double courses of white trim at three separate levels. The effect is amazing. The drawing room, where President and Mrs. Grant received hundreds of guests when they visited the Galighers for two days, is perfect for its period: fluted columns, paneled arches, a great bay window, and quite remarkable cornice with plaster carving of grapes and leaves, of a high order. The Cairo Historical Society is furnishing it with great care to perpetuate its gaslight-era atmosphere.

RENDELMAN HOME (*1865*)
2723 Washington Avenue; open by arrangement; Mrs. Adelaide Rendelman Grieve.

Built somewhat earlier than "Magnolia Manor" by a river captain, this is a three-story mansard-roofed mansion of brick and stone, the stone painted white. It stands in a three-acre park of its own in the midst of the city, with caretaker's house and stables. The entrance door contains panels and fanlight of prismatic glass. A winding staircase with heavy mahogany posts and a balustrade rises to a glass-enclosed "pilot house." Tall doors and window frames are of carved yellow poplar. The parlor and library have a plaster cornice of oak-leaf-and-acorn pattern that looks as though it may have been done by the skillful workmen who executed the cornice in "Magnolia Manor." This pattern is repeated in the border of a large rug whose central medallion depicts the Statue of Liberty. Blue-and-gold stained glass is in the big bay window.

Other houses to note in passing are those of Mrs. Oscar Herbert (1879),

2606 Washington Street; Miss Effie L. Neff, 2009 Walnut Street; Miss Margaret Rust, 703 Walnut; Mrs. George McClung, 603 Walnut; and Miss Sarah Alice Reed (1861), 419 20th Street.

¶ Cantrall

GEORGE POWER HOME AND LAW OFFICE (1850)

At Power Farms, 10 miles north of Springfield; by written request; Mrs. June Power Reilly.

Also known as "Fancy Creek Farmhouse," this pleasant brick country house with wide veranda, set in its ancient grove of maples, is now being occupied by the fourth generation of the family of Judge George Power, who settled in Sangamon County in 1821 and also eight years later built the little white frame courthouse now standing on the grounds. The first seat of justice in the county, it is claimed to be the one in which Abraham Lincoln tried his first case, a suit involving the killing of a dog. The last case that Lincoln filed before he became President was before the judge's son William, who then presided over the county court. George Power, like many another pioneer, came from Kentucky and began life here in a log cabin. It was not until almost thirty years later that he was able to realize his dream of a spacious dwelling built of brick like those he remembered from his Kentucky boyhood. In the meantime both the prairies and the Indians had been tamed. Little has been changed in this homestead. Its heirlooms and the mementos of its famous visitors have been cherished by the family. We could not offer you a better example of the way of life of a worthy pioneer family who gained their local importance the hard way.

¶ Carmi

GEN. JOHN M. ROBINSON HOUSE (1816)

110 South Main Cross Street; by appointment only; Miss Mary Jane Stewart.

One of the oldest houses in the state, it has been called a "living museum" by John Drury, historian of Illinois houses. Miss Stewart's grandfather bought the house in 1835 from John Craw, one of the earliest settlers in White County. It was built as a log house and served as courthouse for several years in its earliest days. General Robinson added wings to the log house and no doubt covered it with clapboard at the same time. A portico, a hooded doorway in the wing, and a white fence set this low dwelling quite apart from its surroundings, for Carmi was a busy town even then, during the oil boom. General Robinson spent eleven years in Washington as Senator from Illinois and much of the furniture in the house today was purchased while he was in the East. The general's father-in-law was James Ratcliff, a tavern-keeper here, one of whose distinguished guests was Abraham Lincoln who was campaigning for Harrison at the time. Lincoln was connected with the family more closely than this, however, for General Robinson's brother-in-law Edwin B. Webb was said to have been a rival of Lincoln's for the hand of Mary Todd and was incidentally the last Whig candidate for governor of Illinois. There are so many interesting heirlooms in this house that space does not permit cataloguing them. But in a rosewood secretary you can see original letters of Lincoln, William Henry Harrison, and Henry Clay, and an autographed copy of a speech of John Quincy Adams to John M. Robinson.

¶ Carrollton (*on Route 67, 32 miles north of Alton*)

BLACK HOMESTEAD (1823)

202 East Walnut Street, 2 miles west on Route 208 and then south ⅝ mile; 9 to 11 and 2 to 4, daily, or by appointment; Robert T. Black.

The land here was registered in 1821 by the owner's grandmother, and the deed, signed by President Monroe, hangs on the wall today. It is the oldest brick house in Illinois north of East St. Louis, and, when it was built, it stood conspicuously fine among the little group of log cabins that formed the hamlet, surrounded by open prairie. It was built facing east, but years later a new road was surveyed in back of it, and so it ended facing west. Later a frame addition with a deep overhang was added across the front, making it look much like a Southern plantation house with its two-story columns and balustraded second-story gallery. The rooms are large and there are fifteen of them, with many fireplaces. This is a comfortable family home with some furniture and relics of the wars still here.

¶ Cedarville (5 miles north of Freeport on Route 20)

JANE ADDAMS HOMESTEAD (1849)
On request by letter or phone; fee nominal; Henry J. Haldeman, Box 3, Girard, Kansas.

Jane Addams of Hull House was born here. Built of brick, the family house is pleasantly rural in appearance, with a recently added porch. The interior has several fireplaces and fine woodwork and floors. The furniture is of interest because much of it was there when Miss Addams was a child in this village. In back of the house is a bank barn (1848) put together with wooden pegs; next door, a brick building once the Addams's general store. Inside of this last is a buggy in which Jane drove to hear the Lincoln-Douglas Debates.

¶ Galena

Like many another booming river town, Galena's prosperity disappeared with the advent of railways, leaving a number of notable pre-Civil War mansions whose style is sometimes linked with the name of Gen. U. S. Grant, who was in fact for some years a resident of Galena, as will be noted. A yearly "open house" is held here in September under the auspices of the First Presbyterian Church. About eight homes are shown, most of which are open to you through the *Guide* year around. Write to Mrs. Walter Ehrler or the church for further information on the tour.

ELIHU WASHBURN HOUSE (1830s)
908 3d Street; on written request, small groups only, May and early June; Mrs. Frank T. Sheean.

The most imposing and handsome Greek Revival house in town, it was purchased by Mrs. Sheean's family from the Washburns seventy-five years ago. Elihu Washburn was General Grant's Minister to France. In 1861 Grant drilled Galena's first company of volunteers on the lawn, captained by Augustus Chetlain, who became a famous general in the war. At one time the Indians occupied this lawn once a year when they came to trade and receive government rations.

CHALATAIN ACRES (1836)
Route 20, 2 miles west of town; by written appointment, June, July, and August; 50 cents for the First Presbyterian Church; Mr. and Mrs. W. Clifford Stauss.

The original log cabin put up in 1826 by Louis Chetlain, a Swiss settler, is still part of the structure of this house. Ten years later he enlarged it to its present size. It is the oldest farmhouse standing in northern Illinois. It passed out of the Chetlain family only when the present owners bought it in 1943. They restored it without any important change. It is a long, white clapboard house with a deep pillared porch and an open gallery above. The three dormers are reminiscent of early clapboard houses in Virginia. Perhaps the porch was added later. The name of the house, by the way, is not misspelled here but appeared this way in the deed by mistake, and the owners left it so. The furniture is in keeping, much of it heirloom.

GEN. JOHN E. SMITH HOUSE (1845)
807 Bench Street; write or phone (350) for appointment, except in winter; Mr. and Mrs. Louis I. Nack.

A one-story-and-basement house built of red brick on a stone foundation, this is a good example of Middle Western Greek Revival. It has nice proportions and some charming detail, which includes a very pleasant portico supported by fluted Ionic columns. John Smith was a Galena jeweler who later became a staff officer for General Grant. The house is furnished with many old Galena items and several from the Duncan Hines home in Kentucky.

MINER'S COTTAGE (1838)
901 4th Street; open on request; Miss Katherine Delihant.

This is a double stone cottage which once belonged to miners working at nearby Muddy Hollow. Each side has three rooms and two fireplaces which have been unchanged. The original floors and windows are also there. Some of the furniture is old Galena, pine and maple, and all is in keeping with its simplicity.

MELVILLE HOUSE (*before 1840*)
1009 3d Street; on written request;
Mr. and Mrs. Walter Ehrler.

This was originally a double house occupied by Maj. Thomas Melville and his married daughter. Major Melville was Herman Melville's favorite uncle, and the author of *Moby Dick* spent the summer of 1840 in this house. Remodeled fifty years ago into a single dwelling, both halls were thrown together at the time which gave the house a new spaciousness. Three of the main rooms are furnished with antiques, largely early Galena Victorian and Empire. There is a collection of glassware.

NORRIS HOUSE (*1853*)
3 miles west on Route 20, then south 1 mile on Norris Lane; on written request;
Miss Katherine and Mr. Ralph Norris.

A rosy-brick home with wide eaves supported by brackets and tall double windows, the whole house is typical Galena of the period when it was built. The furniture has been used by the Norris family for three generations and there are many local articles, among them such kitchen equipment as dasher churns, wooden molds, and a fine old cookstove. This is the real thing.

THE ROCK HOUSE (*antique shop*)
(*c. 1830*)
Virginia Fitzgerald.

An interesting stone house with stone window lintels and corner quoins, used as a shop. Can be seen any time.

The bracketed overhang of the roof gives considerable character to the General Grant house in Galena.

GENERAL GRANT HOUSE (*1857*)
Bouthilier Street; daily 9 to 5 except holidays; State of Illinois.

Grant came here some years before the Civil War and clerked in his brothers' leather store for six hundred dollars a year. The store is still at 120 Main Street, as is the plain little house where he lived with his wife and four children until the war. As a graduate of West Point, Grant volunteered at once and was commissioned a Colonel. When he returned to Galena, world-famous, the people here purchased the Alexander Jackson House by a subscription of sixteen thousand dollars, furniture and all, and presented it to the hero. The Grants intended to live there permanently, but three years later they were settled in the White House. The house today is much as it was when they lived in it. Most of their furniture has been retrieved and its personal interest is further enhanced by the fact that it represents so well the manner in which a prosperous and important family lived in the Middle West at that period. The exterior of the brick house, with its corner porch and unusually deep overhanging eaves, is pleasantly unpretentious.

¶ *Kankakee*

DR. A. L. SMALL HOME (*1855*)
Eighth Avenue and Water Street; Saturday and Sunday afternoons 2 to 5, and by appointment; Kankakee Park District.

Dr. Small not only carried on his country practice from this trim two-story limestone house of the prairie, but, being a horticulturist of note as well, surrounded his house with many acres of nursery and arboretum. The house is therefore far from being the sole attraction. One of the doctor's six children born in the house became the late Governor Len Small of Illinois, of whom there are many mementos here. The parlor, dining room, and office are as the doctor left them when he died.

¶ *Kaskaskia*

PIERRE MENARD HOME (*1802*)
50 miles southeast of St. Louis; daily; state of Illinois.

Kaskaskia was the first capital of Illinois,

and Pierre Menard, its first Lieutenant Governor, built this lovely Louisiana-like house after he was appointed Judge by Gov. William Henry Harrison. It is a spacious raised cottage with a long, sweeping roof projecting out over a gallery with delicate columns. The windows (with original hand-pressed French panes) which open onto the gallery are unusually large. The delightful old house contains a few of the Menard belongings, among them old Pierre's flute and flageolet, his barber chair, his embroidered vest, and his mahogany chest. In one room is an elegantly carved mantel, said to be a French import. The stone kitchen is interesting, with its enormous fireplace and its water basin carved out of a huge piece of rock. The Randolph County Historical Society is about to furnish it.

The Pierre Menard home near Kaskaskia is one of the Mississippi River houses that show the influence of the early French cottage architecture brought up from Louisiana.

¶ Marengo

ANSON ROGERS' HOUSE (1846)

East Grant Highway (Route 20); open as a dress shop called "Coach and Four" with "Coach House" in rear (modern) operating as restaurant; Delmar and Marjorie Stevens.

This fine Greek Revival house has fortunately suffered few changes, except for the building in its rear. The house is of wood on a stone foundation, with six impressive supporting columns. Most of the original woodwork, the fireplace, and the mantels remain as they were. The house is furnished with antiques throughout.

The ORSON P. ROGERS HOUSE (c. 1846) stands nearby and is built similarly. It is used by tenant farmers at present.

¶Nauvoo

MANSION HOUSE (1841)

Open daily.

The pilaster decorations across the front of this house give it a kind of Greek Revival elegance. It is one of the few homes in this country on record which was built according to divine revelation. Often referred to as the "Joseph Smith House," it is now a Mormon shrine. At nearby Carthage is the old jail in which Smith was murdered, now something of a shrine as well.

The houses in Nauvoo "have a quality almost Dutch" in Talbot Hamlin's opinion. The BRIGHAM YOUNG HOUSE (1840), with its stepped gables and its interesting general composition, he finds "especially Continental in flavor."

¶ New Salem

NEW SALEM STATE PARK

(a completely restored village of the 1830s)

Daily, 9 to 5, except Christmas, New Year's Day, and Thanksgiving Day; staff of Park Guides, Department of Conservation, Division of Parks and Memorials of Illinois.

This is a reconstruction of the town in which Lincoln spent six of his formative years. Arriving by flatboat in 1831, he remained here to take an active part in the life of the village as postmaster, store clerk, and surveyor. Thirteen log cabins, plus the Rutledge Tavern, a school and church, and ten shops and stores have been reproduced and fitted out appropriately. The furnishings include many articles used by New Salem citizens of the time, such as wheat cradles, flax shuttles, and dough and cornmeal chests. Doctors' offices and cobblers' shops contain early implements; stores, bolts of old calico and other staples of the period. Vegetable gardens, flowers, and trees have been planted to re-create accurately the village scene as it was. At the homes of the two doctors, herbs used for medicinal purposes are grown in the gar-

One of the most interesting houses at New Salem State Park is the Onstot Cooper Shop of early log construction, in which Lincoln studied his law books by the light of the open fire.

dens, just as they were by wilderness medicos. There is only one original building—the Onstot Cooper Shop, built 1835, the shop in which Lincoln studied Blackstone, Shakespeare, and Burns by the light of Cooper's burning wood shavings. The whole village, in its humble simplicity, constitutes a moving memorial to one of the world's great men. There are overnight accommodations at the Wagon Wheel Inn and in several nearby towns.

¶ *Ottawa*

VALLEY VIEW (*1842*)
2011 Canton Road, North Bluff; by phone or written request; Mrs. Philip S. McDougall.

Abraham Lincoln visited here frequently. His host, a wealthy Kentucky aristocrat, Judge T. Lyle Dickey, was a political foe, though reputedly a great friend. He served as an officer in the Mexican and Civil Wars and was an Illinois supreme court justice. In spite of various enlargements, the house retains quite a bit of original character. The furniture is mostly English.

JOHN HOSSACK HOUSE (*1854*)
210 West Prospect Avenue; by written request to Mr. Philip H. Godfrey.

A grand old house of the plantation type, its deep double galleries with their well-proportioned square columns in widely spaced rows of six give it an impressive and yet comfortable appearance. The hip roof is crowned with a small railed-in plat-

form which is little more than a decoration but may well have served John Hossack as a lookout—for this house was a well-known stop on the Underground Railway.

¶ *Quincy*

GOV. JOHN WOOD HOME (*1835*)
425 South 12th Street; weekdays 10 to 12, Mondays and Wednesdays 2 to 5; Historical Society of Quincy and Adams County, Mrs. Edna Williams (curator).

John Wood, one of the early Governors of Illinois, came here from Cayuga County, New York, where the Greek Revival was going strong. This accounts for the style of the house that he built here in Quincy after he had made his fortune. In it are the governor's Civil War pistols and the sword and medicine book his surgeon father carried in the Revolution. Among the fine furnishings is a chandelier of French drop crystals which once glistened in the great salon of a Mississippi River steamer.

¶ *Springfield*

ABRAHAM LINCOLN'S HOME (*1839*)
8th and Jackson Streets; daily, 9 to 5, except Thanksgiving Day, Christmas, and New Year's.

This is the only house that Lincoln ever actually owned. Sold to him ready-built by the Reverend Charles Dresser, who had married the Lincolns in 1842, it cost only fifteen hundred dollars in cash, with a mortgage of nine hundred dollars. After two years of married life spent for the most part in boardinghouses, the Lincolns settled here with their little boy, Robert Todd. When built in 1839, the house was a one-story-and-a-half cottage. It was later enlarged. Some historians say Mrs. Lincoln had the second story raised during one of her husband's absences. The house is constructed of native hardwoods: framework and floor are of oak, lathes and weatherboarding of hand-split hickory, and door and window frames of black walnut. The Lincolns lived here for seventeen years, except for the year he was sent to Congress, when it was rented to Cornelius Ludlum for ninety dollars. Three of Lincoln's sons were born here; one died here. When the Lincolns went to Washington in 1861, they sold their house furnishings to their tenant, who subsequently took them to Chicago and lost them there in the fire. Some Lincoln pieces may be seen now on the first floor, but for the most part the house has been furnished from the homes of friends and relatives who lived in the town during Lincoln's time.

BENJAMIN S. EDWARDS HOME
(*1833*)
700 North 4th Street; daily, 2 to 5;
Springfield Art Association.

When the early part of this house was built by Dr. Thomas Houghan, there was not another house in sight. Benjamin S. Edwards, who was to become the third Governor of the state, had the simple farm-

This is the Lincoln home in Springfield, of which the front parlor is shown on page 222, now preserved as one of the most personal of Lincoln memorials, a gift to the state from the President's son.

house transformed into a most romantic and imposing Italianate villa, remodeled in the 1850s. Its flat hip roof and wide overhanging eaves, its Corinthian-columned veranda, and the ornamental cupola are all the height of a fashion that was veering away from the Greek Revival. Lincoln once spoke to a crowd from an upper window. At that time the house was the center of the town's social and political activity, and the 1850 atmosphere has now been beautifully restored in the furnishings which are those of a wealthy and prominent citizen of the period and place. The wing which houses the Springfield Art Association, a separate building, conforms to the style of the house.

This is the house that Judge George Power built thirty years after starting life in Illinois in a log cabin. Elsewhere on the grounds is the tiny court house in which Lincoln is said to have tried his first case.

When the Tallman house was built at Janesville before the Civil War, it represented the utmost in Middle Western magnificence, and it is regarded today as the state's most ambitious Victorian mansion, and is so restored and preserved. On the opposite page, by contrast of transplanted Colonial, is the old Indian Agency house at Portage.

WISCONSIN

¶ Southwestern Wisconsin: Prairie du Chien; Cassville; Mineral Point ¶ Southern Wisconsin: Portage; Cooksville; Milton; Janesville; Beloit ¶ Southeastern Wisconsin: Watertown; Wauwatosa; Milwaukee ¶ Northeastern Wisconsin: Sheboygan; Greenbush; Neenah; Kaukauna; Green Bay

*W*HAT the early houses of Wisconsin, at least the ones listed here below for visiting, lack in numbers is more than made up for in variety and surprise. The range is wide indeed between the 1776 Tank Cottage of wattle and daub, at Green Bay, and the elegant Italianate Tallman Mansion of the 1850s, at Janesville—and in between the two a lot of Wisconsin history was made. And at Green Bay, who would expect to encounter from the outpost period there as chaste an example of Greek Revival as the Cotton House? Towns like Cooksville are numerous in New England, but what about these New England houses clustering around their village green out here in Wisconsin? And where else in the country will you come across a group of Cornish stone cottages, built long ago by immigrant miners from Cornwall? The answer is: nowhere but here in Wisconsin.

¶ Southwestern Wisconsin

¶ Prairie du Chien (where Route 18 crosses the Mississippi by toll bridge to Marquette, Iowa)

VILLA LOUIS or HERCULES L. DOUSMAN HOUSE *(1843)*
> *Take Villa Louis Road at toll bridge; daily 9 to 5, May 1 to October 31; 50 cents and 10 cents; State Historical Society.*

The history of this amazing mansion is closely connected with the early career of the whole territory, for the builder of the house served as confidential agent for the John Jacob Astor interests. Dousman delivered hundreds of thousands of dollars in goods to the Indians and white trappers, and in return received millions of dollars in pelts. His intuitive understanding of the Indians and his reputation with them for honesty gave him enormous influence. When in 1844 he married a great beauty, Jane Fisher Rolette, he was already a millionaire; and what he built on an Indian mound above the river for his bride was a two-story brick house on Georgian lines, large and luxurious. His wife named it "Le Château Brillante," for when she arrived here after their honeymoon, five hundred candles were burning for her on the glassed-in front porch. This porch of the early house has been preserved, but little else. The Georgian lines disappeared under the Victorian remodeling undertaken by Madame Dousman in 1872, four years after her husband's death, when the outside walls were clad in yellow Milwaukee brick and a third-floor ballroom was added. The heirs of the family lived in the house until 1934 and assisted in its restoration as a Victorian period piece when it was taken over by the State Historical Society. Many of the heirlooms were brought back to the house by the family, and today it represents a perfect picture of ornate comfort, just as if a wealthy and hospitable family of that era lived there.

BRISBOIS HOUSE (1808)
On river front; daily, 9 to 5; 30 cents and 10 cents; John Cornelius and Mrs. Louise Root.

In 1781, following the trail of Marquette and Joliet, Michael Brisbois, a young Canadian baker, came down the Mississippi to what was then an Indian village called Prairie of the Dog, named for the chief of the Fox Indians, who lived there. Since "Prairie" later became one of the great fur marts, Brisbois was destined to prosper. In 1808 he built his plain but ample cut-stone dwelling on an Indian mound on the river front; and the house stands today much as it did when it was built—one of Wisconsin's oldest landmarks. The last descendant of Michael died here in 1935, leaving most of the original family furnishings still in the house. Strong and simple, and heated by four fireplaces,

it furnishes an excellent picture of how life was lived by a prosperous trader in those early times. This story it tells better than the Dousman House nearby, for though Brisbois was well known, his career was not exceptional. Apparently he continued to bake bread; he also farmed and traded furs like everyone else. Of peculiar interest is the fact that his asparagus beds are still producing. The Indians told him of the new plant that had been brought over from England and was growing at Lake Pepin, and he sent his son there to get plants.

¶ *Cassville (about 30 miles south of Prairie du Chien via 133)*

STONEFIELD-NELSON DEWEY HOMESTEAD (c. 1850)
In Nelson Dewey Memorial Park; open 9 to 5 daily, May 1 to October 31; Wisconsin Conservation Department.

The first Governor of the state (1848–1852), Nelson Dewey, was born in Lebanon, Connecticut, came to Cassville in 1836, and prospered. After his governorship he bought the entire village of Cassville and decided to develop on this two-thousand-acre tract a kind of plantation, self-sustaining, with all its dependencies. Something went wrong, however, and Dewey died a poor man in 1889. His wine cellar, smokehouse, barn, and servants' quarters, built of stone in a kind of sharp French Gothic style, are still standing, maintained as a crafts museum. The residence, a brick mansion that was swept by fire in 1873 and reconstructed, is furnished with many of Governor Dewey's possessions.

¶ *Mineral Point*

TRELAWNY, PENDARVIS HOUSE, POLPERO, and NEWLYN (c. 1835)
Open daily; Robert Neel and Edgar Hellum.

These four houses in this astonishing village, where Cornish tin miners came in the 1830s after hearing of the Wisconsin lead mines, are built of local buff sandstone and are much like the ones the miners left behind in their native Cornwall—face or smooth stone used in front and around the windows and doors, the rest rough. The walls are eighteen inches thick and the fireplaces niched at the corners. In winter wood stoves were also used for heating. The stubby chimneys are red brick and the roofs of split-pine shingles. The first three houses have been furnished with interesting and authentic old pieces, effectively arranged to create a "lived-in" look; "Newlyn" is a guest house. The re-creation of a workmen's community is as unusual as it is interesting. You can eat a Cornish dinner if you stop for a while, or take your tea with saffron cake, plum preserves, and scalded cream.

¶ Southern Wisconsin

¶ Portage

AGENCY HOUSE or KINZIE'S HOUSE (1832)

At Fort Winnebago; daily, 9 to 5:30; 35 cents and 15 cents; Colonial Dames.

In 1830 when John Kinzie brought his New England bride here close by Fort Winnebago, their furniture had to be taken over the rapids of the Fox River, and much of it arrived water-soaked. Kinzie had been sent out by the government to take charge of the Winnebago Indian Agency here at the portage, where the Indians in large numbers were already government charges. Very neat and New England-looking, the house, although of frame, had brick fill for insulation. Jefferson Davis made some of the furniture for the house while he was a prisoner at the fort, one talent of his which is little known. Mrs. Kinzie tried to make it a place of hospitality for both Indians and voyageurs; her piano was the marvel of the settlement. Later in life she wrote an account called *Waú Bun,* now published by the Colonial Dames there.

SURGEON'S QUARTERS (1826)

Fort Winnebago, across canal from Indian Agency; daily 10 to 5 and Sunday and holiday afternoons Memorial Day to Labor Day, during May by appointment; 35 cents and 15 cents; D.A.R.

The house is built of hand-hewn logs, the adze marks plain to be seen. The shape was evidently meant to be defensive, with two ells shielding the door. Support for

original floors are tamarack logs. The quarters are furnished with appropriate austerity.

¶ Cooksville (25 miles southeast of Madison on 38)

A COLLECTION OF EARLY HOUSES (1848–1856)

The town stands on a piece of land transferred to Daniel Webster by the United States government in 1837. Webster sold it in 1848 to Dr. John Porter of Massachusetts, who had it plotted out like a New England village, arranged around a green. Several of the homes around the green which date from that period are still occupied today, and although some of them are built in the Gothic Revival mode, then coming into fashion, the whole effect is oddly New England, with prim gardens and old shade trees. The people of the town, conscious of their unusual heritage, staged their first "open house" in 1949 under the auspices of the Rock County Historical Society. For further information it might be best to write to Mr. Miles T. Armstrong, who operates the Cooksville Store and owns one of the houses himself. There are about five houses in all, dating from 1848 through 1856, and they are well cared for. Mr. and Mrs. Armstrong are willing to be of help to anyone wishing to visit some of them, since the tour is not held regularly. Typical houses here are the MORGAN HOUSE (1848), Classical Revival; the ROBERTSON HOUSE (1850), modified American Gothic (owned by the Armstrongs); the DUNCAN HOUSE (1848), Classical Revival; and the HOXIE HOUSE (1852), American Gothic.

¶ Milton

MILTON HOUSE and GOODRICH LOG CABIN (1844)

Daily, 10 to 5; 50 cents and 10 cents; Milton Historical Society.

The house is an early inn of unusual concrete construction, with a unique hexagonal three-story lobby. The inn and cabin were connected by an underground tunnel and together were an important station for escaping slaves. They are being restored and furnished appropriately by the local historical society.

¶ Janesville

LINCOLN-TALLMAN HOUSE
(1855–1858)

440 North Jackson Street; daily 9:30 to 5 and Sundays and holidays 1 to 5, May to November; 40 cents and 10 cents; city of Janesville.

In 1859 Abraham Lincoln spent a weekend here in the thirty-three-room mansion of William Morrison Tallman, which had been completed two years before. Built at a cost exceeding forty-two thousand dollars (paid in gold) and designed in the style of an ornate Italian villa, it was Wisconsin's showplace at the time. Lincoln addressed the Republican Club Saturday night, attended church with the Tallmans Sunday, and left for Springfield the next day where three weeks later he announced his candidacy. Could he have suspected that his wealthy host had built his mansion with

Octagonal houses keep cropping up all over the country—not many so notable as this famous one at Watertown.

special features to aid escaping slaves, and that the house was already one of the most important stations on the Underground Railway? At that time Lincoln did not advocate the violation of the Fugitive Slave Act. His friend Tallman, an ardent abolitionist, was the first person to present to Congress a petition for freeing the Negro; a man of both courage and vision, he had been twice mobbed for his speeches against slavery. Coming from Rome, New York, to Janesville, a frontier village, he had grown wealthy on Western land. He owned one tract alone of 1,700,000 acres in Texas. His house reflects his wealth—three floors, sixty feet in height to the top of its cupola. Built of Milwaukee pressed brick, with arched double windows and elaborate Italianate carving, and both baroque and rococo in style, its heavy mass is architecture at its most exuberant. A heating plant as well as fireplaces, running water in four bedrooms provided by drainage from the roof, gaslights and speaking tubes, and dumb-waiters for the servants were luxuries never before heard of on the frontier at this period. Two carved walnut doors open from the drawing room into a conservatory whose windows are topped with crescents of colored glass. The oriel window on the second floor in the east hall, with its bright panes, served as a signal for fugitive slaves who were coming up from the Rock River. Slaves stayed in the basement, where there were beds and food for them, unless there was a search, when they were hidden in the attic by way of secret staircases or spirited out and sent on their way again. The carriage house, which now serves as a museum for the Rock County Historical Society, is similar in style to the house. The house has been restored to its original Civil War appearance.

¶ Beloit

RASEY HOUSE (1848)

517 Prospect Street; daily 9 to 5, Sundays 1 to 5; 25 cents; D.A.R.

Built of cobblestones picked up in Turtle Creek by the college students at nearby Beloit in 1848, the house was sold right after it was erected in order to raise funds to roof and put windows into the first building on the Beloit campus.

The Kilbournetown house in Milwaukee marks one of the western reaches of the Greek Revival.

¶ Southeastern Wisconsin

¶ Watertown

OCTAGON HOUSE (c. 1854)

Daily 1 to 5, Sundays and holidays 10 to 5; 40 cents, 30 cents, and 15 cents; Watertown Historical Society.

The invention and originality displayed in the design of this house make it one of the best octagonal houses in the country. Of cream-colored Milwaukee brick, it is crowned with four chimneys. It has eight rooms to a floor—fifty-seven altogether with halls and closets. The owner John Richards, a lawyer from Hinsdale, Massachusetts, came to Watertown when it was a village and stayed to see it boom. The staircase is spectacular, rising to the fourth story in a tightly curled spiral; the climb is made easy by the well-dimensioned treads and risers. The third floor was designed to shelter some of Mr. Richards' mill hands. Sixty-three doors have been counted in the house. The narrow balconies running the whole way around the house had to be removed for safety, but the society plans to restore them. The furniture, of the gaslight era, is all virtually intact, with the original wallpapers and carpets.

¶ Wauwatosa

LOWELL DAMON HOUSE (1844–1845)

2017 Wauwatosa Avenue, Sundays, 2 to 5; Milwaukee County Historical Society.

As typical a piece of Colonial architecture as can be found in the entire state. The man who built it was a cabinetmaker who also made buggies that lasted a lifetime. His house reflects his rare abilities. It contains various collections of antiquarian interest.

¶ Milwaukee

KILBOURNETOWN HOUSE (1844)

In Estabrook Park; 2 to 5 Sundays only; Milwaukee County Historical Society, Colonial Dames (custodians).

Here is another unexpected Greek Revival temple from the pioneer period. Built by Benjamin Church, an early architect and builder, long before Milwaukee existed, it is a small house with great style featuring four fluted Ionic columns. The low wings, each with its own door and window, outlined in a chaste molding decoration, complete a picture of fine proportions and perfect restraint. As usual, the Colonial Dames have done well by its furnishings.

¶ Northeastern Wisconsin

¶ Sheboygan

TAYLOR HOUSE (c. 1848)
½ mile west of city on Route 23;
Sheboygan County Historical Society.

This is a picturesque foursquare Italianate residence with an immense cupola, a strange edifice to have been built as a farmhouse in the country. Judge Taylor was a notable of the neighborhood; his house, a prominent local landmark, is furnished as a museum, whose aim is to preserve the history of the county.

¶ Greenbush

WADE HOUSE (1850–1851)
Route 23, in state park, 6 miles west of Plymouth; daily 9 to 5, May 1 to October 31; 50 cents and 10 cents; Kohler Foundation, Inc.

Located now in a state park, this place was originally Stage Coach Inn on the plank road from Fond du Lac to Sheboygan and was built by Sylvanus Wade, who brought his family here in 1844 when it was still Indian country. It is a typical spacious country tavern, with heavy square pillars and a roofed second-story gallery. It has been furnished with great attention to the details of the period and very well done indeed, even to the proper carpets, china, and stoves.

BUTTERNUT HOUSE
(same period as Wade House)
In state park near Wade House.

West of the Wade House, Sylvanus helped his son-in-law Charles Robinson to build this charming Greek Revival abode. That Robinson was a carpenter is very evident. It is a story-and-a-half house with a cupola and a recessed porch which divides the front and carries around the corner, odd and very stylish in appearance. The severe cupola crowns a flat-hipped roof neatly. Altogether, this is quite a model of unsophisticated originality in adapting Greek Revival to personal needs and desires. It is furnished as a family would have done at the time it was built. Other buildings are being restored, and the entire site is being returned to its original landscaping, planted with butternut trees, sugar maples, wild

crab apples, and the high-bush cranberries which grew there. This was the project of the late Mrs. Herbert V. Kohler, and much of it was carried out by her.

¶ Neenah

DOTY GRAND LOGGERY (c. 1845)
5th and Lincoln Streets in Doty Park; daily 9 to 12 and 1:30 to 5, Saturdays, Sundays, and holidays, 1:30 to 5; city of Neenah.

This was the home of James Duane Doty, territorial Governor of Wisconsin from 1845 to 1861.

¶ Kaukauna

GRIGNON HOUSE (1838–1839)
On banks of Fox River, just off 41; open all the time; 25 cents; Kaukauna Historical Society; William Wolf (curator).

Known as "The Mansion in the Woods," it was built here on the banks of the Fox River by Charles A. Grignon, son of the pioneer fur trader, Augustin. He brought his workmen as well as most of his materials from Buffalo, New York, and the house is reminiscent of the simple and sometimes somber Greek Revival houses that are scattered all over that section of New York State. With its balustraded open gallery at the second-floor level and its portico, it is M. Grignon's adaptation of the new fashion in building in the East. The solid-cherry stair rail and the handsome carved newel post and banisters in the house were brought from New York City, the final stage by canoe up the river. It was Charles's great-grandfather Charles de Langlade who was regarded as the founder of the first permanent settlement in Wisconsin, and it was he who married the sister of the Ottawa chieftain. The Charles who built the house could sit on the long balcony of his white clapboard mansion in the woods and watch the camping grounds of the Indians, who paddled up and down the Fox River below him. He lived, alas, to see the advance of industry and with it the withdrawal of his ancestors from the river. The house is three stories with twelve rooms that now, largely through the efforts of its curator, have been restored even as to much of the original Grignon furniture. During restoration the original log cabins were found under the edge of the bluff where Charles was born.

¶ *Green Bay*

TANK COTTAGE (*1776*)

Union Park; daily 10 to 5, Sundays and holidays 2 to 5; 50 cents and 10 cents; city of Green Bay.

This farmlike home of wattle and daub is the oldest in the state. The various owners could give a complete picture of the way the state was settled and how it grew. While the Great Lakes region was still under British control, a French fur trader named Joseph Roi built himself a cabin here with a huge fireplace, which may still be seen. Roi, who could neither read nor write, represents those intrepid French explorers and traders who first braved the wilderness which was then the Mississippi Valley. Why he built of wattle and daub is unknown, for it was a method seldom used in these crude cabins, nor was it in general use in France. However, the method (stuffing the inner and outer walls with twigs and leaves held together with mud clay) is interesting architecturally because it was so rare in our own early buildings. It was Nils Otto Tank, a missionary from Norway, who made a house of the cottage, clapboarding and plastering it and adding the two sloping, shedlike wings which give it its interesting lines. In the Tank Cottage, whose mistress, Madame Tank, was a wealthy and aristocratic Hollander, her Dutch heirlooms may still be seen, as well as her paintings and silver.

The Tank cottage at Green Bay is not only by far the oldest house still standing in the state but one of the most ingratiating early farmhouses to be found anywhere, its furnishings as fascinating as its story.

FORT HOWARD SURGEON'S QUARTERS (c. 1817)

Kellog and North Chestnut Streets; Tuesday to Saturday 10 to 5 and Sundays and holidays 2 to 5, May 1 to November 1; 50 cents and 10 cents; city of Green Bay.

This building and the hospital near it were once a part of the old fort but were moved here for preservation. It was the home of Dr. William Beaumont, whose discoveries, made at the fort on Mackinac Island, Michigan, (see page 221) were continued here. The house contains Beaumont's possessions, furniture, china, pictures, and library.

COTTON HOUSE (1840s)

2632 South Webster Avenue, Allouez; daily 10 to 5 except Mondays, Sundays 2 to 5; donation; Brown County Historical Society.

As an example of pure Greek Revival on a modest scale, its wide siding painted white, the house is interesting if rare in these parts. It was built by Capt. John Winslow Cotton, whose early home was in this very hamlet.

The Cotton house at Green Bay has an unusual recessed Greek Revival portico formed by its advancing wings.

INDEX

PHOTOGRAPH CREDITS

MASSACHUSETTS Page 3, Wayside Inn: Samuels; page 5, Harrison Gray Otis House: Society for the Preservation of New England Antiquities; page 5, Paul Revere House: Samuel Chamberlain; page 7, Henry W. Longfellow House: Frank O. Branzetti; page 8, Royall House: Samuel Chamberlain; pages 9, 10, Gore Place: Ezra Stoller, Ladies' Home Journal; page 11, Lyman House: Dwight O'Hara; page 16, Strawberry Hill: Zaharis; page 17, Lee House: Ezra Stoller, LHJ; page 20, House of Seven Gables: Haskell; page 21, Derby House: National Park Service; pages 23, 24, Parson Capen House and Fairbanks House: Samuel Chamberlain; page 25, Jabez Wilder House: Arthur C. Haskell; page 28, Adams Mansion: Ralph H. Anderson; pages 29, 32, 33, 35–38, Harlow House, Sturbridge Country Store, Narragansett Historical Building, Parson Ashley House, Frary House, Hall Tavern, Old Manse and Storrowton: all by Samuel Chamberlain; pages 40, 41, Shaker Farm: Ezra Stoller, LHJ; page 42, Thomas Cooke House: Samuel Chamberlain; pages 44, 45, Dell House and Nantucket: Ezra Stoller, LHJ.

NEW HAMPSHIRE Page 49, The Warner: Samuel Chamberlain; page 50, Gov. John Langdon House: Kingsbury Studio; page 51, Richard Jackson House: Samuel Chamberlain; pages 52, 54, Franklin Pierce House and Fort Acres: Eric M. Sanford; page 55, Ocean-Born-Mary House: L. M. A. Roy; pages 58, 59, Orford: Samuel Chamberlain.

MAINE Pages 60, 71, Ruggles House: Ezra Stoller, LHJ; pages 61, 62, 64–66, Hamilton House, Lady Pepperrell House, Sarah Orne Jewett House, and Holmes House: all by Douglas Armsden; page 67, Tate House: Ezra Stoller, LHJ; page 71, Field House: Douglas Armsden.

VERMONT Pages 73, 80, Dutton House, Shelburne: Ezra Stoller, LHJ.

RHODE ISLAND Page 88, Eleazer Arnold House: Laurence E. Tilley; page 89, Hunter House: Ezra Stoller, LHJ; page 92, John Brown House: Rhode Island Historical Society; page 93, Carrington House: Ezra Stoller, LHJ; page 94, Nathaniel Greene Home: L. E. Wagner; page 96, Barnum House: Laurence E. Tilley; pages 97, 98, Hunter House and Vernon House: Preservation Society of Newport County.

CONNECTICUT Pages 100, 102, Bonnet Hill Farm: Ezra Stoller, LHJ; page 101, Glebe House: Connecticut Development Commission; pages 106, 108, Denison House and Stonecrop: Ezra Stoller, LHJ; page 111, Buttolph-Williams House: Meyers Studio, Inc.; pages 112, 114, 118, Webb House, Royce House, and Nathan Hale Homestead: all by courtesy of Connecticut Development Commission.

NEW YORK Pages 120, 126, Rock Hall: Ezra Stoller, LHJ; pages 120, 149, Campbell-Whittlesey House: Society for the Preservation of Landmarks in Western New York; page 123, Dyckman House: E. P. McFarland; page 130, Home, Sweet Home: Ezra Stoller, LHJ; page 133, Philipse Castle: Laurence D. Thornton; page 139, House of History: Ezra Stoller, LHJ; page 142, Hasbrouck House: Cortlandt V. D. Hubbard; page 145, Constable Hall: Fynmore Photos; pages 146, 147, Fenimore House and Farmers' Museum: New York State Historical Association; page 150, Eastman Birthplace: George Eastman House, Inc.

NEW JERSEY Pages 154, 169, Homeland: Ezra Stoller, LHJ; pages 155, 156, Zabriskie–von Steuben House and McKonkey Ferry House: Department of Conservation and Economic Development; page 161, Boxwood Hall: M. W. Barish; page 161, Mead Hall: Peter A. Juley & Son; page 162, Ford Mansion: Ralph H. Anderson; page 164, Dey Mansion: Nathaniel Ewen; pages 168, 170, Indian King Tavern and Hancock House: Department of Conservation and Economic Development.

PENNSYLVANIA Pages 172, 184, Pottsgrove: Ezra Stoller, LHJ; page 175, Powel House: Cortlandt V. D. Hubbard; pages 176, 177, Rooms from Millbach: Philadelphia Museum of Art; page 180, Morris House: Ezra Stoller, LHJ; page 180, Upsala: Cortlandt V. D. Hubbard; page 182, 1704 House: Theodore B. Hetzel; page 186, Wheatland: Frederic S. Klein.

OHIO   Page 194, Mower House: Columbus Dispatch Photo; page 195, President's House: Marietta College; page 196, Matthews House: Hunter Studio; page 199, Headley Inn: Ohio Power Company; page 203, Glendower: Harold Rueppel; page 205, Sinton-Taft House: Taft Museum.

INDIANA   Page 209, Posey House: Wallace Studio; page 211, Shrewsbury House: Metzger & Metzger; page 213, Harrison Mansion: Read Studio.

MICHIGAN   Pages 215, 220, Mackinac Island: Emerson Dufina; Sanford House: Bernie Photographs.

ILLINOIS   Pages 212, 225, 228, 230, 231, Lincoln Home, Saucier House, Grant House, Menard House, Onstot Cooper Shop: all by courtesy of Illinois Division of Parks.

WISCONSIN   Page 237, Kilbournetown House: Milwaukee Journal; pages 239, 240, Tank Cottage and Cotton House: R. S. Sivesind, State Historical Society.

ABOUT THE AUTHORS

It would not be unnatural if the readers of the *Guides* were to wonder what kind of a house the Pratts live in. It is an old house but not very old, having been built by Jonas Calf in 1845. It stands in the rolling country of Bucks County, Pennsylvania, where all the old houses are built of the native fieldstone. In this case the walls are a monolith, two feet thick, plastered on both sides, and prone to sweat indoors in hot humid weather. In the moldings throughout there is a certain delicacy, bespeaking a natural sense of nicety in the farmer-builder. There is no elegance, to be sure, but there is feeling. The house was probably built in two sections—simultaneously, the Pratts suspect—and the second section was to accommodate a married son. As functional for its time and place as any modern design, it is still prized for its excellent utilitarian qualities and the peacefulness of its appearance. To compare it for distinction with most of the houses listed in the *Guides* would be presumptuous. But anyone who has an interest in simple farm dwellings, simply adapted, is welcome to visit it by written appointment in April and May when everything about the house looks its best.

Dorothy Pratt was born in Rochester in the midst of a city and countryside redolent with Greek Revival mansions and cobblestone houses. Richard Pratt was born near Harrisburg, between the Pennsylvania Dutch counties of Lebanon, Lancaster, and Berks, and the Scotch-Irish county of Cumberland, in a region where the great masonry barns are masterpieces of American building. He has been architectural and garden editor of the *Ladies' Home Journal* for the past twenty years. Since 1944, one of his magazine projects has been the well-known Regional Series of Early American Homes on which he and his wife have worked as a team, finding and photographing the houses and writing about them. This fine color series resulted in *A Treasury of Early American Homes* in 1950 and *A Second Treasury of Early American Homes* in 1955, on which the Pratts collaborated.